Fed Up

The Federal Government's War on America

By Derk Palfreyman

Green Ivy Publishing
1 Lincoln Centre
18W140 Butterfield Road
Suite 1500
Oakbrook Terrace IL 60181-4843
www.greenivybooks.com

ISBN: 978-1-944680-92-3

Contents

Chapter 1

Those who refuse to study history are destined to repeat it.

[1]

FED UP was written to inform the reader of facts relating to the federal government's war on America's values, morals, religions, and education. In short, the federal government has declared war on traditional America.

This war is a result of the backdoor policies of communism. However, my research has led me to believe that there is a larger picture. Dr. Bella Dodd, a former member of the National Committee of the United States Communist Party of America, stated: "I think the communist conspiracy is merely a branch of much bigger conspiracy."

Dr. Dodd is not alone in her belief. Dr. Carroll Quigley, Professor of history at the Foreign Service School of Georgetown University claims personal knowledge of elitists who are really pulling the strings on the world stage. He addresses this in his book, *Tragedy and Hope.* He writes, "It is too late for the 'little people' of the world to turn back the tide."[2]

My personal belief is that Dr. Quigley is wrong. I believe there is still time to turn back the tide. Regardless of whether communism is the goal or just the vehicle, if we defeat the vehicle, we defeat any ultimate system using it as vehicle.

To overcome this pollution of our freedoms, we must first become better informed. We need to know the limits of power, and who is asserting that power. American's need to understand what is legal under our Constitution and what is not. As a people, we need to recognize this movement for what it is. It is a war against traditional America, religion, and freedom.

---

1   A misquote of George Santayana: "Those who cannot remember the past, are condemned to repeat it" (*The Life of Reason*, 1905).

2   The Naked Capitalist, Skousen, W. Cleon, Private Edition, 2197 Berkley Street Salt Lake City Utah,1970 Page 1-4

The results of this war on American values are manifested in the enslavement of the many Americans who have become entrenched in the welfare system and fallen prey to the propaganda and the religion of the Left. The religion of the Left is based on a deep and abiding faith in the sanctity of the state. They believe the constitution is flawed, and the United States is responsible for all the calamities of the world.

Most traditional Americans, Libertarians, Republicans, Democrats, Independents and affiliates of other political parties have a deep and abiding love of personal freedom. This freedom includes allowing others the right to their personal beliefs and practices as long as they do not directly infringe upon the freedoms of others.

Throughout our history, we have elected both saints and villains as representatives of our great Republic. One of our downfalls has been to disregard character as the most important attribute of elected and appointed officials.

When the United States Supreme Court overturns two centuries of precedent rulings concerning freedom of religion, and rules against First Amendment rights to freedom of speech and religion, we begin to see the fruits of this critical war.

When the courts assume the right to make laws, and congress has neither the guts nor backbone to stop these lawless acts of assumption, it is time to replace those in power. It is time to impeach Supreme Court Justices who attempt to circumvent the legislative process by making laws or rulings that are inconsistent with the powers granted them under the Constitution.

When a Supreme Court Justice declares a penalty to be a tax, he has assumed authority, which he does not possess. A tax cannot be imposed by the Supreme Court or any other public entity. The authority to raise revenue is a power given only to the House of Representatives. This was the case with the Affordable Care Act, which will be discussed in detail later in the book.

Americans have become increasingly concerned about the overreach of government agencies. These non-elected agencies exercise powers that are not granted to them under a constitutional government. Non-elected agents of the government never answer to the people. As these appointed agencies become increasingly powerful, the American people find their freedoms rapidly eroding. These agencies do not fear the people because they do not face elections; therefore, there is no accountability either individually or collectively.

Even our elected representatives are so deeply entrenched that they rarely fear the people. Congress enjoys only about a 10 percent approval rating, and yet somehow, year after year, we as citizens continue to re-elect incumbent congressmen at a rate of 80 to 90 percent.

Since the early 1970s, America has murdered over fifty million unborn babies. The people who lead the charge for more abortions are the same people who shut down entire industries to save an insect, fish, or bird which they consider endangered.

In recent years the diminishing of humanity has been manifest in the tidal wave of mass murders.

Congress has been derelict in its duty to stop and impeach a runaway president who has proved to be nothing more than a petty tyrant. People have been murdered because of the direct actions and or inaction of President Barack Obama and his administration. Our healthcare has been ruined and our economy is on the brink of imploding, and yet almost no one is talking impeachment. Almost no one in Congress has stepped up to stop President Obama and his Royal Presidency.

Those few Republican legislators who have stepped up and attempted to stop the insane overspending and overreach by the President and Congress have been castigated by their own party. When Senators Ted Cruz and Mike Lee stepped up to defund Obama Care, the likes of Republicans Orin Hatch and John Boehner, sided with Harry Reid and President Obama and conspired to marginalize Lee and Cruz.

America is on a collision course, and fast becoming a socialist or even a communist government. If the communists succeed in removing our constitutional government, we will lose the rule of law and with it, our rights as a free people.

America will cease to be free and America will cease to be the defender of freedom the world has come to know. In the words of Abraham Lincoln: "America is the last best hope"

Chapter 2

Government Systems

Religion, Patriotism, Education and Freedom are the foundation of self-government known as a Republic. Ignorance, Secularism and Slavery are the deceitful tentacles of Socialism and Communism.

Communism and Fascism are not left and right of each other but both espouse the views of the far Left, progressives, and liberals. The Democratic Party has been hijacked and is now the political arm of the progressive and communist movement in America and around the world. Unfortunately, the mainstream Republican Party is not far behind in espousing these same views that will destroy the United States if it is not stopped.

Communism and Fascism are the parties who use the tools of finger pointing to gain favor in the political arena, and to enslave the people. They are the agencies who use the leverage of food to control and force the capitulation of the people to fall in line with their political ideals.

Communism and Fascism both believe in social engineering and espouse the views of socialism. They oppose private ownership or control of businesses, and private ownership of property. Property includes your home, bank accounts, vehicles, all personal property, and your children.

Both oppose the rights of the individual, the rights of free speech, and the right to own weapons. They believe you work for the state and the state will decide what you need and receive. They want to control what you drive, how far you drive, and your medical care.

Followers of Fascism and Communism seek to destroy the U.S. Constitution along with your civil rights. These systems control the people of their regimes by forcible suppression. In Russia, it is the GRU or the KGB; in Germany under the iron hand of Hitler, it was the SS or Gestapo. These organizations hunt down any and all dissidence, arrest and send them off to labor or death camps. History is replete with the death and suffering of tens of millions of these countries citizens who were imprisoned and murdered under these ruthless rulers and their systems of government.

In the United States, we have a myriad of regulatory agencies now under a large umbrella called "Law Enforcement." These agencies are being trained to kill Americans. When President Obama was on the campaign trail in Colorado Springs, July 2, 2008, then Senator Obama stated.

"We cannot continue to rely on our military in order to achieve the national security objectives we've set. We've got to have a civilian national security force that's just as powerful, just as strong, just as well-funded."[3]

Why did candidate Obama think he needed an internal army? Follow the wording closely.

"To achieve the national security objectives we've set."

It is to check the people, and keep them in line. Tyrants always have to use force against their citizens to keep them in line with administrative objectives. To create an internal army just as strong and just as well funded as the military. Congress was a willing partner to the Brown shirts of America it has been covered under the harmless blanket of the term Law Enforcement. These new Law Enforcement officers are not the traditional sheriff, police, or peace officers who we have seen in the past, solving crimes and protecting citizens.

These strong-arm agencies are the United States Government's version of German SS Troops. They are funded through the benign names of Department of Homeland Security (DHS) and Federal Emergency Management Agency (FEMA) and

3   http://www.creators.com/opinion/joseph-farah/obama-s-civilian-national-security-force.html

other agencies under their control. President Obama learned well from his mentors, Hitler and Stalin. To control the people, an internal police force is necessary.

America is looking to sheriff departments across the nation for leadership in legitimate law enforcement. The sheriff is the only elected law enforcement official and because of this, they are accountable to the people.

One of the outstanding sheriffs who uphold the U.S. Constitution and enjoy outstanding support from constituents is the outspoken Sheriff Dave Clarke from Milwaukee County, Wisconsin. He told his constituents to get a firearm and get trained so they can defend themselves until the police get there.[4] Sheriff Joe Arpaio of Maricopa County Arizona is known as "the toughest sheriff in America." Almost all Sheriffs in the West and many from otherwise liberal states such as New York and Florida are rising to do their duty for the people and not obtrusive governments. Many of these sheriffs have signed a pledge opposing subversion of their citizen's constitutional rights. In Colorado, sheriffs refused to enforce unconstitutional gun laws. Sheriffs from across America are the last bastion against the bastardization of law enforcement.

Federal agency overreach

Recognizing the danger to liberty these rouge agencies possess, we need to step away from CNN and ABC news. The following event did not fit the narrative and was at first almost non-existent as far as the mainstream news media was concerned.

Bunkerville, Nevada, April 7 through April 12, 2014. Rancher and grazing land steward, Cleven Bundy was in a twenty-year dispute with the Bureau of Land Management (BLM). Over the past fifty years, the BLM had driven most of the ranchers in the area from their grazing lands. The rights of the ranchers to utilize these

---

4   Prison Planet, Sheriff Responds to Attacks over Second Revolution, By Steve Watson, February 21, 2013

western grazing lands had been recognized by the federal and state governments as a right for almost 150 years, not just a privilege.

From the late 1930s to 1993, the Bundy family had paid their yearly grazing fee assessments to the BLM. Under BLM statutes, assessed grazing fees had to be used to improve the land for grazing. The BLM had not been using the fees to improve grazing feasibility but instead used the fees paid by these ranchers to destroy the ranching industry and drive the ranchers from their property by continually cutting the number of livestock that could be grazed and removing traditional grazing lands from the trust.[5][6]

Mr. Bundy claimed he did not recognize the authority of this federal agency to administer century-old grazing lands which constitutionally should have been turned over to the State of Nevada within a short time of Nevada being granted statehood.

Mr. Bundy cited the U.S. Constitution and told the BLM he would pay fees to the state of Nevada but believed he was not beholden to the federal government.

U.S. Constitution Article 1, Section 8 restricts the federal government from owning property of a state except for a ten-mile square area for the seat of government, and for forts and arsenals.

All states shall be entitled to the same privileges as the several states. All new states would enjoy the same privileges as the original thirteen states at the time of the writing of the Constitution; including title to all property within the state except as the law provided for certain federal ownership.[7]

The eastern states had their land released to them shortly after attaining statehood. This allowed them to profit from the resources of their state lands.

---

5 http://www.blm.gov/wo/st/en/prog/grazing.html
6 http://www.blm.gov/wo/st/en/info/regulations.html
7 US Constitution Section 1 article 8-9

However, the western states have never enjoyed this same privilege. The average amount of land owned by the federal government east of Colorado is from 11.8 percent to 1.2 percent

In the West, it is a different story. The state with the least land owned by the federal government is Montana at 29.9 percent. The states with the highest federal land ownership are Nevada 84.5 percent, Utah 57.4 percent, and Oregon 53.1 percent. Because of this disparity in land ownership it places the federal government in conflict with the Constitution. To be in compliance, the federal government needs to deed these lands back to the states. [8]

This conflict was just another in a long line of federal government overreach and enforcement that the corrupt federal courts have unconstitutionally upheld.

On April 7, 2014, armed with a court order, the BLM began a roundup of Bundy's cattle. The BLM began by closing over 600,000 acres of public land to all citizens. In the wide-open desert of southern Nevada they set up an insultingly small area as a First Amendment protest area.

The Bundy family and others came and protested. The paranoid BLM had set snipers on a high point sighting down on the protester area. The protesters refused to stay in the unlawful protest area.

Unlike protests on the Left with OWS, these people came on their own. No one paid them to drive to southern Nevada. The protestors did not throw rocks, or bottles at the officers. They did not defecate on police vehicles. They did not destroy property or interrupt commerce.

BLM troops, in the spirit of Selma, Alabama in the 1960s, deployed tasers, threatened the protesters with dogs, and arrested

---

8   http://bigthink.com/strange-maps/291-federal-lands-in-the-us Accessed April 22, 2015

and abused the unarmed protesters. [9] [10]

The BLM court order did not allow for the BLM to roundup the cattle on the range. Because cattle are private property, the BLM is required by law and by BLM statutes to default to the local county sheriff for enforcement of the court order. [11]

On Saturday April 12, the Bundys—and many Americans— had had enough with this insidious overreach and abuse by BLM Storm Troopers. The 400-plus BLM officers were met Saturday morning by over 1000 unarmed demonstrators. The BLM were given orders to fire on unarmed demonstrators if they did not disband or if they advanced on BLM positions.[12]

The game changer came with the arrival of hundreds of militia from several states. These law abiding and lawful militia men came well-armed with the objective to protect the Bundys and other protesters from the massacre that the BLM had promised to inflict on them. [13]

On the afternoon of Saturday, April 12, the BLM, citing congressional pressure from constituents, the safety of BLM officers, the safety of citizens, and the belated intervention by the County Sheriff, announced they would disband the roundup and leave the area.

After the BLM made their exit, the Bundy Family and the press found a wake of destruction left by these supposed stewards of the public trust. U.S. military men would have been court marshaled if they had trashed and abused a combatant's property as

---

9   http://www.history.com/topics/black-history/selma-montgomery-march

10   Authors Note: Selma, Alabama, 1965, democratic governor George Wallace deployed troops and dogs on protestors who were on a legal march from Selma to the state capital to encourage black people to register and vote.

11   http://4thst8.wordpress.com/2014/07/08/sheriff-now-confirms-blm-had-no-place-to-take-bundys-confiscated-cattle/

12   Talking points, Bundy Ranch Still trying turn BLM standoff spark into a national fire. Dylan Scott May 9, 2014

13   -Washington Post, "The long fight between the Bundys and the federal government from 1989 to today," by Jaime Fuller, January 4, 2015

the BLM had done to the Bundys' private property. These federal SS troops acting under orders from their superiors and like Russian and Gestapo troops in WWII illegally destroyed everything in their path.[14] [15] [16] [17] [18]

Paramilitary police are dangerous enough to a free society; but when compared to armed federal agencies, with huge egos and almost no oversight, this rule-by-agency is akin to rule by tyranny because there is no electoral oversight.

Following is a short list of other raids conducted against U.S. citizens by these unlawful federal law enforcement agencies.

January 20, 2012: SBA (Small Business Administration) Conducted a SWAT raid on company because SBA changed the rules of a loan and failed to notify the client. No charges were filed against the client or the illegal raiders.[19]

2011: FDA (Federal Drug Administration) Conducted a SWAT raid on an Amish Farm for selling raw milk. The farm was later found to be in compliance with state law. [20] No charges were filed against the illegal raiders.

June 2011: Department of Education conducted a SWAT Raid against Kenneth Wright's home where, in front of his children, they handcuffed him as though he were a dangerous felon who had committed a murder. The agents were looking for fraud information

---

14   Human Events, BLM Accused of Trashing Bundy Ranch after Nevada standoff, By John Hayward, April 17, 2014
15   http://www.foxnews.com/politics/2014/04/16/feds-accused-leaving-trail-wreckage-after-nevada-ranch-standoff/ Accessed June 25, 2014
16   http://www.foxnews.com/politics/2014/04/16/feds-accused-leaving-trail-wreckage-after-nevada-ranch-standoff/)
17   Authors Note: There are many fine and dedicated BLM field officers and other federal employees who work hard to assist the people and businesses that they interact with; however, most of these agencies, with the blessings of Congress, have assumed powers they do not possess.
18   U.S. Constitution Section 1, Article 1.
19   Arkansas Business, Federal Agents Sued after Raiding Bottled water…, By Arkansas Business Staff, Monday March 11, 2013
20   Reason.com, Raw Milk Raid on Amish Farm, Nick Gillespie, May 16, 2011

about Wright's ex-wife.[21] What was the Department of Education doing in a criminal fraud investigation?

January 2006: Salvatore Culosi Jr., an unarmed optometrist suspected of being a bookie, was shot and killed by a SWAT officer when the officer's weapon accidently discharged. No charges were filed against the officer.[22]

Justice begs the question: what are the Small Business Administration, Federal Drug Administration, Department of Education, EPA, Federal Housing Administration and dozens of other non-police federal agencies doing with SWAT teams when they do not have legitimate police authority?

Destroy the viability of military veterans

The second tier of a fascist, communist ruler is to destroy any military members past and present who might oppose killing and subjugation of the nation's citizens. Tyrants and Dictators always kill off or at least fire established military leaders, especially generals and commanders.

Paranoid about revolution and the Russian Czar, Stalin murdered thousands of his generals to make certain they could not move the people against his murderous regime. Stalin in turn killed educators and tried to rid the country of all religious people and symbols.[23]

Pol Pot of Cambodia, in a little over three years (1975 to 1979), attempted to kill all of that country's military people, doctors and educators, then denuded the country of any signs or symbols of their history and religion so that the people would not have religious or historic effects to remember the country they had lost to this

---

21   Washington Post, Education Department Agents raid California Home, By Elizabeth Flock, June 8, 201

22   Washington Post, Metro, Sawat Tactics at Issue after Fairfax Shooting, By Tom Jackman, January 27, 2006

23   http://russiapedia.rt.com/of-russian-origin/stalins-purges/

ruthless dictator.[24]

President Obama has already started this raid on the military and religion. He has been retiring and firing conservative generals and leaders. The Obama regime has been blasting and diminishing Christianity and all religion except Islam in the military.

Under the Obama regime the military has restricted chaplains from distributing bibles, and all but forbidden religious discussion among the rank-and-file soldiers.[25]

On October 17, 2013 soldiers attending a pre-deployment briefing at Fort Hood reported they were told that evangelical Christians and members of the Tea Party were a threat to the nation and that any soldier donating to those groups would be subjected to punishment under the Uniform Code of military justice.[26]

Is President Obama following the founding fathers and seeking personal liberty for the people, or does he follow the footsteps of Hitler and Stalin in suppressing citizen liberties and stamping out all opposition?

Under Hitler, the police were uniformed the same as the SS and other troops. The German police were no longer the protectors of the people but just another arm of federal storm troopers. In the U. S., police SWAT teams dressed in military gear are becoming a common sight on the streets of our cities.

The constant presence of paramilitary police on American streets has changed our perception of police. Instead of being perceived as protectors of the people, they are fast becoming the superiors of the people. In place of proper respect, the police are feared and hated. In the seventeen hundreds, Alexander Hamilton

---

24   Surviving the Killing Fields, (Basic Books 1987) by Haing Ngor
25   WND, Purge Surge: Obama fires another commander, By F Michael Maloof, November 4, 2013
  Front Page, Obama's War on the Christian, "Extremist" Threat, By Joseph Kent, October 25, 2013
26   Fox News, Does the army consider Christians, Tea Party a terror threat, By Todd Starnes, October 23, 2013

warned about the constant police presence and how they would become superiors instead of protectors of the people.[27]

The face of communism

Centralized government, or communism, is the desired outcome of progressives and liberals. These are self-described as the "Far Left." These groups are neither liberal nor progressive. They have hijacked the terms to make themselves sound softer. If they were to declare who they are as COMMUNISTS, only the 20 to 30 percent of the extreme Leftists and communists in this country would vote for them. They prey on the uneducated and or uninformed to keep their power and their minions in office. Communism and fascism always end with the same results. After the people have been disarmed, subdued and conquered, dissent is no longer tolerated.

Private ownership of firearms, freedom of the press, freedom of assembly, freedom of religion, and the rule of law are rights taken in rapid secession. Starvation, or at least food shortage, is implemented to enslave and keep the populace in line with party policy.

The genocide and murder of large elements of the population follows when dictators and parties have absolute power. With no bill of rights or constitutional protections, nothing stands in the way of wholesale slaughter of the people by dictators. Following are examples of fascist and communist dictatorships who were some of the most heinous murderers of all time.

---

27   The Federalist Papers,(Alexander Hamilton, 2003) page 42

Country	Time period	Number murdered
China	1946 to present Chairman Mao/and successors	49 to 78 million people
Red Russia	1900 to 1946 Stalin/ and successors	50 to 60 million people
Germany	1935 to 1945 Hitler	12 million people
Belgium	1886-1908 Leopold 11	8 million people
Japan	1900 to 1945 Emperor Hirohito	5 million people
Cambodia	1975-79 Pol Pot	1.7 million people

Of these seven countries alone, over 165 million innocent victims were murdered in cold blood. All of these counties, except Japan (who were earth worshipers) were dedicated atheist regimes. They all targeted church clergy for murder to stop the spread of any religious expression. All of these countries confiscated the firearms from the people to maintain control.[28]

Cambodia 1975-1979

In Cambodia, Pol Pot murdered two out of every eight Cambodian citizens. In 1975, the people of Cambodia were driven out of the cities. With little or no food, they were forced onto communal farms in the country-side, which in reality were forced-labor concentration camps. The people were required to work with little food and almost no medical attention. Men and women were rounded-up for the slightest supposed infraction, raped, brutalized and murdered in ways that are unimaginable. Young, old, men, women, and children were generally brutalized before their murders. Just as in the German Concentration camps, pregnant women were

---

28   Worst Genocides of the 20th and 21st Centuries by Piero Scaruffin. http://www.scaruffi.com/politics/dictat.html

often the target of the most brutal sadistic murders of all.[29] [30] [31]

These brutal murders were committed by the Khmer Rouge between 1975 and 1979. This number pales to the numbers murdered by Stalin and Hitler. However, in percent of population it was one of the highest per capita. These were citizens of the mother country, not invading armies.[32]

Japan 1935-1945

Japanese soldiers were encouraged and schooled to be more brutal than soldiers of any other nation in modern history. On December 13, 1937, Japanese soldiers entered the city of Nanking China. The soldiers, encouraged by their superiors, engaged in what came to be known as the Rape of Nanking. The soldiers brutalized, and murdered 90,000 Chinese POWs then turned their brutality to the civilian population and murdered over 210,000 unarmed civilians.

Total deaths in Nanking exceeded 300,000 of a city of only 600,000. Every other person in Nanking was murdered by the brutal Japanese Imperial Soldiers. The Japanese soldiers were under orders to inflict the greatest amount of pain and suffering possible before finally killing their victims.

In a month and a half, from mid-December 1937 to the beginning of February 1938, it is estimated that every woman between the ages of eight and eighty, including pregnant women, were brutally gang raped multiple times then murdered to ensure the victims could never testify against the perpetrators.[33]

29   About.com, Pol Pot Leader of the Khmer Rouge, By Michael Richards
30   Surviving the Killing Fields, (Basic Books 1987) by Haing Ngor
31   Photos of the Cambodian killing fields may be found at www.google.
com/search?q=photos+of+the+killing+fields&rlz=1C1ASUT_enUS437US440&es_
sm=93&tbm=isch&imgil=wtnUH-n0e52FrM percent253A percent253Bhttps
percent253A percent2
32   www.google.com/search?q=photos+of+the+killing+fields&rlz=1C1AS
UT_enUS437US440&es_sm=93&tbm=isch&imgil=wtnUH-n0e52FrM percent253A
percent253Bhttps percent253A percent2
33   The History Place, Genocide in the 20th Century, copyright @ 2000 The

Could the United States become another Russia, Germany, or Cambodia? Take off the rose-colored glasses, America. Not only could it happen, but the pieces are being put in place to ensure it happens. Take for example this quote from the oldest-ranking member of the House of Representatives, John Dingell (D-Michigan): "It takes a long time to do the necessary administrative steps that have to be taken to put the legislation together to control the people." [34]

John Dingell has been in the House of Representatives since 1955. By 2014, he had been in the house for over sixty-two years.[35]

This is one more reason no one should be allowed to stay in the people's house for an extended amount of time. To John Dingle, the people are no longer constituents but are subjects to be controlled.

In March of 2013, Florida Atlantic University, Professor "Deandre Poole" required students to write the name Jesus on a piece of paper and place it on the floor. Then he required the students to stomp on the paper. One student, "Ryan Rotlela," picked up the paper and told the professor the assignment was insulting and offensive. Rotlela took his concerns to Professor Poole's supervisor. Not only did the supervisor not take action against professor Poole, but student Rotlela was promptly suspended from the class.[36] Poole went on to explain: "If we are going to live peacefully in society, then we have to be able to create settings where we can engage in these types of conversations."[37]

"Peacefully in society." What is this guy smoking? This man is nothing short of a race bating, God-hater. This lesson is designed to inspire hate for a specific segment of society, Christians. The

---

History Place http://www.historyplace.com/worldhistory/genocide/nanking.htm

34   News Talk WJR Radio with Paul W. Smith, 3/23/2010, John Dingell (D Michigan)

35   http://en.wikipedia.org/wiki/John_Dingell

36   Huffington Post, Deandre Poole Keeps FAU Job after "Stomp on Jesus "Controversy, By Tyler Kingkade, June 24 2013. http://www.huffingtonpost.com/2013/06/24/deandre-poole-fau-stomp-on-jesus_n_3490263.html

37   Huffington Post, Deandre Poole Keeps FAU Job after "Stomp on Jesus "Controversy, By Tyler Kingkade, June 24 2013

complicit supervisor explained that the assignment was a lesson in debate; however, there was no debate. Discussion was not allowed; dissenting viewpoints were not allowed. If the student protested, he was suspended from the class.

The truth is, Professor Poole and his supervisors are nothing less than racist bigots, and a despicable disgrace to their profession and the human race. Any honorable institution would have fired Poole immediately.

Too many universities have become so bigoted and hate-filled; they will do anything to destroy any semblance of morality and Christianity. Where is the uproar for fairness in education? Where is the concern for the individuality of students? Where are the protectors of the offended? If this assignment had been to step on the face of Dr. Martin Luther King Jr., Mohammad, or President Obama, there would not only have been outrage but rioting on the campus. Professor Poole's life would have been threatened and possibly taken.

Outrage by students and the immediate firing of the professor would have been an appropriate response to this insolent bigot. However, it has become just another example of the lack of tolerance by the Left and communists in America. If America does not wake up, the progressive communists will completely disassemble our liberties and the Constitution. This was not free speech; this was communist, fascist hate-speech, and another nail in the coffin of a free constitutional republic.

In 1938, "Time magazine" named Adolf Hitler "*MAN OF THE YEAR.*" At the time, Hitler's campaign of intimidation and murder against the Jewish people in Germany was well known. It was also known that Hitler was pressuring parents to take their children out of Christian schools and enroll them in "Hitler Jugend" (Hitler Youth) where the children were indoctrinated in anti-Christian anti-family beliefs and values.

German children were taught to hate Catholics, Christians

and Jews. Children were required to inform authorities if parents, friends, or relatives spoke against the Nazi regime or Hitler. Church groups were infiltrated and their members punished if they spoke against the Nazi Party. The German people became paranoid and reclusive because of fear of retaliation for any misspoken words.

They lived in abject fear of speaking to friends or family. Germans pulled their shades down to stop the prying eyes of the Gestapo. The invasion of privacy and freedom to think or speak was so imprinted on the minds of the people that after WWII, many German people who came to America would keep their window shades pulled down in their homes for the rest of their lives.[38] [39] Communism and Fascism rule by compulsion; rulers arrest or kill those who show defiance.

Ten steps to establishing a dictatorship

Naomi Wolf wrote *The End of America*, where she outlines the ten steps through which all nations establish a dictatorship.

1. Create an internal/external threat that terrorizes the populace.

2. Create secret prisons with torture.

3. Create a paramilitary force (examples: TSA, DHS, FEMA, BTFA and all other federal agencies who are now designated as Law Enforcement and who are not traditional police).

4. Single out ordinary citizens as troublesome persons.

5. Establish surveillance of citizens groups and ordinary citizens. Examples are the IRS targeting of conservative groups and the NSA cyber spying.

---

38   (Information gained from personal interviews with Eugen and Helene Hechtle who lived through the Hell of World War II as German citizens. Eugen and Helene migrated to America in 1952 to escape the scourge of Socialism in Germany. Eugen died 1999, Helen died 2012

39   America The Last Best Hope Volume 11, By William Bennett page 148, Paragraphs 2-4

6. Detain and release citizens without formally charging them with any crime. (This has been "legalized" under Obama's NDAA and was passed by a willing congress, both Republican and Democrat.)

7. Target key individuals who are well-known, popular figures. (Such as Rush Limbaugh, Glenn Beck and other conservatives.)

8. Restrict the press. (To keep in the good graces of the government, the American mainstream media has become a willing partner in defending a corrupt government.)

9. Redefine dissent as treason. (The FBI has warned that people who "stockpile food" and or ammunition might be terrorists!)

10. Subvert the rule of law. (President Obama has been making up his own laws and lying to an illiterate American public. He uses unconstitutional executive authority to make laws without the approval of Congress.[40])

We need to be involved in this Great Republic and not only as bystanders. We need to hold our elected officials accountable for the votes they make and the legacy they leave behind. If your phone number is not flagged by your congressmen or congresswomen, you are not involved enough.

Only those who vote and are involved have a right to complain.

---

40   Huffington Post, Ten steps to close down an open society, by Naomi Wolf April 24, 2007 / The Guardina, Fascis America 10 easy steps, Naomi Wolf, Monday April 23, 2007

Chapter 3

Fascism and Communism are two sides of the same coin.

Communism and fascism are intolerant common sisters with the same intent: domination of industry, product, and property, enslavement of the people, and control of the human spirit. It is rule by force and tyranny. The people have no stipulated rights under these forms of government, for there is no rule of law.

Fascism defined

Fascism is "a political philosophy, movement, or regime (as that of the fascistic) that exalts nation and often race above the individual and that stands for a centralized autocratic government headed by a dictatorial leader, severe economic and social regimentation, and forcible suppression of opposition."

Communism defined

A theory or system of social organization based on the holding of all property in common, actual ownership being ascribed to the community as the whole or to the state.

A system of social organization in which all economic and social activity is controlled by a totalitarian state dominated by a single and self-perpetuating political party. [41]

Both communism and fascism promise to solve problems quickly through command and control. Command always ends in violence to obtain the control.

The prevailing method for fascists and communists is to accuse the opposition of what they themselves are guilty of.

In 2010, when the Tea Party Patriots achieved national attention by taking many elections nationwide, establishment Republican and liberal progressives in the U.S. government and the mainstream news media did what all fascist and communists

---

[41]   Dictionary.com, May 29, 2015

do when their power is questioned. They started a campaign of character assassination to destroy people who held a different vision for America.

The establishment did not attempt to debate the Tea Party Patriots, they would not engage in a healthy exchange of ideas for, or against a policy or law. The treatment of Sarah Palin (vice presidential candidate, 2008) was despicable. Dislike her politics if you choose, but since when did it become stylish to degrade women and attack them with vicious lies?

MSNBC's Martin Bashir said the following about Sarah Palin "idiot, dunce, someone should defecate in her mouth." Other things said about Sarah Palin by major news outlets are so despicable they are not fit to be spoken, let alone printed.[42]

These hate-filled comments are indicative of the Left, who have no standing in a standard discussion but depend upon the instrument of hate not debate.

These radical communists have broken ties with the original intent and principles of America's Founders and the Constitution. They did everything in their power to paint the Tea Party with their own brush. This portrayal was not reporting news; it was an unveiled attempt to create hate against a specific group of people who do not see the world as liberals do. Where is the tolerance for opposing points of view? These are the same liberals who are supposed to be the party of tolerance and love.

The progressive communist media and corrupt government officials deceptively created an image of the Tea Party in their words as "out-of-step with America," racist, dangerous, militant, and advocating the violent overthrow of the United States Government.

For months, this deception was targeted at the American people. The myth that the Tea Party was responsible for the eruption

---

42   Media Buzz, By Howard Kurtz, Martin Bashir Quits at MSNBC over Palin slur, December 5, 2013

of violence against blacks, women, gays, Jews, and any other group who are non-white American males was hammered at Americans day and night by the mainstream media.

For all the deception, the media could never find a single link connecting the Tea Party patriots to any of the wild accusations they had made.

Tea Party Patriots

Who are the Tea Party Patriots and why do they drive the progressives so crazy.

The Tea Party is not so much a party as a way of thinking. It has a very real mix of Republicans, Libertarians, and even some Democrats, women, whites, blacks, Hispanics, Asians and many other races who understand the dangers our country is facing.

The common belief of these patriots is that our country is losing her roots, there is a very real danger of America's moral collapse. If a constitutional America is to continue, we need to return to the founding principles of our forefathers.

The Tea Party does not have a specific leader whom the Left can target. The Tea Party is about a system of beliefs by an ever-growing number of people who have chosen to educate themselves on the Constitution and basic American values and principles. This self-education is becoming the biggest nightmare of all for the American Left.

The Tea Party is a true grassroots party that rallies without money or help from any political machine. It has already made a deep imprint in the American political landscape and threatens to continue to do so.

In 2010, the Tea Party held The Restoring America rally on the Mall in Washington DC. At the conclusion of the rally, National Parks Department cleanup crews picked up less than fifty gallons of trash and refuse left behind by this massive rally, which was attended by an excess of over a half-million Americans from across the country. The stewardship these patriots showed for the National Mall was indicative of their love for America.

Two months later, One Nation held a rally at the Washington Mall. This was the Democrat answer to the Tea Party. One Nation was attended by only a few thousand people, but the Parks Department picked up truckloads of trash left by the One Nation group.

Occupy Wall Street and The One Nation rally were organized by the same people who lecture America on everything from green living, global warming, and Earth First. Opposite of the Tea Party, this group showed their disrespect for our country by trashing the National Mall. [43]

Unlike the Tea Party, One Nation had to bribe participants to go to the rally. Bribes included free bus rides, free Metro fare cards, free tee-shirts, and free lunches. Many of these were donated by the NAACP, Steel Workers Union, AFL-CIO, and even the screen Actors Guild.

It was estimated that the free incentives offered to One Nation participants was in excess of over a million dollars to get just a few thousand people to show up.[44, 45, 46]

Participants of Restoring America were not bussed in by Unions or other groups. There were no free lunches or free tee-shirts. These patriots came from across America at their own

---

43   http://dailycaller.com/2010/10/03/liberal-one-nation-working-together-rally-leaves-lincoln-memorial-ridden-with-trash-much-dirtier-than-glenn-becks-restoring-honor-rally/ Accessed March 30, 2015

44   Breitbart, Astroturf? Thousands given Free Bus Rides by Unions and AACP to one Nation Rally, By Kristinn Taylor and Andrea Shea King, September 27, 2010

45   http://www.theblaze.com/stories/2010/10/03/

46   www.google.com/search?q=Restoring+America+rally+2010&rlz=1C1AS UT_enUS437US440&espv=210&es_sm=93&tbm=isch&imgil=h2-lvJOFQaTx8M percent253A percent253Bhttps; http://www.google.com/search?q=photos+of+crowd+a t+one+nation+rally+at+the+mall&nord=1&rlz=1C2ASUT_enUS437US456&tbm=isch &imgil=LUWYsV8DNRfe4M percent253A percent253Bhttp percent253A percent252F percent252

expense to show their patriotism and love for America, not to burn flags and defecate in public places. There was a marked difference in the reverence and respect the Restoring America Rally showed for the nations property at the National Mall and the disrespect and desecration of this national monument left by the One Nation rally.

Restoring America was not made up of angry white men as the media had hoped. It was a cross-section of America, all patriots of diverse gender, ethnic, and religious backgrounds. This was truly a rally of the people. There were no fights, drugs, rapes, or murders.

Why the lack of violence? These patriots follow the constitution and believe in the rule of law. They are not the radical, violent, fringe element that is portrayed by the media. Tea Party Patriots simply believe in limited government as prescribed by the Constitution. They are not fringe, they are centrists, and they believe in America.

Given the respect for law which attendees at Tea Parties events and Pro-gun rallies have, President Obama could have walked unattended through any of these rallies and been safe from injury or harm. This is because these people understand and truly believe in law and the sanctity of life. Although President Obama represents everything opposite of the Tea Party, they respect his right to have a different opinion for America.

Who is Occupy Wall Street?

While the progressives were searching under every rock and failing to find any evidence that the Tea Party was engaged in any of the violence or hate they had charged them with, the mainstream media was expounding the virtues of Occupy Wall Street (OWS).

In January of 2011, Representative Gabriel Gifford (D-Arizona) was shot and wounded at a Democrat rally in Arizona. The communist myth-media went wild. Without any evidence, the media purposely and with malice conjured up a story that the shooter was part of the "dangerous Tea Party" and that ex-vice presidential hopeful, Sarah Palin was the real problem. She had incited the violence.[47]

Although these accusations would later prove to be a complete fabrication, no apology was ever offered for this blatant assault on these real American patriots. No apology ever to Sarah Palin who, it was later proved, was all but unknown to the shooter.

The shooter, twenty four year old Jared Lee Loughner, had no ties or commonality with the Tea Party or any of their beliefs. However, he did have common ties with the far-Left. Loughner had studied the *Communist Manifesto*, *Mein Kamph*, and other Leftist material. He was closely associated with the beliefs of One Nation.[48] This information was almost non-existent in the media and was hidden on Page 10, if published at all.

In 2012, twenty-two-year-old Oscar Ortega Hernandez approached the Whitehouse fence and fired eight shots at the Whitehouse. The media frenzy immediately associated Hernandez with—who else?—the Tea Party. An investigation later found Mr. Hernandez had praised al Qaeda leader, Osama bin Laden. According to the Secret Service, Hernandez was connected with Occupy Wall Street, and had sympathies for the violent overthrow of the United States. This is the same strategy and action taken by President Obama's friend and supporter Bill Ayers. Ayers was a member of the Weather Underground, a militant anti-American group. In the 1970s Bill Ayers bombed the Pentagon and NYC Police department.[49] [50] [51]

---

47   Daily News, Sarah Palin now in cross hairs: by James Gordon Meek, January 10, 2011

48   ABC News, What does Jared Lee Loughner Believe? By Brian Montopoli, January 10, 2011, http://www.cbsnews.com/news/what-does-jared-lee-loughner-believe/

49   The daily caller, Bill Ayers Defends Weather Underground, By Patrick Howley, May 6, 2013

50   Authors Note: The unrepentant Bill Ayers not only walks the streets of America as a free man, but until the mid 2000s, he was employed by the University of Illinois at Chicago.

51   http://www.biography.com/people/bill-ayers-380916#media-attention-during-the-2008-elections

This vital information of who was influencing Hernandez was quickly extinguished by the mainstream news outlets. In fact, after Hernandez's true sympathies were discovered, it suddenly became unimportant to CNN, MSNBC and the other news outlets that Hernandez had connections with OWS, or the fact that Hernandez himself described the White House attack as a terrorist attack. Of course when Hernandez's true political sympathies were discovered, he was excused as deranged and angry.[52]

OWS, is an unofficial arm of the Democratic Party, just as the Ku Klux Klan had been an arm of the Democratic Party from the 1860s and as recently as the 1970s. OWS was a party protected and advanced by President Obama as "mainstream America." Supporters of OWS include the American Nazi Party, Louis Farrakhan, white supremacist David Duke, Socialist Party USA, the Council on American-Islamic Relations, and many other anti-Semitic groups. These groups are advocating the violent overthrow of the United States, violence against Jews, and violence against anyone they considered the 1 percent, also known as "The Rich." From the earliest protests there were anti-Jewish signs and slogans, such as "Wall St. Jews," and "Jewish Billionaires."[53][54]

In 2011 and 2012, OWS was responsible for extensive property damage to both personal and government properties and the intentional interruption of commerce. The cost of these demonstrations across the nation was in the tens of millions of dollars. Many cities saw traffic and businesses brought to a standstill for weeks or months. Multiple cases of drug offenses, rape, violence, and murder were reported.[55] Police were spit on and police vehicles damaged and defecated on. In many cases, city officials excused

52   Yahoo News, Idaho man who fired eight shots at White House pleads Guilty, Reuters, September 18,2013 http://news.yahoo.com/idaho-man-fired-eight-shots-white-house-pleads-171039947.html

53   The Weekly Standard, Obama on Occupy Wall Street: "We are on their Side," by Daniel Halper, October 18, 2011

54   Commentary Magazine, Occupy Wall Street and the Jews, by Jonathan Neumann, Jan 1, 2012

55   The Wall Street Journal, The Dark Side of the War on the one Percent, by Ruth R. Wisse, Feb 3, 2014

these actions by participants, and no arrests were made of these violent criminals.

Los Angles racked up a bill in excess of five million dollars in special police protection, garbage cleanup and property damage. New York City costs were over three-times that of California and were estimated in excess of seventeen million dollars. These costs did not include the cost of the interruption of commerce, which cost millions of dollars in lost revenue to the same citizens who provide goods and services to these cities and their citizens.[56]

OWS protests were reminiscent of *Kristallnacht*, "Night of Crystal." *Kristallnacht* protests took place on nights of November 9 and 10 of 1938. Throughout fascist Germany, Austria, and other occupied German countries, the Nazi party, Storm Troopers, and Hitler Youth with the blessings of the government rained down violence on Jewish businesses, breaking out windows, and plundering and destroying Jewish property. The German police were under orders not to protect German-Jewish citizens and their property from those lawless criminals.

A similar scene was played out in many American cities with the OWS protests. Police were ordered not to interfere with the protestors while they targeted and destroyed private property.

This was only the beginning of the terror to come to German Jews. From 1935 on, Jews were targeted by the fascist German government, similar to the way the "1 percent" is being targeted by fascists in OWS.

With the blessings of President Obama and the Democratic Party, the lawless OWS movement is similar to the initial tactics the Nazis and Stalinists used in Germany and Russia under their ruthless fascist and communist dictators in those countries that created hate and animosity against specific citizens.[57]

---

56   US News, NBC News, Cities: Occupy Protestors cost taxpayers Millions, By Miranda Leitsinger, May 11, 2012

57   http://www.ushmm.org/wlc/en/article.php?ModuleId=10005201

Big Labor and leading Democrats support Occupy Wall Street and the hate it fosters.

Stephen Lerner, a former official of the (Service Employees International Union) SEIU, spoke to students at Pace University about a plan to "destabilize" the country. Lerner, described by Ezra Klein in the Washington Post as "one of the smartest organizers in the labor movement," suggested various means of "bringing down capitalism," including civil disobedience, mass defaults on mortgages and student loans, strikes and large-scale protests."

Organizer Stephen Lerner advocated efforts to "bring down the stock market" and to "interfere with the ability to be rich." Lerner stated that unions alone would not be able to affect such a ground-shaking movement. "We will need students and community groups to take the lead, to provide cover for organized labor." [58]

Lerner is no crackpot dummy. He is deadly serious about taking down and destroying America and using the power of unions and unsuspecting youth and students to obtain redistribution of wealth. Lerner's idea, of redistribution of wealth only applies to others. His wealth will translate into power. Under Lerner's ideal system, we will have two classes of people. Ultra Rich and Ultra Poor, the all-powerful and the powerless.

The spring from which OWS flows is poison. Lerner and other labor activists have been involved in the protests from the beginning. They want to create mayhem, or in his words, "disrupt how the system operates." He wants to distract Americans from their real problems—and the failings of the Obama administration—while at the same time rebuilding the power of the unions. All those hapless students and community activists blocking traffic and interrupting the commerce of America are nothing but expendable tools for the

---

58   http://www.foxnews.com/opinion/2011/11/21/for-big-labor-occupy-outbursts-are-carefully-nurtured-strategic-weapon/

Marxist Communist Party.[59] [60] [61]

Make no mistake, Stephen Lerner, his followers, and funders will destroy the United States if he can continue to push his unsuspecting minions to do his bidding. OWS never was the spontaneous protest it was professed to be. From the beginning, it was organized and well funded. It was dedicated to disrupting the commerce of the United States with violence and open rebellion. Remember, the Obama administration not only condoned OWS but encouraged it. [62]

Unions are an intricate part of the vehicle to destroy the United States and the capitalist system. SEIO President Mary Kay Henry said:

"The importance of Occupy Wall Street can't be measured by any set of demands. What's more important to understand are the values that unite the protesters and their authentic understanding of what has gone wrong in our economy."[63] [64]

Ms. Henry's statement tells us a lot and nothing about OWS. In multiple press interviews with OWS participants, they showed no continuity of interest or values, or any understanding of the economy they were protesting.

In personal interviews by the author with OWS participants the parties I interviewed could not give a single coherent or cohesive answer as to what they were protesting. The only answer was that they were protesting the rich. When asked how much money was

59   Discover the networks, Stephen Lerner, By Matthew Vadum October 10, 2011, http://www.discoverthenetworks.org/individualProfile.asp?indid=2525
60   Author's Note: Nazis is the common name for "Socialist Worker Party." In Germany, Nazis used the labor unions to facilitate Nazi rule under Adolf Hitler, just as the labor unions are being used by Learner and others to disrupt and destroy the United States.
61   http://www.abovetopsecret.com/forum/thread709027/pg1 Accessed Jan/9/2016
62   Business Insider, Caught on tape: former SEIU Official reveals plan to destroy JP Morgan, By Henry Blodget, March 22, 2011.
63   http://townhall.com/columnists/carlhorowitz/2012/03/31/occupy_wall_street_springboard_for_seiu_organizing/page/full
64   http://www.dailymail.co.uk/news/article-2046586/Occupy-Wall-Street-Shocking-photos-protester-defecating-POLICE-CAR.html

too much, there was no denomination given. The only answer was, "too much is too much."

It is hard to take a group seriously that cannot express a valued reason for the protest and that brandishes signs urging:[65] "Shoot Sperm Not Bullets, Close Corporate Tax Loopholes, Tax Religious Groups, End the Wars, Legalize Weed and Bring Back Arrested Development".[66]

OWS protests are not protected under the free speech clause of the First Amendment because of their violence against persons, property and the interruption of commerce. The right of assembly as stated in the First Amendment is "The rights of the people to peaceably assemble." [67]

OWS did not peaceably assemble to address grievances against the government. They assembled to disrupt the legal enterprise of businesses, restrict traffic and cause public discontent. They destroyed property both private and public. Knowing the truth about Occupy Wall Street, and The Tea Party Patriots, the Leftist mainstream media continues to spread insidious lies and hatred by attempting to further disparage the Tea Party, labeling them "fascists."

It is of paramount importance to understand political systems before engaging your mouth, pen, or video camera and showing your ignorance in the hope that the people are too stupid to understand terms used to describe those you disagree with.

---

65   The Daily Mail, Stinking up Wall Street: Protesters accused of Living in filth as shocking picture show one demonstrator defecation on a Police Car, By Hannah Roberts, October 9, 2011
66   http://www.dudelol.com/occupy-wallstreet-protest-signs/
67   US Constitution 1st Amendment.

Fascism

Examine OWS and the Tea Party, see which one is following in the footsteps of Fascism and which one is espousing the principles of liberty and personal freedom? Which group is using underhanded tactics to try to take down any opposition? Which group really stands for centralized government and which group for personal freedom?

Fascism is often used by the mainstream media to describe any group who espouses opinions not in step with the beliefs of the political Left. Fascism is portrayed as the "Far Right". In truth, Fascism is far Left; it is intrusive and limits personal freedom.

The Tea Party is not the political group who is requiring you to pay for someone else's healthcare, dictating what you can eat or drive or where to live. They are not the party who drives business into bankruptcy by over-regulation, and thereby devastating the job market.

Who is the governing party who picks and chooses winners and losers in businesses such as Solyndra, the now broke wind energy company? Who is the party who taxes people and business out of world competition? That would be the Democrats and their minions in OWS.

Chapter 4

Constitutional Republics and Capitalism

"Governments are instituted among Men, deriving their just Powers from the Consent of the Governed." —Thomas Jefferson, Declaration of Independence

Governments should reflect the will of the governed. They should provide security and safety so that citizens may raise families, and carry on commerce with relatively little intervention from government powers, foreign or domestic. These are the basic tenants of a healthy Constitutional Republic.

Republics are designed to protect the people from government overreach. The United States Constitution, when followed, allows more freedom to the people than any other formal form of government. The Constitution mandates rule by law. The sister of the republic is capitalism. It is the only system in which common citizens may change their station in life and obtain wealth by serving others and not by plunder.

"The smallest minority on earth is the individual. Those who deny individual rights cannot claim to be defenders of minorities."[68]

Democracies vs. Republics

Democracies do not have constitutional boundaries to protect the basic rights of citizens and boarder on mob rule because they are governed by the whims of simple majorities. Democracies leave minorities without constitutionally protected rights. They are volatile; often changes of power come with each election. These changes can be manifest by abuses to minorities and the losing party who have no lawful recourse once their party loses power. Because there is no rule of law, these governments are unstable as water, have short life expectancies, and almost always end with murder under aggressive tyrannical rulers.[69]

---

68   Ann Rand; Russian emigrant 1929-1979, author of *Atlas Shrugged*
69   The Freeman, Democracy's Road to Tyranny, By Erik Kuehnelt-Leddihn, May

Constitutional Republics rule by reason of Constitutional law, which protects individual rights. It does not matter which party is in power. If the republic is being properly executed, the rule of law is supreme; it prevents hostile takeovers by restricting the actions of the majority, or the government. Under a republic, the party in power cannot arbitrarily decide to restrict or rescind the Constitution or the rule of Law.

Republics are often miss-spoken as democracies. In fact, progressives and communists around the world have intentionally referred to Republics as Democracies. It is not because they have miss-spoken or do not understand the difference. It is a reference with malice to convince an unlearned populous that we live under the rules of democracy and not under a republic.

Because of the knowledge and education of our Founders, they understood the difference between democracies and republics and they carefully crafted a Constitutional Republic.

Modern thinkers of today would have us believe that winning an election allows the prevailing party to rule without reference to established laws. Just three days after President Obama's inauguration in January of 2009, Obama stated: "Elections have consequences"[70]

President Obama made this statement suggesting that because he had won a presidential election he had authority to do anything he wanted without regard to the rule of law. Over the coming years, President Obama would follow this line of thinking and would become the most abusive and repressive President in the history of the United States. President Obama would rule as a dictator and not as President. He would ignore Congress and our weak Congress would allow him to rule as if they did not exist. President Obama made this statement to congress in 2014:

> One of the things I'll be emphasizing in the meeting is the fact that we are not just going to be waiting for legislation; in order to make sure that we're providing Americans the kind of help

1, 1998

70   http://www.washingtonpost.com/wp-dyn/content/article/2010/10/25/AR2010102502408.html

that they need. I've got a pen and I've got a phone. And I can use that pen to sign executive orders and take executive actions and administrative actions that move the ball forward. [71]

This reckless attitude of self-serving superiority over the people was one of the realities the Founders realized in the disposition of man. Even good men can be corrupted by power and the superiority of attitude it breeds. This was one of the reasons the Founders choose a republic over a democracy.

In a proper functioning republic, Congress, comprised of both Democrats and Republicans, should do their constitutional duty and impeach any president who begins to assume powers he does not possess, or who starts acting as a dictator and circumventing the congressional process.

By the nature of their structure, Constitutional Republics purposely make the legislative process lengthy and slow so that laws can be properly vetted before being brought to a vote for passage or defeat. Deadlock or the slow process of debate is a positive, not a negative attribute of government. Deadlock means that our congress is working and not just becoming a rubber stamp for tyrannical Executive or Judicial branches.

A glaring example of dismissing the vetting process is The Affordable Care Act. This law was one of the most perversely passed laws in American history. The Affordable Care Act, also known as "Obama Care", was passed by an illegal act of the Senate.

Senate Majority leader Harry Reid (D-Nevada) had to change Senate rules to pass the measure by a simple majority rather than the sixty votes as prescribed in the Senate rules. All was going as planned in the Democrat-held Senate until Senator Edward Kennedy (D- Massachusetts) had the audacity to die on Harry Reid and President Obama.

After his death, Kennedy was replaced in a special election by Scott Brown (R-Massachusetts) this threw a wrench in the works because now Senate Democrats were one vote short. Harry Reid

---

71   : http://dailycaller.com/2014/01/14/obama-declares-congress-redundant-ive-got-a-pen-and-ive-got-a-phone-video/#ixzz30cjOcmCp

and the Democrats dominating the Senate simply changed the rules again and used what is called the Reconciliation Rule. This rule is to be used only for budget items and requires only fifty-one votes.

Because laws require sixty votes in the Senate using the Reconciliation Rule, the Senate illegally passed the bill by only fifty-nine votes.

Alcee Hastings of the House Senate Rules Committee stated, "We're making up the rules as we go along."[72]

Furthermore, the House and Senate bills were not the same bill. The paranoid Senate leadership knew the House would not pass the bill as it was written in the Senate, so Harry Reid and the Democrats simply ignored the House bill and passed their own version as though the House version did not exist.[73]

Under provisions of the Affordable Care Act, the President, Congress, and many other government officials exempted themselves from this intrusive legislation; however, under the Constitutional Republic, all citizens and officials, elected and non-elected, are bound by the rules of law as prescribed in the Constitution. It was the intent of the Founders that all people including government officials be subject to any law legally enacted.[74]

There is no prevision in the US Constitution for any elected officer or official to be exempt from any laws governing the people. When President Obama or any other official changes or picks and chooses which laws they will enforce, they are in contempt of the same Constitution they swore to uphold.

"If, to please the people, we offer what we ourselves disapprove, how can we afterwards defend our work? Let us raise a standard to which the wise and honest can repair. The event is in the hands of God" (George Washington's 1787 Statement to delegates to the Constitutional Convention). [75]

---

72   http://www.crawfordbroadcasting.com/Vecchio_Archives/How percent20Obamacare percent20Became percent20Law.pdf

73   The Washington Post, The house has voted 54 Times in four years on Obamacare, By Ed O'Keefe, March 21, 2014

74   Article 4 Section 1 Clause 1 US Constitution

75   http://www.faithofourfathers.net/washington.html

The free market

"If all men were angels we would need no government" (Federalist Papers, Number 10) [76]

"Prior to Capitalism the way people amassed great wealth was by looting, plundering, and enslaving their fellow man. Capitalism made it possible to become wealthy by serving your fellow man." Walter E Williams.[77]

From the invention of the Steam engine to the latest computer, the riches obtained by the inventors have been dwarfed by the benefits to the common man. This is the legacy of capitalism, the ability to provide a richer life for oneself while serving others.

The government's role in a constitutional republic is extremely limited. The federal government exists to protect the several states from hostilities from other nations. It is given the power to declare war and protect the country. The other constitutional purpose is to protect individual rights, stop illegal monopolies, protect patents, and protect the rights of people to keep the profits of their labor, whether employees or employers.

Free market, or capitalism, is the right to try, the right to buy, the right to sell, and the right to fail.

Anyone who has owned or managed a business—from a lemonade stand to a corporate giant—soon learns the lessons of customer satisfaction and finances. If you produce a bad product or service, if costumers are not happy, the business will fail. If a product sells for less than the cost to create it, the business will fail. In a free market system, competitors will continue to find better ways to serve customers with better and safer products at lower costs. Established businesses need to be fluid and smart to see changes and adapt to them or go broke. This is called competition. It is what drives inventions and innovation.

---

76   The Federalist Papers, (Alexander Hamilton, 2003) page 42
77   http://www.goodreads.com/quotes/685945-prior-to-capitalism-the-way-people-amassed-great-wealth-was

In a communist or socialist society, business is owned and controlled by the government. When government owns and controls business, where is the incentive that drives improvements and inventions? In a socialist society, there is no competition to drive innovation. Without competition, productivity slows, quality decreases, and prices generally inflate. Russia has long been the pirate of the world, stealing secrets from the West. Why should an individual work to invent a product if the proceeds of the invention will be confiscated by the state? In recent years, China has switched much of their socialist economy to a free market capitalist system. The results have been an explosion of prosperity in their economy.

One of the frauds that have been perpetrated on the American people is the sanctimonious assumption that working for a nonprofit company is superior to working for a for-profit company. What does a nonprofit company do? What do they create? How are they contributing to the economy? If the employee of a nonprofit company really believes they are superior to those who work for profit companies, why do these employees require compensation for their work?

Most nonprofit companies do not produce products that create new money, or services that make life better for the common man.

With the exception of the few companies who truly give compassionate service, almost all other nonprofit companies are tax shelters who pay their chairmen and chairwomen some of the highest compensation in the world. Most employees, whether they work for a profit or nonprofit company, expect to be paid for their time and labor.

Any money paid to an employee above the basic expenses of survival, also known as food and shelter, is profit. Almost all workers are paid a profit on their labor; this allows the employee to save for retirement and make upgrades in their living standard.

Most nonprofit companies pay little or no tax. Most are

service by nature. They themselves produce nothing. If a company is truly nonprofit, how does it grow and contribute to the overall health of the economy of the country. Many nonprofit companies pay exorbitant wages to CEOs, who are almost non-existent as far as actively running the company or entity. The following are examples of so called nonprofit companies and the compensation paid to their CEOs.

Company	CEO	Salary per year
Good Will	Marck Curran	$2,300,000.00
Sloan…Cancer Inst.	Peter Scardino MD	$2,207,147.00
UNICEF	Caryl M Stern	$1,200,000.00
Wild life Conservation Soc.	Steve E Sanderson	$1,163,666.00
United Way Worldwide	Brian Gallager	$1,035,347.00
American Red Cross	Marsha J Evans	$651,957.00
The United Way	Brian Gallagher	$375,000.00 [78][79]

The following are true non-profit organizations

Salvation Army	Todd Bassett	$13,000
American Legion	National Commander	$0
Veterans of Foreign Wars	National Commander	$0
The Vietnam Veterans	National Commander	$0

78   http://www.charitywatch.org/hottopics/Top25.html
79   http://urbanlegends.about.com/library/bl_charities_salaries.htm

St Jude's Research Hospital 100 percent of donations go to treatment of children

Ronald McDonald House 100 percent goes for housing of parents attending their critical children in hospitals

Lions Club International 100 percent for medical missions around the world[80]

The last seven companies on this nonprofit list pay little in financial compensation but pay great benefits in personal satisfaction. In addition to these companies, there are also tens of thousands of Americans who volunteer for little or no financial compensation in their communities to man their local ambulance, fire, search and rescue and other essential organizations. Many search and rescue volunteers personally pay almost all of their own expenses to save the lives of others. These are truly nonprofit, but few people turn to these organizations for a career.

For-profit companies pay money to taxes, investors, and labor. These are the companies producing the goods, services, and products we use every day. These are the businesses feeding the world, building the cars, building our homes, making clothes, cell phones, computers, and the list goes on and on. Ironically, these are the companies that are kicked around, over-taxed and over-regulated by federal and state governments. In spite of this targeting, they continue to make our lives better, cleaner, and healthier. These companies invent products that keep our air and water the cleanest in the world.

Very few things of great importance have been invented by government. However, government loves to create oversight. The wheel was not invented by government. Here is a list of items created by the private sector which government had no hand in but now want to regulate.

1. Time zones were created by the railroads. Prior to the coming

of the railroads as we moved across United States and the world 12:00 noon was where you were when the sun was overhead. With the coming of the railroad schedules had to be precise, so under the direction of the private sector, time zones were established in 1883. However, it was not until 1918 that congress officially adopted the time zone system. This time zone system would eventually be adopted around the world into twenty-four time zones. Without time zones, modern travel would be almost impossible.[81]

2. Canning of produce and meats was invented by a French confectioner and adopted by food companies to stop spoilage. This decreased the loss of products, which increased profits. With canning, products could be shipped and stored long after their normal shelf life would have expired. When adopted by governments, it made it possible for armies to fight with little regard to where the food was grown. Canning cut waste and created a clean and healthy food supply for the masses of humanity.[82]

3. The steam engine was created by a private inventor, Robert Fulton, not the government. This invention shrunk the world, increased productivity, made life better for millions, and was the gateway to modern cheap electricity, which manifestly improved the lives of everyday people.[83]

4. The internal combustion engine was a pollution cutting invention and the key to abating world hunger. With the internal combustion engine, the grain belt in America and other areas of the world now has the ability to produce enough food to feed the world. Clean fuels such as natural gas replaced

81   http://www.history.com/this-day-in-history/railroads-create-the-first-time-zones, http://www.timeanddate.com/time/time-zones-history.html , Accessed March 15, 2015

82   http://nchfp.uga.edu/publications/nchfp/factsheets/food_pres_hist.html, Accessed March 15, 2015

83   http://www.pbs.org/wgbh/theymadeamerica/whomade/fulton_hi.html Accessed March 15, 2015

wood and coal for heating and cooking, air conditioning, the harnessing of electricity, home insulation, electric lights, and the list goes on including almost everything we use in our daily lives. These were invented by individuals, not governments.

5. Almost all diseases were discovered and their cures found by private institutions. In 1855, Cholera was proven to be a waterborne disease by Dr. John Snow. In the 1880s, Louis Pasteur proved through Germ Theory how germ pathogens could be transmitted through water. This was the beginning of attention to water purification. It started in the private sector.[84]

Personal liberty, morality and government by the people are the founding principles of America. These principles in a capitalist system are the components allowing the poor to prosper and take themselves from poverty to prosperity.

The Patriot Act and the dismemberment of the Constitution

On September 11, 2001 Muslim extremists skyjacked four passenger jets. They flew two jet liners into the Twin Towers in New York City. Another was flown into the Pentagon. A fourth airliner was brought down when the passengers realized that the plane had been hijacked was going to be crashed into an important U.S. building. These patriotic heroes chose not to comply with the demands of the hijackers. A group of men on the plane rushed the skyjackers, which led to the jetliner crashing in a Pennsylvania field rather than into its intended target.

In response to the 9-11 attack, President George W. Bush passed the Patriot act. This response did stop some further terrorist actions, but at what cost to freedom? Decisions made in the political world often create a domino effect that is hard to break away from. The Patriot act was one of those dominos that has created one of the largest breaches of personal liberty America has ever witnessed.

84   http://www.epa.gov/safewater/consumer/pdf/hist.pdf

Under the Patriot Act President Bush created the Department of Homeland Security (DHS). The DHS was sold to America as a clearinghouse for terroristic information which was to be disseminated to law enforcement. This author was also duped by the assumption that the government could be trusted with this much sensitive information.

It wasn't long before DHS had taken on a life of its own. Along with the National Security Agency (NSA) in 2015, it is capturing your personal text messages and phone numbers. NSA is also monitoring, collecting, and storing personal emails from American citizens.[85] Collecting this information is a clear violation of at least the first and fourth amendments. The patriot act and the legislation following it have devastated personal liberty.

The Patriot act opened the door to the National Defense Authorization Act (NDAA). This act was passed and signed into law in December of 2011. Surprisingly, it had strong bipartisan support in both the House and Senate; President Obama signed this Act into law on New Year's Eve, 2011.

In 2012, America would see the most far-reaching laws against our personal civil liberties. This legislation allows the arrest, detention, and murder of American Citizens on American soil without warrant.[86] This act is a violation of the First, Fourth, Fifth, Sixth Seventh and Eighth Amendments.

This controversial act has been roundly criticized as unconstitutional by groups on both the political Left and Right. Of greatest concern was Section 1021 granting the United States military authority to exercise police powers on American soil. Upon order of the president and at his sole discretion, agents of the military are empowered to "detain until the end of hostilities anyone the president believes to have substantially supported al Qaeda, the

---

85   The Guardian, NSA collecting phone records of Millions of Verizon Customers, By Glenn Greenwald, June 6, 2013

86   http://en.wikipedia.org/wiki/National_Defense_Authorization_Act_for_Fiscal_Year_2012

Taliban, or associated forces."

In September 2012, Judge Katherine Forrest concluded that Section 1021 "failed to pass Constitutional muster because its broad language could be used to squash political dissent." In a statement clearly directed to lawmakers, she added:

"Section 1021 tries to do too much with too little – it lacks the minimal requirements of definition and scienter that could easily have been added, or could be added, to allow it to pass constitutional muster." That is, Congress failed perhaps deliberately– to define 'substantial support' of terrorist groups or describe those activities which might be construed as crossing the legal line. And no law may be enforced if those to whom it applies are unable to clearly understand what a violation of that law entails.[87]

If the courts were to apply this same logic to the IRS code and the Affordable Care Act, both would be ruled unconstitutional because a law could not be enforceable if it is not clear to those to whom it applies.

The Patriot Act and DHS are custom-built for any president or upstart tyrant who chooses to abuse his power by monitoring anything and everything the people say or do. Of course, the follow-up course of action is always punishment of all who dare to oppose the controlling regime.

The Tyrannical abuses of the IRS targeting conservative groups during the 2012 elections should have been a wakeup call for all Americans. Remember, if the party in power can use a segment of a law or an agency to punish or intimidate American citizens, no citizen is safe. Power and parties change, the people you are abusing today may be the rulers tomorrow.

All Americans, Democrat and Republican need to demand that this abuse of power be stopped and those who authorized it imprisoned.

87   Western Journalism, Judge Strikes down NDAA, rules Obama must obey Constitution, By Doug Book May 19, 2012

Power corrupts and absolute power corrupts absolutely

In 2014 as the investigation into the IRS scandal unfolded, there was stonewalling and lying from the President on down. Shortly after the scandal became public knowledge in 2012 President Obama told news organizations that his first knowledge of the targeting was when he saw it on news reports. The President said it was outrageous and those involved would be brought to justice.[88]

The Whitehouse and IRS officials laid the blame on a local IRS branch that targeted groups without the knowledge of their superiors. In the 2014 IRS investigation, this information was found to be false. The trail of lies led to the top IRS official, Lois Leaner. Strong evidence suggests President Obama lied to the American people; he had known about the abuses long before he acknowledged them.

On February 1, 2014, President Obama changed his stance on the IRS when he said there was "not even a smidgen of corruption at the IRS." President Obama was saying this as the FBI and Justice Department was actively investigating the IRS targeting allegations. The President went on to try to defend his earlier debunked statement that the targeting was only done by a local office.

If it did not seem corrupt enough, picked to head up the investigation was Democrat donor and Obama supporter, Barbara Bosserman. The House Oversight and Government Reform Subcommittee wanted to know why Bosserman, who obviously had a conflict of interest, was heading the Committee.[89]

This is how tyrannical governments work. There is no rule of law that officials are held accountable to. If the constitution were

---

88   CNN politics, Obama: Alleged IRS political targeting Outrageous, CNN Washington Bureau, May 14, 2013
89   The Christian Post, Republicans, Reporters ask About FBI Investigation into IRS after Obama claims not a smidgen of corruption' By Napp Azworth, February 5, 2014

being strictly followed, this president and the IRS officials would be in prison. Because of the absolute corruption in Washington by both the Democrats and establishment Republicans, nothing of consequence will be done about this or any other scandal perpetrated by President Obama and his minions. President Obama and the Democratic Party have continued to stonewall the investigations and call it a witch-hunt that is racially motivated.[90]

Taxation without representation

In 1776, America fought a devastating war with her mother country, England. One of the major reasons for this war was the requirement that the people pay taxes while not being allowed to be involved in decision making, or even to vote for governors and other stewards of the people. The governors made rules that violated the basic tenants of personal freedoms of the people. The people were given no recourse in the courts or in the ballot box to challenge these rules.

There is great danger in amassing power in unelected officials. In the United States today we are allowing unelected officials to make laws and act as judge, jury, and executioner in the performance of those laws while the people have little recourse in court and none at the ballot box. Federal agencies such as the Environmental Protection Agency (EPA), Federal Emergency Management Agency (FEMA), Bureau of Land Management (BLM) and all other acronym agencies were created by lazy congresses and tyrannical presidents. They are all constitutionally illegal. These agencies make laws and create and collect fines and penalties. The Constitution does not prohibit agencies from existing as advisors to congress; however, after the preamble, the first order of business of the U.S. Constitution is as follows: "All Legislative Powers herein granted shall be vested in a Congress of the United States, which shall consist of a Senate and House of Representatives."[91]

---

90   Newsmax, Congress: Obama Stonewalling IRS Probes, by Greg Richter, May 10, 2015
91   United States Constitution, National Center for Constitutional Studies, 2nd addition 2005, Article 1, Section 1

There is no provision for congress to delegate this sacred power of making laws. Every law, good or bad, almost always restricts freedom. This is why congress is charged with this special power; they are accountable to the people.

As soon as an agency makes a single rule or regulation, it is in violation of the law. When any attempt is made to impose fines or penalties, they are in direct violation of Article One Section Seven of the Constitution: "All bills for raising revenue shall originate in the House of Representatives"[92]

These agencies are running rough-shod over the American People. They are without accountability, they cannot be voted out of office, and the judicial system is so corrupted that it is almost impossible to win a court case against them.[93]

The EPA and a mass of other federal agencies are ruling our lives at their leisure. They are doing the Government's business in the war on America with impunity. These agencies shut down industries, impose fines, and generally raise hell in the lives of the American people, who rarely have any judicial recourse.

These agencies are not accountable to the people. They are not voted into office, yet they wield the same power as elected officials. They tax and regulate as though they had been placed in office by a majority of the populace who unanimously agree with their programs. However, this is not the case.

The case for taxation without representation is made now through these illegal government agencies.[94]

---

92   United States Constitution, National Center for Constitutional Studies, 2nd addition 2005, Article 1, Section 7
93   Washington Times, EPA Facing fire for armed raid on mine in Chicken Alaska: By Valerie Richardson, October 11, 2013
94   The Heritage Foundation, From Administrative State to Constitutional Government, By Joseph Postell, PHD, Dec 12, 2012

Chapter 5

The Constitution of the United States of America

For years, America had been a festering boil and now in 1775 it was about to pop. Her mother country had imposed unfair taxes, and army regulators rode rough shod over the people. Searches were made without warrant and the people were required to quarter (provide food and shelter with no reimbursement) to soldiers of the British Empire.

On April 19, 1775 the match that would set fire to the tinder was struck. British Commander General Gage marched his soldiers twenty miles from Boston to Lexington with the intent of gathering all firearms from the American arsenal at Concord. At Lexington and then at Concord, the British met resistance from American minutemen. At the Old North Bridge in Concord the first shots of the Revolutionary War were fired. After a series of bloody engagements, the British started their twenty-mile retreat to Boston. While en route to their destination, they were continually fired upon by minutemen waiting in ambush. At the conclusion of the battle, the British had 273 casualties, Americans casualties numbered only ninety-three. The shot heard around the world had been fired, and the American Revolutionary War had begun.[95]

A little over a year later, on July 4, 1776 representatives of the thirteen American Colonies voted unanimously in favor of a Declaration of Independence. It was signed by fifty-six of the leading men in America. These men would come to be known as the Founding Fathers of America. This formal claim for independence threw America headlong into a war with the most powerful army and navy in the world. If they failed to be victorious, the fate of the signers would have been torture and death.

By 1787, it had been twelve years since the thirteen colonies formally declared independence from England. They had been governing under the Articles of Confederation. This form of

---

95   http://www.nps.gov/mima/north-bridge-questions.htm Accessed Jan 9, 2015

Government had proven wholly inadequate to the governing of the nation. The State Representatives concluded that it was better to write a new constitution than to attempt to repair the fallacies of the original Articles of Confederation.

The writers of the United States Constitution did not write the document as we see legal documents written today. It was not written to hide information and confuse the people. It was not written with a hidden agenda. Quite the opposite: it was written in simple language, a language the common people with a frontier education could read and understand.

The U.S. Constitution is the oldest and most concise constitution in the world. It is the supreme law of the land and all other laws are subservient to it. A simple but complete document, it encompasses the rules of our government. The entire document is about 4400 words and can be read in under an hour by a person with an adequate eighth-grade education. The Constitution is a document insuring freedom and liberty for the people by the restrictions it places on the federal government.

Unlike almost all governments before, and since, the American Constitution was unique in that it restricted government to the will of the governed; not the governed to the will of government!

The genius of the document is its simplicity, balance, and self-healing abilities. Self-governance requires self-interest which is not to be confused with selfishness. Self-interest allows charity, goodness, and virtue to be rewarded. Selfishness encourages greed, covetousness, and lawlessness.

Except for those rights specifically outlined in the Constitution, the federal government is restricted to the will of the states.[96] Hence, we are called the United States plural, not a United State, singular. The States is plural because we are an entity with divisions of power among states and federal government. Each state is sovereign unto its self. The Founders understood the tendency of man to seek power, even when that power is restricted by the laws

---

96   United States Constitution, National Center for Constitutional Studies, 2nd addition 2005, Amendment 10

and the will of the people.[97]

Governmental powers always gravitate to the center. To accomplish this, governments move power and responsibility away from the people and local governments by establishing federal entities to address local issues. An example of this gravitation is the federal intervention in education, healthcare, welfare services, and natural resources within state boundaries.

It is ironic and indicative of this overreach that the federal government wants to take personal responsibilities from the people and states but fails to administer the money of the United States as required of Congress under Article 1, Section 8.

"Congress shall have power ... to coin money, regulate the value thereof, and of foreign coin." [98]

The Constitution

The first item addressed in the Constitution is the power to legislate. It is explicate: all legislative power, or the power to make laws rests with congress. There is no provision for Congress to delegate this power.

The second order of business in the Constitution dictates how representatives are chosen. Called the Lower, or Peoples, House, these representatives are chosen by direct vote of the people from their respective congressional districts. It is the lower house that is vested with the power to purpose legislation for taxation and revenue.[99] Because they control the power of the purse, these representatives have to face their voters every two years. At these two-year intervals, the informed or uninformed voter can choose either to re-elect or reject these representatives.

Article 1, Section 2 is often misquoted by knowledgeable people who haven't read the text or for political purposes; they

---

97   Federalist Papers, Bantam Dell, Random house, 1982 Federalist, 15 Hamilton, Page 86, 87
98   United States Constitution, National Center for Constitutional Studies, 2nd addition 2005, Article 1, section 8
99   United States Constitution, National Center for Constitutional Studies, 2nd addition 2005, Article 1, section 7

intentionally misquote the section to disturb and/or incite their audiences. Attorney Benjamin Crump, attorney for the family of Michael Brown, erroneously claimed the constitution declared "African Americans were to be considered only three-fifths of a man."[100] [101] Mr. Crump is not the first to make this false claim of racism by the Founders.

Al Sharpton and numerous so-called black leaders have also incorrectly quoted this section. However, this section never mentions Blacks, Negros, African Americans or, any other race. It instructs how to count the whole number of people for the purpose of congressional representation. This section was intentionally placed in the constitution to temporally satisfy the southern slave states, but to bring about the eventual eradication of slavery. Article One, Section Two, Clause Three reads, "According to their respective numbers, which shall be determined by adding to the whole number of free persons, including those bound to service for a term of years and excluding Indians not taxed, three fifths of all other persons."[102]

It should be noted that the "all other persons" phrase does not mention blacks or slaves. With great compassion and exactness, the exclusion mentions only all others who are not free men. Determining representatives this way insured the South would suffer a handicap when counting citizens for representation, thereby depriving the region of votes until the slaves became free men.

Slavery

Lincoln called it, "the rattlesnake under the table of the Founders."

In 1787, involuntary servitude, or slavery, was an acceptable practice and was allowed in almost every nation in the world. Since

---

100   http://www.twitlonger.com/show/n_1s5v36a Accessed Jan 9, 2016
101   Author's Note: Ferguson, Missouri, 2014: Eighteen-year-old Michael Brown was being questioned by police because he fit the description of the suspect in a recent robbery. Michael assaulted the investigating officer and tried to take his gun. A fight ensued and Michael was shot and killed by the officer.
102   United States Constitution, National Center for Constitutional Studies, 2nd addition 2005, Article 1, Section 2

the beginning of recorded history, slavery had been practiced in various forms of severity in almost every nation on earth.

The ultimate goal of the Founders was to abolish slavery in the United States. The Founders outlined the constitution with a provision including self-serving events, which in time would prove favorable to the South to abolish that horrific institution.

Slavery was a tremendous obstacle for those who were writing the American Constitution. The Founders agreed "all men", whether they be white, black, yellow, or red, were meant to be free, and "all men" were created equal by their creator. However, in 1787 there was strong opposition in the American South against abolishing slavery. This opposition was led by congressional Democrats, especially those from the southern states. The Founders believed that if the slaves were not counted as full citizens for the purpose of congressional representation, eventually there would be enough overwhelming congressional votes in the free North to abolish the barbaric practice in the United States.

Constitutional balance includes three Branches of Government:
- Executive: President
- Congressional: Consisting of the upper and lower houses
- Judicial: Supreme Court

The Congressional Branch

The lower house is designed under the Constitution to represent the people of each individual legislative district in a state. House representatives only serve a term of two years. This direct representation of each voting district keeps the house closer to the people. For this reason, it is called "the People's House."

This is where every vote counts. A large metropolitan area may hold a majority of the population of the state; however, because of legislative districts, the outlying areas and counties of the state are also represented.

Every two years, each representative has the opportunity to

be re-elected or rejected by the people from his or her own district. Legislative district voters should take this opportunity to meet or personally listen to all of the representative candidates during the voting process.[103] This is the voting public's opportunity to change or keep a given course followed by their public officials. [104][105]

All bills for revenue are to originate in the Lower House. The lower house holds the purse strings of the federal government. If the executive implements or authorizes plans, orders, or agencies which the house believes are not constitutional or in the best interest of their constituents; it is not only their right, but their sacred duty and obligation to refuse to fund that order.[106] This is called "balance of power."

Upper House

The Senate was designed to represent the state to the federal government. Under the original Constitution, senators were voted in by the state legislature, not by popular vote. This made the senators responsible to the states, not to the federal government.[107]

The 17th Amendment changed the election of senators from appointment by the state legislature to a popular vote by the populace of the state. This act severely diluted the delicate balance of power written into the constitution by making both houses elected by direct popular vote. Because a senator is now voted in by the entire state, it is possible for a few large cities to dominate a senatorial election, thereby diluting the voice of those in less populated or rural areas. By changing the way senators are elected, we now have representatives of the federal government to the state rather than representatives

---

103   US Constitution Article 1: Section 2
104   http://fcnl.org/resources/newsletter/oct07/do_emails_and_letters_to_congress_work/ accessed Jan 9, 2016
105   Author's Note: The greatest impact an individual can have on the representative process is by calling or writing their congressmen directly. It is estimated that each letter or call represents about 10,000 constituents. Only about 5 percent of constituents ever contact their congressman.
106   US constitution Article 1 Section 7
107   US constitution Article 1 section 3-6

from the state to the federal government.[108]

This amendment brought us closer to a democracy and further from a republic or representative government as established under the U.S. Constitution.

The Executive Branch / President and the Electoral College

Article 2, Section 1 of the Constitution dictates how a president will be elected and what his duties are to the office.

The Electoral College was designed to empower the people in presidential elections. Each state was allowed the freedom to establish how their Electoral College would be implemented, but the original concept was to have the vote of each legislative district represented, not a "winner-take-all" for the state. This district or electoral vote allowed the rural counties to be equal with the larger cities in casting a vote for president. If the Electoral College was correctly implemented, each state would hold the same importance to every presidential candidate. The results would be better representation of all the people at the federal level.

If a state had ten representatives and two senators, that state would be allowed twelve electoral votes. If four districts voted Democrat and six voted Republican, these would be counted respectively to each party. The two senator electoral votes would have reflected the conscience of the state representatives.

The office of President is a sacred trust. It is given to a person who has been voted into that office to do the work of all the people of the United States. The Constitution requires that before he is allowed to execute his authority in the office of President he must take the following oath found in Article 2, Section 1, Clause 10 of the United States Constitution: "I do solemnly swear (or affirm) that I will faithfully execute the Office of President of the United States, and will to the best of my ability, preserve, protect and defend the Constitution of the United States."[109]

---

108   US Constitution Article 1: Section 3 / Changed by the 17th amendment 4/8/1913
109   United States Constitution, National Center for Constitutional Studies, 2nd

By taking this oath, the President has sworn to uphold and protect the Constitution not the government, but the Constitution. The Founders understood the weakness of man and the strength of the Constitution.

Abuse of executive orders

Almost all Presidents have used executive orders for what we might call light or regular house cleaning. These orders have traditionally been used to add or change administrative personnel, changing of directives within a regulatory branch, or clarification of an existing law.

The executive branch does not possess the constitutional authority to use executive orders to make, break, or substantially change any law.

In 1952, President Truman's government order 10340 was contested in the Supreme Court with Youngtown Sheet & Tub Co. verses Sawyer. President Truman attempted to put all steel mills in the United States under government control. The Supreme Court ruled the order invalid because this amounted to a law, and "all laws" have to originate in Congress, not in the executive branch. Following are some examples of executive orders that are treated as laws but were not properly executed under the Constitution.[110]

- EXECUTIVE ORDER 10995 allows the government to seize and control the communication media. (1962 President Kennedy)
- EXECUTIVE ORDER 10997 allows the government to take over all electrical power, gas, petroleum, fuels and minerals. (1962 President Kennedy)
- EXECUTIVE ORDER 11000 allows the government to mobilize civilians into work brigades under government supervision. (1962 President Kennedy)
- EXECUTIVE ORDER 11004 allows the Housing and Finance Authority to relocate communities, build new

addition 2005, Article 2 section 1 clause 10
110   Youngstown sheet & Tube Co. V Sawyer, 343 U.S. 579 (1952) https://supreme.justia.com/cases/federal/us/343/579/case.html

housing with public funds, designate areas to be abandoned, and establish new locations for populations. (1962 President Kennedy)

- EXECUTIVE ORDER 11921 allows the Federal Emergency Management Agency (FEMA) to develop plans to establish control over the mechanisms of production and distribution, of energy sources, wages, salaries, credit and the flow of money in U.S. financial institution in any undefined national emergency. It also provides that when a state of emergency is declared by the President, Congress cannot review the action for six months.111 112 (1976 President Ford)

Americans, regardless of political affiliation, Democrat, Republican, conservative or liberal: beware! This order, 11921 is custom-made for a ruthless dictator. When put into action, our republican form of government will become non-existent. We will lose all of our civil rights. These types of executive orders allow a president to become a dictator with no controls or oversight. The complacency of Congress in allowing these orders to go unchallenged shows complete disregard for the rule of law and the sacred protections of the people under the Constitution.

When Presidential Executive orders are not questioned or stopped by Congress, Congress becomes an enabler and paves the road to tyranny. As previously discussed, the President is not allowed to make any law. It is the role of congress to take time and properly evaluate all potential laws.

The slow and occasionally heated debates of potential laws— often called, "gridlock"—are not the nemesis to constitutional law that the press, and government authorities claim it to be. This is the constitutionally prescribed and methodic process of making laws is the legal mechanism to slow the growth of Government and control potential laws, so they can be properly vetted before becoming ratified.

---

111   at http://www.snopes.com/politics/obama/executiveorders. asp#sKAZbhJxjpe4sldU.99
Reference: https://www.votetocracy.com/blog/79/understanding-executive-orders-and-the-powers-they-grant
112   US Constitution Article 1: Section 1

Judicial Branch

Of the three branches of government, the judicial branch was designed with the least power. "Judges both of the supreme and inferior courts shall hold their offices during good behavior"[113] The judicial branch has neither the right to make laws, nor the power of the purse to tax or fund legislation.

It was obvious that good character was of supreme importance in the selecting of judges. Supreme Court Justices are nominated by the President and are required to be ratified by Congress.

For years, the Supreme Court has been making rulings that are inconsistent with the U.S. Constitution, which they have sworn to uphold. The courts have been making laws by becoming activist courts. Any time a judge becomes a court activist and rules against the letter or spirit of the Constitution, they should be immediately removed from office because they have shown bad behavior in failing to uphold the Constitution.

When a Justice throws the U.S. Constitution under the bus and regards the constitutions, and laws of other countries above the United States, it is time to impeach that judge. For example, in 2012, when Justice Ginsburg told Egyptian authorities, "I would not look to the U.S. Constitution if I were drafting a constitution in the year 2012," her comments are consistent with her disdain of U.S. Law and the Constitution.[114] The Justice stated to the Egyptian ministry she "weighs foreign law as well as U.S. law when forming a legal opinion."[115]

In these statements, Justice Ginsburg has shown a general hostility toward the U.S. Constitution, which she has sworn to uphold and defend.

From the 1962 ruling against prayer in school to the 2012

---

113   US Constitution Article 3: Section 1

114   http://www.foxnews.com/politics/2012/02/06/ginsburg-to-egyptians-wouldnt-use-us-constitution-as-model/

115   http://jacksonville.com/forums/rants-raves-forum/2012-02-06/ginsburg-wouldnt-use-us-constitution-model, researched February 23, 2015

ruling in favor of the Affordable Care Act, Congress has turned a blind eye as the courts assert power by ruling from the bench. The courts, not finding any opposition, have run rough-shod over the Congress and the will of the people. In recent years, the Supreme Court has almost become an extension of the executive branch or office of the President.

Over the years, the Supreme Court has made some illegal rulings which were not consistent with the spirit or letter of the law of the Constitution. Just because the Supreme Court makes a ruling does not make it correct. An example of an unconstitutional ruling would be the slave case of Dread Scott.

The 1857 slave holder, John Sandford took his slave, Dread Scott to the free state of Illinois. Once in Illinois, where slavery was illegal, Dread Scott sued for his freedom. After court battles lasting almost ten years, the United States Supreme Court ruled that Mr. Scott would remain a slave and had no rights as a free man.

In the fifty-page court opinion, US Supreme Court Justice Taney, a Democrat, ruled: "Dread Scott was not a United States citizen and because of his race could never become one… that as a black man, Scott was so inferior (that he Dread Scott) had no rights which the white man was bound to respect"[116]

In the case of the 2012 Affordable Care Act, there was a provision for a penalty to be assessed for citizens who did not buy health care. U. S. Supreme Court Justice Roberts changed the wording of the legislation from penalty to tax.[117] This word change calling the penalty a tax is a direct violation of the restrictions placed on the judicial branch by the Constitution. By using the word tax Justice Roberts created a law that included a tax. Roberts should be impeached for assuming power that he is not vested with. This violation of ethics constitutes "bad behavior."[118] As discussed earlier, bad behavior by a justice is an impeachable offence.

---

116   America the Last Best Hope, Volume 1, Bennett, William J, Nelson Communications Inc, Pages 293, 294
117   Forbes, The Obamacare "Tax" That Chief Justice Roberts Invented is Still Unconstitutional, by Ilya Shapiro, May 12, 2014
118   US Constitution Article 1: Section 1

Chapter 6

The Bill of Rights

The most important minority in a nation is the individual.

After the signing of the Constitution on September 17, 1787, there were numerous amendments proposed to clarify to future generations both the spirit and intentions of the Founders regarding the rights of a free people and the individual states. These rights are not bestowed by man but are described by the Founders as God-given liberties, or rights. They were added to the Constitution as a clarification that God-given rights are not given by government and, therefore, cannot be taken by government. It is regrettable that many Americans regard these rights as negative liberties. This misconception is due to the restrictions that the Bill of Rights places on the federal government to ensure the rights of a free people.

The Bill of Rights constitutes the first ten amendments to the Constitution. As in the Constitution itself, the language of the amendments is simple; there is no ambiguity. Of the 160 amendments originally proposed to the Constitution, only ten were considered essential to be incorporated in the original document.

Of the original ten amendments the first and second were placed as a priority because enforcement of all other amendments, and the Constitution itself hinged upon the right of the people to keep the government in check. With freedom of speech and the ability of the people to keep and bear arms and ammunition they could defend the country against all enemies, both foreign and domestic.[119]

The right of the people to peaceably assemble

Amendment I

"Congress shall make no law respecting an establishment of religion, or prohibiting the free exercise thereof; or abridging

---

119   http://www.constitutionfacts.com/us-constitution-amendments/fascinating-facts/

the freedom of speech, or of the press; or the right of the people peaceably to assemble, and to petition the government for a redress of grievances."

The right of free speech for or against the government is a sacred trust. The people have the right to protest against the government without fear of reprisal by the Department of Justice, the President, or the Internal Revenue Service (IRS).[120] [121]

With the right of protest, the people are also required to be responsible. The right of protest does not allow protesters the right to destroy private or public property, nor to interrupt public commerce. Slander is not a protected right to yell fire in a crowd to cause a disturbance or panic is not protected. Simply put; your first amendment right ends, where my nose begins.

Religious freedom protects the right of the individual to choose where, what, and when to practice religious beliefs. This provision was designed to prevent the government from mandating what to believe or what religion could be practiced. The government is restricted from establishing or favoring one religion over another.

Religion is any belief system whether God-based or secular. Therefore, any belief system that is forced on the people or given preferential treatment by the government is unconstitutional.

In recent years, the federal government has been invaded by Christafobs.[122] Christafobs are those who have a meltdown any time Christian-based teaching or prayers are allowed in public places, especially in public schools.

Contrasting points of view are not tolerated by Christafobs, and they continually cry foul anytime the name of Christ is mentioned,

---

120   http://www.huffingtonpost.com/2014/08/02/lois-lerner-crazies_n_5644376.html

121   Author's Note: During the presidential elections of 2012, Lois Leaner was the Director of the Internal Revenue Service (IRS). Under her direction and instructions, the IRS targeted conservative groups, delaying applications for proper tax status. Ms. Leaner also ordered targeted audits on persons who gave money to Republican candidates. Learner's biased auditing slowed or stopped funding for conservative groups. These delays gave an unfair financial advantage to democratic groups, thus possibly changing the outcome of a national presidential election.

122   Christafob: a fear of anything Christian

especially in public school. Secularism, abortion, homosexuality, and climate change have replaced Christianity as the religion of choice in government funded schools. Secularism and its tenants are religions, sanctioned, and worse, mandated by the government in public schools. The use of the public schools to teach this religion is a complete bastardization of religious freedom as prescribed in the Constitution.

The first amendment was not written as a prohibition of God-based religion but as a prohibition of government to interfere with religion.[123]

Amendment II

"A well-regulated militia, being necessary to the security of a free state, the right of the people to keep and bear arms, shall not be infringed."[124] [125]

The right to bear arms is not a privilege given by government but a basic human right given by our creator. According to an opinion of the United States Supreme Court, bearing arms by the people is not only a right, but an obligation.

The Second Amendment does not exclude military weapons. Quite the opposite: the original intent was to include weapons "common" to the military, so the people could be called upon at any time to protect and defend the country and the Constitution from all enemies whether foreign or domestic.

The term, "militia" was understood by the Founders as all males between the ages of sixteen to sixty. It did not refer to what is now the National Guard or any other regular military entity. It was an army of the people. The U.S. Supreme Court made this very clear in the landmark opinion of the court in United States v. Miller, 1939.

---

123   US Constitution, 1st Amendment
124   US Constitution, 2nd Amendment
125   US Constitution, Article 1, Section 8, Clause 15

Opinion of the court

"The signification attributed to the term Militia appears from the debates in the Convention, the history and legislation of Colonies and States, and the writings of approved commentators. These show plainly enough that the Militia comprised all males physically capable of acting in concert for the common defense . . . when called for service these men were expected to appear bearing arms supplied by themselves and of the kind in common use at the time (Page 307 U.S. 180).

"The possession of arms also implied the possession of ammunition, and the authorities paid quite as much attention to the latter as to the former.

"Reserving to the States respectively, the Appointment of the Officers, and the Authority of training the militia . . . the citizens are required to supply their own firearms and ammunition in a type which is common to military standards (underlining added).[126]

"Clauses intended to insure the possession of arms and ammunition by all who were subject to military service appear (sic) in all the important enactments concerning military affairs. Fines were the penalty for delinquency."[127]

In this case, the Supreme Court makes it clear that it is the responsibility of the government to make certain that arms and ammunition common to the military are available and in ample supply to the common people.

This ruling also made clear that each state is responsible for training all adult males in military tactics. In our modern world that would include all interested females. States which do not offer some type of advanced training for its citizens are delinquent in their obligation to the nation. Government officials of any state restricting

126   US Constitution Article 1 Section 8 clause 15
127   http://supreme.justia.com/cases/federal/us/307/174/case.html United States Supreme Court, United States v. Miller, 307 U.S. 174, No 696, Argued March 30, 1939, decided May 15, 1939

gun and ammunition ownership in any way are in violation of the same constitution which they have sworn by solemn oath to uphold.

It was clear to the Founders that it was not productive to have people with antiquated arms and little or no ammunition. It should not be a surprise that most weapons common to the military look like military weapons. AR-15, AK-47, AR-10 rifles and 9mm, and 40cal semi-automatic loading pistols with detachable large-capacity magazines would be common to the military, and therefore, it is required by the Second Amendment that the people have access to and possess these types of arms and ammunition. Failure to possess updated weapons and ammunition is a violation of the law.

Therefore, any state, city, or federal entity that restricts or restrains these rights without due process, is in violation of the law. Due process includes restrictions placed by the courts on a specific individual because of an abuse or crime committed by that individual, which would restrict a certain right. However, this standard can only be applied to a convicted criminal where the state can show compelling evidence as to why a person should be restricted. [128]

Amendment III

"No soldier shall, in time of peace be quartered in any house without the consent of the owner, nor in time of war, but in a manner to be prescribed by law."

Prior to the Revolutionary War, the American colonists were often required to house and feed the British soldiers who were residing in the area. This was a great imposition to the people, which the Founders believed was an infringement upon the rights of free men.[129]

Amendment IV

"The right of the people to be secure in their persons, houses,

---

[128]   Author's Note: Most gun laws border on insanity. We restrict persons from firearms that may fire a 200-grain projectile, but allow that same person to drive a tanker truck that could be used as a 50,000-pound flammable projectile.

[129]   The Wars of America, Leckie, Robert, Castle Books 1998, Pages 83-87

papers, and effects, against unreasonable searches and seizures, shall not be violated, and no warrants shall issue, but upon probable cause, supported by oath or affirmation, and particularly describing the place to be searched, and the persons or things to be seized."

The fourth amendment insures that people would be secure in their homes and effects. Warrantless searches are a violation of the law. Without this protection, the police could invade your home at any time on what is called a "fishing expedition" to see if they can find any violation with which to arrest and prosecute you.

Peace officers can legally search your home or business only under certain conditions:

1. After presenting a judge with evidence that a law has been broken, and investigation reveals there is probable cause to believe evidence of a specific type is in your home or place of business, a judge is required to discern if the warrant meets the legal requirements.[130]

2. In the event of hot pursuit in which a suspect is actively fleeing police, the police have authority to follow the suspect into his residence or business; however, the right of hot pursuit needs to be expedient and cannot be unduly delayed.[131]

3. If the police know of a serious offence possibly endangering the lives or health of persons, or of evidence which will probably be destroyed if immediate action is not taken.[132]

4. Without a warrant, the use of aerial drones for surveillance is a blatant violation of the Fourth Amendment and should be vigorously prosecuted as a violation of civil rights.

5. Without a proper warrant, recording or keeping any records of phone, email or any other electronic device owned by U.S. citizens is a clear violation of the Fourth Amendment. Any government entity or personal caught using electronic surveillance without a specific warrant should be prosecuted to the fullest extent of the law.

---

130   Utah Criminal Code 77-23-210
131   Utah Criminal Code 77-9-3:A /
132   Utah Criminal Code 77-7-6:A-B

Amendment V

"No person shall be held to answer for a capital, or otherwise infamous crime, unless on a presentment or indictment of a grand jury, except in cases arising in the land or naval forces, or in the militia, when in actual service in time of war or public danger; nor shall any person be subject for the same offense to be twice put in jeopardy of life or limb; nor shall be compelled in any criminal case to be a witness against himself, nor be deprived of life, liberty, or property, without due process of law; nor shall private property be taken for public use, without just compensation."

Self incrimination

The Founders had seen the results of so called justice running over the basic rights of the people in Europe, England, and even in America. People accused of a crime were often forced to admit to crimes they had not committed. The use of force to obtain a confession was accomplished by torture. The accused would be forced to consider that the pain of denying a crime may be worse than the pain inflicted for restitution for the crime, hence the expression: "They put the thumbscrews to him." Thumbscrews were used to compress the thumbs until the pain was so intense that the accused would admit to most anything.

The Founders believed that accused persons should have the personal agency to choose to confess or deny crimes they were charged with. They also believed that no person in the justice system should have to testify against his or herself.

Double jeopardy

The Founders believed it was unjust and immoral for a person to be tried twice for the same crime. All evidence in a trial both for and against the accused should be assembled prior to its presentation to the jury. If a person is found not guilty of a crime, he cannot be tried again for that crime even if pertinent evidence is discovered at a later date.

This provision has been circumvented, by allowing different government entities to try a person twice for the same crime. This happens when the suspect is tried by the state courts and later tried for the same crime under federal statutes.

Private property

The Founders had a great respect for private property, for without the safety of private property, there can be no personal freedom or equity of law. Private property includes personal possessions, money, and real estate. The Founders believed private property ownership was a God-given right that should not be infringed upon except in cases that included a compelling public interest.

Any private property taken for public use must be compensated for at, or above market value. The personal right to property has been abused by all entities from local cities and counties, to the federal government.

When a government entity changes the usage of property, restricts traditional use, or takes any private property, without compensation and without a compelling public interest, this is a violation of individual civil rights. When a government agency designates private property as wetlands and restricts the traditional or designated use, the owner should be compensated. If the owner is not compensated, it is a violation of the Fifth Amendment.

The government is rarely challenged for violating private property. When they are challenged, the courts are stacked against the people. Most courts assume that government has the authority to take lands, and it is up to the property owner to prove otherwise. With each suit these agencies win, they become more abusive of American citizens.[133]

Amendment VI

133   http://insideclimatenews.org/news/20110531/epa-greenhouse-gas-ruling-endangerment-finding-texas-lawsuit, Referenced February 25, 2015

"In all criminal prosecutions, the accused shall enjoy the right to a speedy and public trial, by an impartial jury of the state and district wherein the crime shall have been committed, which district shall have been previously ascertained by law, and to be informed of the nature and cause of the accusation; to be confronted with the witnesses against him; to have compulsory process for obtaining witnesses in his favor, and to have the assistance of counsel for his defense."

The right to a speedy trial

The right to a speedy trial is important so that evidence does not go stale. Time is of the essence to prevent innocent persons from lingering in jail for an undue amount of time, and so the accused would not be kept in a state of uncertainty. It also serves justice to have the person either exonerated or condemned in a timely manner for the crime he or she is accused of.

Trials should be scheduled after hot tempers have cooled, but before evidence and passions have become so cold that the desire for justice has been lost. In our present system, trials for grievous crimes such as rape and murder are often postponed so long that people lose the passion for justice for the victims.

Public trials are the mechanism that best serves the accused and ensures proper treatment and fairness by keeping the justice system as transparent as possible. The right to face ones accusers and question them is paramount if justice is to be served in the courts of any land. Without this right, how could a person truly defend themselves?

The right to information about the nature of the crime is the only way defendants can prepare a proper defense against charges made against them. The right to counsel is the privileges of having an attorney defend the accused. This protects the defendants and insures that they are given every opportunity to prove their innocence.

National Defense Authorization Act

In 2012, Congress passed and President Obama signed in to law the National Defense Authorization Act. This act stripped American citizens of their civil rights under the First, Fourth, and Sixth Amendments. Section 1021 of this act gives the President the right to have American citizens arrested without warrant, deny them the right of council, and to detain them indefinitely.

"Section 1021 allows for the 'indefinite detention of American citizens without due process at the discretion of the President.' This section has been challenged as a violation of constitutional principles and the United States Bill of Rights. The indefinite detention clause has been broadly denounced nationally and internationally."[134]

In 2015, Senator Mike Lee (R-UT) wrote legislation to rescind these obtrusive elements of the NDAA. At the writing of this book, it has yet to be voted on.

Following are some of the civil rights violations now legal under NDAA:

The First Amendment, protection of free speech: if the President or other officials decide they don't like what you have said or written, you can be arrested.

The Fourth Amendment, insuring against warrantless searches: the government can now invade your home, office, vehicle, cell phone, or computer without warrant and arrest you, based only on suspicions and not probable cause.

The Sixth Amendment: under NDAA, U.S. citizens are not entitled to a speedy trial. In fact, they are not guaranteed a trial. The government is not required to have your accusers questioned by you. Between President Obama and the Congress, who needs an enemy?

---

134   https://www.aclu.org/blog/tag/ndaa

Congress needs an extreme makeover. We need congressmen and woman with backbones, both Democrat and Republican, who are not afraid to stand up for proper government to stop this erosion of our God-given rights. Both parties are guilty of complicity with this legislation. Each person, regardless of political alliance, should fact check to see how their representatives voted on this infringement of American liberty.

In a rare move, thirteen senators evenly split, six Republicans, six Democrats, and one independent voted against this tremendously intrusive bill.

This is a list of those who voted against this massive overreach.

Democrats

Dick Durbin (D-Ill)   Ben Cardin (D-Md)   Al Franken (D-Min)

Tom Harkin (D-Iowa)   Jeff Merkley D-Ore)   Ron Wyden(D-Ore)

Bernie Sanders (I-Vt)

Republicans

Jim Risch (R-Idaho)   Rand Paul (R Ky)   Mike Lee (R-Utah)

Jim DeMint (R-S.C.)   Mike Crapo R-Idaho) Tom Colburn
                                        (R-Okla) [135]

Amendment VII

"In suits at common law, where the value in controversy shall exceed twenty dollars, the right of trial by jury shall be preserved, and no fact tried by a jury, shall be otherwise reexamined in any court of the United States, than according to the rules of the common law."

---

135   http://www.dailykos.com/story/2011/12/18/1046736/-National-Defense-Authorization-Act-13-Senators-voted-NO#

Trial by jury

The Seventh Amendment holds provisions for a trial by jury. Jury trials were designed to have the accused to be tried by their fellow citizens to insure the best avenue for justice and to derail the government from imposing fines or prison time without due process of law.

This amendment is also circumvented by the NDAA.

Amendment VIII

"Excessive bail shall not be required, nor excessive fines imposed, nor cruel and unusual punishments inflicted."

Cruel and unusual punishment

Under the provisions of the Eighth Amendment, citizens of the United States enjoy rights against excessive bail and cruel and unusual punishment. Bail is the monetary amount required to temporarily release a prisoner prior to trial.

Excessive bail would include any bail which was excessive considering the crime committed. Consider a suspect on a first-time offense for shoplifting 200 dollars in merchandise. If the judge were to set bail at 10,000 dollars this would constitute excessive bail considering the offense committed.

Cruel and unusual punishment, as known by the Founders, included the common practices of the Europeans, such as debtor's prison, excessive bail, and fines that could never be paid. Cruel and unusual punishment was what the Founders had witnessed in European counties and what the British had in mind for the Founders if the rebellion had been unsuccessful.

If the Founders had been caught and punished by the British, the punishment could have included maiming, torture, evisceration of the prisoner by cutting and ripping out the internal organs and burning them while the prisoner was still alive. The Europeans had become infamous for their ability to keep a person alive for extended periods of time while inflicting a maximum amount of pain. This was cruel and unusual punishment as it was understood by the Founders.

The Founders also understood that there were cases in which the death penalty was appropriate and should be mandatory. In the case of murder, and other heinous crimes, capital punishment by a quick death has always been considered a just punishment. For some crimes, capital punishment is the only means of justice for victims and their families.

Amendment IX

"The enumeration in the Constitution, of certain rights, shall not be construed to deny or disparage others retained by the people."

This provision was to clarify that the people may have other God-given rights that are just as sacred even, if they are not specified in the Bill of Rights.

Amendment X

The powers not delegated to the United States by the Constitution, nor prohibited by it to the states, are reserved to the states respectively, or to the people.

Federal restraint

This amendment was to put the federal government on notice that the states, not the federal government, have jurisdiction of anything not specified in the Constitution. The states have been derelict in their duty of keeping the states strong and the federal government reined in.

The federal government takes money from the citizens of the states then returns part of the money in the form of education, highway funds, and hundreds of other programs. These programs always have strings attached, and the money is rarely returned without restrictions.

The federal government is like a drug dealer; after the states become addicted to the funds given them, the government adds more and more restrictions to the money, thereby keeping the states in line.

Most state governors are too scared to tangle with the federal government to keep them in check. It was the states who made the federal government, not the federal government who made the states.

The Constitution: a divinely inspired document

The Declaration of Independence and the Constitution of the United States are divinely inspired documents, so declared the writer and signers. John Adams worked tireless hours with Jefferson and others who authored the documents.

Declarations of John Adams

In a letter to his wife, Abigail Adams, dated July 2, 1776 speaking of the Declaration of Independence, Adams said, "It ought to be commemorated as the Day of Deliverance by solemn acts of devotion to God Almighty."[136] Twenty-two years later in 1798, to the officers of the First Brigade of the Third Division of the Militia of Massachusetts, Adams said, "This Constitution is only applicable to a religious and moral people."[137]

In another letter, he wrote: "A Declaration setting forth the causes, which have impelled us to this mighty revolution and the reasons that will justify it in the sight of God and man." [138]

Thomas Jefferson

The third President of the United States, Drafter and Signer of the Declaration of Independence stated:

God who gave us life gave us liberty. And can the liberties of a nation be thought secure when we have removed their only firm basis, a conviction in the minds of the people that these liberties are of the gift of God? That they are not to be violated but with His wrath. Indeed, I tremble for my country when I reflect that God is just; that His justice cannot sleep forever; That a revolution of the wheel of fortune, a change

---

136   http://www.masshist.org/digitaladams/archive/doc?id=L17760703jasecond
137   Source: John Adams, *The Works of John Adams, Second President of the United States*, Charles Francis Adams, editor (Boston: Little, Brown, 1854), Vol. IX, p. 401
138   John Adams, by McCullough, David, Simon & Schuster, Page 130

of situation, is among possible events; that it may become probable by Supernatural influence! The Almighty has no attribute which can take side with us in that event.[139]

I am a real Christian – that is to say, a disciple of the doctrines of Jesus Christ.[140]

Are we losing our constitutional protections?

In 2010, Representative Nancy Pelosi (D-CA), while trying to convince congress of the urgent need to pass the Affordable Care Act, Ms. Pelosi made one of the most insane comments ever uttered on the floor of Congress when she stated: "We have to pass the bill so we can find out what is in it."

When asked later why they would pass a bill without reading it, she gave this equally insane answer: "No. What I was saying there is we are House and the Senate. We get a bill. We go to conference or we ping-pong it, and then you see what the final product is. However, I stand by what I said there. When people see what is in the bill, they will like it. And they will."[141]

This has to be one of the most arrogant statements ever made on the floors of Congress. It is something you would not hear from a first grader, but here is a sitting congresswoman telling us we need to pass a law before we read it, so we can find out what is in it.

Using this logic, who would ever sign a major contract without reading it and at least have some understanding of the content? As this legislation has unfolded and Americans now have to live with it, it has become a nightmare. My question for Ms. Pelosi and the Democrat congress that passed it: if Obama Care is such great legislation, then why is it hidden in thousands of pages of rambling regulation that no one can read or understand?

---

139   *Notes on the State of Virginia, Query XVIII,* p. 237
140   *The Writings of Thomas Jefferson, page 385* http://christianity.about.com/od/independenceday/a/foundingfathers.htm
141   Real Clear Politics Video, David Gregory, November 17, 2013

Obama Care, is it really the law of the land?

This landmark legislation was shoved down the throats of the American people by President Obama and an exclusively Democrat congress. There was not a single Republican vote in favor of it. After its passage, it was challenged in the United States Supreme Court. Justice Roberts changed the wording of the text, removing the word, "penalty" and replacing it with the word, "tax".

This millstone around America's neck infamously named Obama Care with its accompanying regulations is already over eleven million words and the regulations are nowhere near complete. It is already over twice the size of the insane United States income tax code.[142] Reading at an average of 100 words per minute, Obama Care would take the reader respectively 115,885 minutes (1,932 hours). Reading eight hours per day, it would take, respectively, 644 days, 92 weeks, or 23 months to read this law.

By comparison, there are 783,137 words in the entire Old and New Testaments of the King James Bible.[143] The Bible can be read cover-to-cover in about 78 hours.

Why is this important to every American? Because to be compliant with the law, citizens need to be able to reasonably interpret the law. It would be impossible for a room full of attorneys to properly interpret this lawless mess called The Affordable Care Act. The average citizen has no chance of reading, let alone understanding this mass of laws and regulations.

The cure for these imposing, incomprehensible laws is simple. No law should be allowed to be longer than the original Constitution, 4400 words. If legislation is really needed, it would stand to reason that the people should be able to understand the law. Any legislation longer than the Constitution is designed to hoodwink and deceive the people.

---

142   CNS News, 11,588,500 Obama care Regs 30x as long as Law, Penny Star, October 14, 2013
143   http://amazingbibletimeline.com/bible_questions/q10_bible_facts_statistics/

Ineptocracy

Ineptocracy is defined as a system of government "where the least capable to lead are elected by the least capable of producing, and where the members of society least likely to sustain themselves or succeed are rewarded with goods and services paid for by the confiscated wealth of a diminishing number producers.[144]

America has ceded her constitutional government to an Ineptocracy. One where the President believes he does not have to answer to Congress or the people. President Obama's famous declaration, "I've got a pen." President Obama says he plans to use his pen to sign executive actions and his phone to convene outside conferences with groups who support his agenda if Congress proves unable or unwilling to act on his priorities.[145] President Obama did not say who these groups would be, but apparently he believes they can sway public opinion in his favor.

President Obama's actions are in direct violation of Article 1, Sections 1 and 7 of the Constitution. This is not how Presidents act. This is the act of a dictator without accountability. The President should be held accountable and impeached for overstepping his constitutional authority.

Staying the course

From time to time, the American Government has made massive mistakes, such as butting into the business of other nations or subverting segments of our own population, but almost all of those mistakes have resulted when our leaders have violated the Constitution. The Constitution was designed to be a guide not only for elected officials but for "We the People." We are as guilty as the worst officials when we fail to read, and study the law of the land, our sacred Constitution.

Once we understand the law, we need to hold our political leaders accountable to those laws. The Constitution is our guide to

---

144   http://www.definition-of.com/Ineptocracy
145   http://www.politico.com/story/2014/01/obama-state-of-the-union-2014-strategy-102151.html#ixzz3C85mREKV

freedom and we should jealously protect it from those who would violate this supreme law of the land. It is not the Constitution that is flawed, but those who administer it.

Chapter 7

Policies that Create War

There are those who start wars, and those who finish them.

There are always those who prey on the weak. They appear in the form of individuals, gangs, and nations. All aggressors display tyrannical attitudes and most want at least three things: dominance, power, and wealth. Wealth can be something as simple as stolen items from a car or as ominous as enslavement of an entire nation and their people.

Because of these aggressors, we are faced with two choices: prepare to defend ourselves, our families, and our nation or be murdered and enslaved. It is the obligation of those who can defend against aggression in all forms to do so.

War and personal dominance are bedfellows. In the case of a single person, or a nation, wars have dominated the landscape of the human experience since the earliest recorded history of man.

In almost every war the United States has fought, there has been an element in society who protests war for the sake of protest. While we respect the rights of protest, it is hard to take someone seriously who protests the nation who is protecting the weak. If the protestors were genuine, they would protest the aggressor nations.

During the Vietnam War, Hollywood starlet Jane Fonda (Hanoi Jane) sided with the North Vietnamese and their communist allies. History confirms that the North Vietnamese communists were the aggressor nation. They were torturing, raping, maiming, and murdering thousands of civilians. During the war, they tortured and killed untold numbers of U.S. prisoners of war.

In 1973, at the conclusion of U.S. involvement in the Vietnam War, congress pulled all funding from South Vietnam and left them to continue the fight alone against the North. North Vietnam continued to be supported and provisioned by Communist China and Russia.

In 1975, after two years of gallant fighting, South Vietnam

fell to the communist North. After the surrender of the South, North Vietnamese Communists went on an orgy of torture, rape and murder in South Vietnam and Cambodia. There were almost twice as many causalities in the two years following the war as there had been during the previous ten years of U.S. involvement.

The North Vietnamese communists who pillaged and murdered the unarmed South Vietnamese refugees was the regime that the anti-war movement and Jane Fonda supported.[146, 147, 148]

Why America fights

America has fought many wars. Some have been more ethical than others. This chapter is not so much about the right and wrong of war, but the factors which bring us to the brink, or immerse us in war.

In Genesis, the first book of the Bible, we find reference to the first recorded murder in written history. Cain killed his brother Able because of jealousy and to obtain the riches that Able possessed. This was only the beginning of the wars for dominance that would prevail and plague man throughout history.[149]

Who are the lovers of war? What nation ever attacked another nation because it was too strong? Few thugs ever attack a well-armed target. From robbers, rapists and murders to foreign nations almost all attackers look for easy, unprepared targets.

In personal attacks the victim is almost always unarmed, and unaware of their surroundings, they are appropriately described as soft targets. In the few cases where attacks are made against known armed victims, or police, these attacks are almost always by ambush. Likewise, it is rare that aggressor nations will attack another nation

---

146   http://www.lzcenter.com/Myths percent20and percent20Facts. html,2014

147   Author's Note: Jane Fonda and her anti-war compatriots are raging liberal Democrats with sympathies and/or ties to the Communist Party. It is also a well-known fact that the Communist Party was a major contributor to the Vietnam anti-war protesters.

148   Modern American Poetry, The Anti-War Movement in the United States, By Mark Barringer, http://www.english.illinois.edu/maps/vietnam/antiwar.html

149   King James Bible, Geneses 4:5-8

who is ready for war with a strong military, and leaders who articulate strength and resolve and are unambiguous about their intentions if attacked. This is called prevention, and it is the cheapest of all wars both in treasure, humanity, and loss of life.

"Being prepared for war is one of the most effective means of preserving peace."

George Washington[150]

Responsibility of leaders

In America we have two main political parties. While I do not agree with all of the ideology of the Republican Party, they have been unfairly portrayed as "War Mongers."

Ronald Reagan was accused by the Left as being a cowboy who was bringing us to the brink of war. Reagan believed that lasting peace could only be maintained through a strong military. He believed aggressor countries would only respect peace if they believed America had the ability and the will to fight to maintain our freedoms.

President Reagan was vindicated when through strength he was able to negotiate the most favorable terms in history for nuclear arms reduction with the Soviet Union. In November 1985, President Reagan met with Russian President Gorbachev in Geneva, Switzerland. Gorbachev said he was willing to give in to all of America's demands on nuclear weapons reduction, with one restriction. The United States had to abandon SDI (Strategic Defense Initiative, or the so called Star Wars program). Reagan shocked Gorbachev when he leaned across the table and forcefully told him "no deal."

SDI was a program undertaken by the U.S. to build a space-based defense system that could defeat Soviet intercontinental ballistic missiles (ICBM). This system scared the Soviets because they understood the implications that if the U.S. prevailed with such

---

150   Historic Documents of the United States, State of the Union speech, George Washington, January 8, 1770

a system, the old balance of power, insured by the idea of mutual destruction, would be severely undermined. The Soviets would lose the scare-factor they had deployed against the West since the end of World War II.

Reagan kept the lines of communication open and talks went on for several more years. In December 1987 President Gorbachev met with President Reagan in Washington DC. At that landmark meeting, Gorbachev signed the most sweeping nuclear arms treaty in history. As part of the agreement, America did not give up SDI.[151]

By projecting strength and not weakness, President Reagan proved to be one of the greatest peacemakers of the twenty-first century. In 1989, that vindication was even more manifest with the fall of the Soviet Union and the Berlin Wall.

President Reagan proved that peace through strength could be maintained and good feelings could be cultivated. President Reagan and President Gorbachev remained friends throughout their Presidencies. U.S. and Soviet tensions remained at an all-time low during the Reagan Presidency. Both men grew to have a friendly affection for each other because Gorbachev recognized that beyond power, President Reagan projected honesty in his personal character. In the reverse, President Reagan honestly liked Gorbachev, reflected in his personal respect that he cultivated for the Russian leader.

Power

Power, when properly projected, used, and controlled is the most consistent way to stop aggression by individuals and or nations. Gang bangers generally do not respond positively to weakness. They love to dominate other gangs and intimidate individuals. The American Indian believed in bravery and treated timid enemies with distain. Believing you can pacify your way to peace and prosperity is rarely achieved because aggressors prey on the weak and timid. History is replete with nations overrun by aggressor nations who were not stopped by kindness. Being prepared as individuals and as a nation is the only way to insure against aggression.

---

151   Newman, Peggy, When Character Was King, Penguin Books, 2002

Democrat policies create war and human suffering

While Democrats may not love war, time and again their policies set us up for war. Six of the eight major wars fought by America were started under or directly following militarily weak Democrat Presidents.

Democrats Woodrow Wilson, Franklyn Roosevelt, Lindon Johnson, Jimmy Carter, Bill Clinton, and Barack Obama; all reduced the military in favor of funding social programs. Under these Democrat Presidents, our military was weakened to the point where other nations lost respect and fear of the United States.

Each time these presidents weakened America's military, our enemies, the enemies of freedom become emboldened and chose these weak times to aggress against the United States or nations we had pledged to protect.

WWI (U.S. involvement 1917-1918): the war was started and fought under Democrat President Woodrow Wilson. He coined the phrase, "peace without victory." After 350,000 American casualties including 116,516 dead, we still did not gain peace; we gained only an Armistice with the Axis powers.[152]

WWII (years of direct U.S. involvement 1941-1945): rightly called a continuation of WWI, the war was started and fought under Democrat President Franklin Roosevelt.

At the conclusion of WWI, Democrat President Wilson, two Republicans, and one more Democrat president demilitarized America. America was sick of war and wanted to bury their heads in the sand and pretend evil no longer existed in the world.

America was in favor of isolationism and didn't seem to grasp the fact that with the advent of internally powered ships, and airplanes, isolationism was no longer an option. It was also a lazy congress and presidents who allowed this unprepared isolationist attitude to go unchallenged.

Our leaders failed to comprehend and counter "defeated"

152   http://www.historylearningsite.co.uk/FWWcasualties.htm 2014

Germany. While the U.S. was cutting her military, Germany was actively rebuilding their war machine.

In the 1930s, Adolf Hitler became the Fuehrer of Germany. With the title, he became all powerful. It was well known by the United States and Britain that Hitler was rebuilding Germany's military war machine in violation of the Versailles Treaty of World War I. Unfortunately, they chose to ignore the buildup. The Western powers knew that Hitler hated Jews, Christians, and anyone who spoke against him, and that he was systematically rounding up and murdering these people.[153]

In 1935, Hitler continued to violate the treaties by creating the Luftwaffe (German Air force). Again, the Western powers were aware of the buildup but chose to stand idly by and do nothing.

In 1936, United States Senator Gerald Nye succeeded in passing a bill which the pacifists in congress believed could prevent war simply by issuing embargos against belligerent countries. Once again, they had chosen to bury their heads in the sand rather than to examine history. The bill was as ludicrous as a gun law that says criminals cannot own guns. It only affects law-abiding people.

While Germany was rebuilding her military, America's government also chose to ignore the decades of military buildup by Japan as well. In fairness to President Roosevelt, he did try unsuccessfully to get Congress to approve appropriations to rebuild America's military. Because of our failure to keep a strong military, America was caught by surprise when WWII broke out even though there had been years of warnings. The cost for being unprepared was 405,399 America soldiers killed. The cost to other nations was millions of lives lost and millions more displaced by the war.

Korea (1950-1953): the war was started under Democrat President Harry Truman. This was the first war in which our leaders chose political expediency over winning. The cost in American lives to achieve a stalemate: over 36,516 American soldiers killed.

The Korean War was brought to closure under Republican President Eisenhower after he made it known to the communist

---

153   Leckie, Robert, The Wars of America, Castle Books 1998 page 676-677

nations he would prosecute the war without inhibition and to use the most appropriate weapons in our arsenals. For the previous three years his predecessor Democrat President Truman had made it equally clear he would respond only to contain the war, not to win it.

At the conclusion of the Korean War of 132,000 North Korean POWs held by U.N. forces over 60,000 chose to stay in the free South and refused to be repatriated back to North Korea.[154]

Vietnam (1964-1973): the war was started under Democrat President Lindon Johnson. This was the second war where U.S. presidents chose politically not to allow the generals to fight a winning war.

The Johnson administration ignored the boots on the ground military leaders. The President and his staffers picked non-strategic targets, effectively tying the hands of the soldiers and inhibiting their ability to fight to win. This allowed the enemy to continue to bring supplies and to continue fighting and killing both American soldiers and Vietnamese citizens.

In 1973, this war was brought to an end under the leadership of Republican President Richard Nixon. In May of 1972, President Nixon started an intensive bombing campaign to stop supplies from being shipped into North Vietnam. Called Operation Line Backer, by October 1972 the operation had brought the North to the peace table.

In December, when no agreement was reached, the North walked out of the Paris peace talks. President Nixon sent an ultimatum to the North Vietnamese to come back to the conference table in seventy-two hours, or else. The North unwisely rejected the demand and President Nixon ordered Operation Linebacker II.

This would be the most concentrated offensive of the war. In the next eleven days, the U.S. obliterated the North's ability to conduct the war. Less than a month later, North Vietnam signed the Paris Peace Accords.[155]

---

154   Leckie, Robert, The Wars of America, Castle Books 1998 page 917-923
155   This day in History, 1972, Nixon orders the initiation of Operation Linebacker 11, accessed June 1, 2015

Had the Johnson administration followed this same tactic, the Vietnam War would have been over with a decisive victory seven years earlier and tens of thousands of lives would have been saved.[156]

The cost for this indecisiveness: 58,209 American lives lost plus tens of thousands of serious injuries which would go on to kill thousands more in the decades to come.

From 1917 to 1973, the total of American serviceman and women who lost their lives under these five Democrat presidents was over 616,947.

Democrat President Jimmy Carter 1976-1980 spent four years cutting America's military budget and apologizing for America. Carter projected weakness to the world. America would soon pay the price for this weak Democrat president.

November 1979, the Ayatollah Khomeini of the Iranian Revolutionary Council thanked President Carter by allowing and later encouraging students to take over the U.S. embassy in Iran. The Iranians took fifty-two U.S. embassy employees and other American citizens hostage, holding them for 444 days.[157] These prisoners were physically and mentally abused; some were told daily that they were going to be killed.

This crisis was brought to an end when Ronald Reagan won the Presidential election in 1980. Ironically the hostages were released literally as President Reagan was being ushered into office on January 20, 1981. Iran apparently got the same memo the Russians received before Reagan took office. The Russian KGB noted in a background paper on Ronald Reagan: "Words and deeds are the same."[158]

President Carter had tried for over a year to obtain the release of the prisoners. Iran had no fear of Carter and no progress toward the release was made under his watch.

---

156   Leckie, Robert, The Wars of America, Castle Books 1998 page 1068-1069
157   http://www.cnn.com/2013/09/15/world/meast/iran-hostage-crisis-fast-facts/ June 2014
158   Bennett William J, America the Last Best Hope, Volume 11, Thomas Nelson 2007, page 485

After Reagan won the 1980 election, Iran tried to negotiate a lengthy release of the hostages, stating it was going to take at least six months before the release could be finalized. Reagan said no to the negotiations. Iran was studying Reagan. They concluded that they did not want to be responsible for the hostages after Reagan took office. It would be fair to say they were scared to death of this no-nonsense Cowboy who believed a strong military was essential to peace. Before becoming president, Reagan quietly projected his willingness to do what was necessary to bring our people home, and Iran complied.

The world knew this was a different president, and not one to be trifled with. President Reagan commanded and negotiated from a platform of strength, not appeasement.[159]

Reagan, with his tough, honest assessment and willingness to hit back at communism led the nation in three small wars. These wars were short and pointed with obtainable goals. Losses under President Reagan:

Grenada:	1983	19
Libya	1986	0
Panama:	1989	40

Including the marine barracks bombing in Lebanon, a total of 425 service men and women lost their lives in the line of duty under President Reagan. While each life is a tragedy, without the strong leadership of President Reagan, the losses could have been hundreds of times greater. The difference was that Reagan had achievable goals. Reagan led with strength, and the military was able to prevail decisively, winning these wars.[160]

President Reagan once again showed the world we are the "shining light on the hill." Instead of hating America, it became fashionable again to love America. World leaders loved and respected Ronald Reagan and the world respected America.

---

159   Bennett William J, America the Last Best Hope, Volume 11, Thomas Nelson 2007, page 482

160   http://www.militaryfactory.com/american_war_deaths.asp. 2013

A few years later with the election of Democratic President Bill Clinton (1993-2001), the U.S. leadership on the world stage took a hit again. President Clinton projected weakness to Al-Qaida and radical Muslim leader, Osama bin Laden. Bin Laden got the signal: the United States would not send a significant response to terrorist acts committed against them. America would soon pay the price for their pacification toward Bin Laden and Al-Qaida.

How America conducts wars

Traditionally, America has developed war strategies based on the strategies, clemency, or degeneracy of our opponents. As Americans, we have historically taken the high ground. While cases may be cited where some American soldiers have acted criminally, generally the American solder has stood head-and-shoulders above all other armies of the world in their treatment of enemy citizens, combatants, prisoners of war, and all detainees.

During the Revolutionary war, American prisoners taken by Britain were detained on special prison ships. Visitors and inmates of these hellish floating prisons appropriately referred to them as "Hell Ships." The death rate from disease alone was phenomenal.

Prisoners kept in the ships' holds were rarely given access to the deck to take in fresh air or clean themselves. The prisoners were given insufficient food, which was often spoiled and rotten. They were bedded in dirty, lice-ridden straw, and human waste was not removed with constancy, which bred decease and vermin. The conditions were deplorable and unacceptable even by the standards of the day. It is estimated over 11,000 prisoners on these ships died of causes unrelated to combat.[161]

By comparison, British prisoners of war were generally fed and treated so well by their American captors that they were not even aggressive about attempting to escape. The conditions for prisoners taken by the Americans were often better than that of the American fighting soldiers.[162]

161   http://www.history.com/topics/american-revolution/the-hms-jersey,2014
162   Bennett William J, America the Last Best Hope, Thomas Nelson 2007, page

During the Revolutionary War Battle of Long Island New York in August of 1776, the battle was poorly planned and executed by the Americans. The battle was turning in favor of the British. Some American troops facing certain annihilation did not have a viable escape route. The American commander made a decision to save his troops from probable slaughter. He had his troops put down their weapons and surrender to the British forces. Unfortunately, these forces were Hessian mercenaries (Germans) commanded by the ruthless German Johann Rall.

When the American troops laid down their weapons and surrendered, the Hessian forces descended on the unarmed Americans bayoneting and slaughtering them without mercy. [163]

By comparison, on December 25 and 26, 1776, just four months after the Battle of Long Island, Washington and his army made the famous night crossing of the Delaware River. The Continental (U.S.) Army attacked these same German troops at Trenton New Jersey. The attack was successful and hundreds of prisoners were taken. These German prisoners of war were amazed when the Americans did not retaliate and slaughter them in like manner.

Washington issued a written order for the 900 captured Hessian Troops:

"Treat them with humanity, and let them have no reason to complain of our copying the brutal example of the British Army in their treatment of our unfortunate brethren . . . Provide everything necessary for them on the road."[164]

After the war, many of these Hessian troops sent for their families and stayed in the United States becoming citizens of the nation who had treated them with such compassion during the war.

90,91
163   Bennett William J, America the Last Best Hope, Thomas Nelson 2007, page 87,90
164   http://www.mountvernon.org/educational-resources/encyclopedia/ battle-trenton / 1776, David McCullough , page 283

Projection of power in preventing war

President Theodore Roosevelt (R) (1901-1909)

For all his flaws, President Theodore Roosevelt—"TR"—understood military power was the best way to insure peace. President Theodore "Teddy" Roosevelt took the navy's new fleet of internal powered ships, known as the Great White Fleet, and sailed around the world to demonstrate that America was a friend to all, but also to put the world on notice that the United States was not to be trifled with.[165] This show of American sea power soundly reinforced his phrase, "Speak softly but carry a big stick." The sixteen ships of America's great white fleet sailed December, 1907 and stopped at major ports around the world. The new U.S. Navy steam powered ships had all been painted white. These ships replaced the last of smaller wooden ships of the navy.[166]

World War I

Kaiser Wilhelm II was born in 1859. He was the grandson of Queen Victoria of England. This is ironic because Wilhelm would eventually declare war on England.

From his childhood, Wilhelm was bright, eager, "born with a chip on his shoulder" and terrified his own parents.[167] By birthright, Wilhelm would become the Kaiser of Germany after the death of his father.[168]

In 1890, Wilhelm forced his Chancellor Otto Von Bismarck

165   http://www.history.navy.mil/library/online/gwf_cruise.htm, 2014

166   Photos of the fleet, www.google.com/search?rlz=1C1ASUT_enUS437 US440&biw=1366&bih=624&noj=1&site=webhp&source=hp&q=great+white+ fleet&oq=Great+white+fleet&g

167   Massie Robert K, Dreadnought, Random House 1991, page 110 / Bennett, William J, America The last Best Hope, Page2,3

168   Photos: Pwww.google.com/search?q=photos+kaiser+wilhelm&rlz=1C 1ASUT_enUS437US440&biw=1366&bih=624&noj=1&site=webhp&tbm=isch &imgil=BGHvlOydvlC4

Trench photos: www.google.com/search?q=trench+warfare&rlz=1C1ASUT_en US437US440&biw=1366&bih=624&noj=1&site=webhp&tbm=isch&imgil=ZO ll0SzXwxLv_M percent253

into retirement. Bismarck, no lover of freedom, was also not on a collision course to make war with Europe or the United States. Bismarck once commented, "There is providence that protects idiots, drunkards, children and the United States of America."

The forced retirement of Bismarck cleared the way for the new Kaiser to work without restraint to make war in the name of Germany.[169] Wilhelm became a student of a book written by American author, Admiral Alfred Thayer Mahan, *The Influence of Sea Power upon History*.

After reading the book, Wilhelm became obsessed with building a navy that made it possible for Germany to grab colonies in Africa, the Pacific, and Latin America. The watchword for the Kaiser's rule was weltmacht oder niedergang (World power or decline). While building his navy, Wilhelm also began building a tremendous land army as part of his scheme to dominate Europe. This would be the first significant war where not just countries would war against each other, but huge coalitions of countries would provide armies in numbers never before known in war.[170]

Russian ruler Tsar Nicolas was Wilhelm's Cousin. Nicolas became uneasy with Germany's conquests and her alliance with Austria. As a means of self-protection Nicolas made an alliance for mutual protection with France and Serbia.

These alliances and coalitions set the stage for the opponents to go to war. All that was needed was the spark to ignite the fires in Europe. There was already distrust and dislike between Austria and Serbia. The spark ignited the fire on July 28, 1914 when seven Serbian Nationalists came to Sarajevo, Austria with the intentions of assassinating Austria's Arch Duke Ferdinand.

While five of the assassins lost their nerve, two followed through with their plans. One threw a bomb which missed its target but the seventh, Gavrilo Princip, stood in the street as the car carrying his target drove within five feet of him, he fired two shots killing the Duke and his wife. The assassination became the excuse for Austria,

169   Bennett William J, America the Last Best Hope, Thomas Nelson 2007, page 4
170   Leckie, Robert, The Wars of America, Castle Books 1998 page 580

backed by Germany, to invade Serbia, who was backed by Russia. Within days, the war had started, and within a few months, it would engulf almost all of Europe.

This war soon developed into The Great War. Later it was classified as World War I and was also called the "Useless and Stupid War."[171]

President Wilson quickly proclaimed the Neutrality of The United States. Wilson and the American people wanted no part of a European war. Wilson not only proclaimed neutrality, but did nothing to prepare for the possibility that America may be engulfed in the war whether she wanted to be or not.

On May 7, 1915, German U-boats working in the Atlantic Ocean fired on and sank the British passenger ship, Lusitania, killing over 1100 passengers, including 128 Americans. President Wilson responded with useless and spineless statements of protest to Germany. When these protests produced no discernible reply, President Wilson sent stronger diplomatic notices of protest. Wilson would continue to send these worthless notices of condemnation for a full year rarely receiving an answer.[172] In addition to his worthless statements of protest to Germany, he stated to America: "There is such a thing as being too proud to fight."

Former Presidents Teddy Roosevelt and William Taft were shocked at the indifference of President Wilson to the willful murder of American citizens by Germany. In the wake of the sinking of the Lusitania, President Wilson continued his refusal to prepare for a war that was coming straight at him and the United States. Democrat Wilson's continued failure to prepare for war contributed to the Kaiser's belief that Germany could attack the United States with impunity.

President Wilson believed it was more important to implementing his progressive social agenda than to prepare for what was fast becoming an inevitable war. Wilson feared his socialist

---

171   http://history1900s.about.com/od/worldwari/p/World-War-I.htm World War I By Jennifer Rosenberg
172   http://www.firstworldwar.com/source/lusitania_germanresponse.htm, 2014

programs could be stalled or even abandon if the United States went to war. In 1915, when he addressed the House of Representatives, Wilson stated: "We must abolish everything that bears even the semblance of privilege or of any kind of artificial advantage." He clearly meant the destruction of the capitalist system and large and small business.[173]

In 1916, President Wilson would run on the platform: "He kept us out of war," but at what cost? Wilson's refusal to prepare for a war would ultimately cost the lives of over 116,000 American soldiers.[174]

In 1916, President Wilson still held the fictional notion that the United States could remain neutral. In a controversial speech that year, Wilson called for "Peace without Victory." Our allies, who were already under siege by Germany, were deeply offended by this statement. While Wilson was continuing his Peace without Victory campaign, Germany was in the process of making secret agreements with Mexico and Japan which included plans to divide the United State among the victors. This agreement was intercepted by the British and was called "the Zimmermann Telegram."

With the revelations of the Zimmermann Telegram, on April 2, 1917 the United States, belatedly and unprepared, declared war on Germany.[175]

World War I would give the world a close up look at evil in the form of weapons of mass destruction. Mounted cavalry had been effectively used for thousands of years. This war would see the last of the Mounted Horse Calvary charge. It would be the first war to use weapons of mass destruction including chlorine gas and fully automatic machine guns that could inflict thousands of causalities in a few minutes. World War I would introduce the world to massive navies, including internally powered ship and air power. The world

---

173   Bennett, William J, America the Last Best Hope, Thomas Nelson 2007 page 13

174   Bennett, William J, America the Last Best Hope, Thomas Nelson 2007 page 10-11

175   Bennett, William J, America the Last Best Hope, Thomas Nelson 2007 page 16-17

and war had changed. It was the first conflict that enveloped the entire world.

On November 11, 1918 after four long years of war, which left over ten million dead in the killing fields of Europe, the war was over; however, it was not finished. It did not end with a conventional unconditional surrender. It ended with a weak Democrat president signing an armistice agreement. President Wilson refused to accept the council of his chief military advisor General Black Jack Pershing. The General pleaded with President Wilson to "let America's Expeditionary Force finish the job."

General Pershing stated: "Germany doesn't know she is licked." Had they given us another week, and we would have taught them.[176] In just a little over twenty years, General Pershing's words would become prophetic with the outbreak of World War II.

Because of the terms of the Treaty of Versailles, Germany was to be saddled with an insurmountable amount of war debt. There was no way Germany could repay the debt. This environment created the fertile breeding ground for a leader who could put Germany back on the road to prosperity. That leader would be voted in as chancellor by the German people in 1933. His name was Adolf Hitler.

World War II

Your enemies will dictate the war you will fight

America fought two world wars against Germany. In both cases, prior to the wars America's leader left an international impression of both administrative and fighting weakness. America and her leaders were living with their heads in the sand as the world came apart around them. Because of technology the days of America's isolationism were gone forever.

World War II was triggered by the age-old desire of absolute power and dominance by a perverted, sick, and ruthless leader; Adolf Hitler. Hitler promised to bring respect to Germany and aid

---

176   Bennett, William J, America the Last Best Hope, Thomas Nelson 2007 page 33-34

her economic recovery. He would become one of the world's most hated men of all time. Hitler was a powerful speaker and when he came to power, he soothed the people. Within a short time, Hitler created such animosity toward Jews, Christians, homosexuals and others that millions of German citizens were rounded up and slaughtered in government concentration camps.

Quotes attributed to Hitler
- "It is always more difficult to fight against faith than against knowledge."
- "As long as the government is perceived as working for the benefit of children, the people will happily endure almost any curtailment of liberty and almost any deprivation."[177]
- "Providence has ordained that I should be the greatest liberator of humanity. I am freeing man from the restraints of an intelligence that has taken charge, from the dirty and degrading self mortification of a false vision called conscience and morality, and for the demands of a freedom and independence which only a very few can bear."
- To conquer a nation, first disarm its citizens. Adolf Hitler, 1933. This quote has been questioned for accuracy; however, the idea is soundly entrenched in the Nazi gun laws of 1938.[178]

The SS troops and Gestapo of Germany could be depended on for inhuman treatment. These human degenerates prided themselves in delivering pain and suffering. They were the commandants of concentration camps. These were the secret police who would take people from their homes in the middle of the night, leaving a trail of rape, torture, and murder.

Germany

---

177   http://www.goodreads.com/quotes/783904-the-state-must-declare-the-child-to-be-the-most
178   Zelman, Aaron, Gun Control Gate Way to tyranny

The War with Germany was fought against a treacherous enemy; however, the everyday solders were generally decent men who believed they were fighting for their lives and their country. Most of the duty soldiers chose to follow the rules of war as outlined by the Geneva Convention. There were cases when the warring combatants of both sides showed mercy and compassion on the opposing army.

Franz Stigler was a German Fighter Pilot. On December 20, 1943, American pilot Charles Brown flew a bombing mission against a German aircraft factory. Brown's B-17 was severely crippled by flak and fighter fire. The B-17 was running on only one of its four engines.

German fighter pilot, Franz Stigler was dispatched to finish off the plane; however, in violation of his orders he took pity upon the wounded men and their crippled plane. Instead of firing on the helpless plane, he escorted it out of enemy air space and returned to his base falsely reporting to his bosses that he had shot the plane down over the ocean. In 1990, Stigler contacted Brown, and the two old adversaries met and remained friends until the death of Stigler.[179]

There were many atrocities committed during the war. Generally speaking, however, when a soldier surrendered in the European theater, there was reasonable expectation he would be treated humanely. Because of this mutual trust in the treatment of POW's, both sides took thousands of prisoners which saved countless lives on both sides. Most POW's were treated humanely and at the conclusion of the war, all would be repatriated to their native country.

Japan

Japan was different enemy. While both Japan and Germany were fighting toward world domination, Japan had been gearing for war with the West for generations. Young children were taught brutality from the earliest days in school. They were also taught that the Emperor was a god.

---

179   http://www.military.com/Content/MoreContent1/?file=dday_0033p1

Military enlistees were desensitized and de-humanized by their superiors who forced them to brutally torture prisoners. New enlistees were taught to brutalize by repeatedly stabbing a bound prisoner. Each time the soldier would make a thrust his compatriots were told to cheer to give positive reinforcement to the soldier. After the session, the soldiers were given further positive reinforcement by being treated to alcohol and prostitutes. Within a few weeks, these normal people became crazed murderers and rapists. The results of this depravity were manifest in the infamous Rape of Nanking China.[180]

Pacific War

Japan's attack on the United States at Pearl Harbor December 7, 1941 was conceived in treachery and deception. Japan planned to have their declaration of war delivered in Washington D.C. at 1:00 pm Eastern time, 7:00 am Hawaii time. The declaration was to be delivered about thirty minutes before Japanese fighters would appear over Pearl Harbor.

Because of the deficiencies of the Japanese translators at their Washington D.C. embassy, the declaration of war was not delivered until 2:20 p.m. Washington time, 8:20 a.m. Hawaii time. The first attack at Pearl Harbor commenced at about 7:50 a.m.

Japan wrongly assumed America was the soft underbelly of the Western powers and would cower from the terrifying events at Pearl Harbor and sue for peace. The aftermath of Pearl Harbor united America with a burning anger to avenge the treachery and their fallen soldiers. Japan found, belatedly, that not only did America not cower, but America would attack and prevail. Because of the sneak attack, America resolved that the only surrender for Japan would be an unconditional surrender.[181]

Because the attack decimated America's battleships in the Pacific—due to America being asleep while Japan was increasing

---

180   http://hellfire-pass.commemoration.gov.au/the-enemy/treatment-of-prisoners.
php
181   Marston, Daniel, War in the Pacific, Random House, Osprey, 2006, Page 230

her military might and the decision to defeat Germany first—it took a year before America could barely slow the advance of the Japanese.

The Japanese did not believe in surrender and had nothing but distain for anyone who did. The Japanese soldiers were commanded to commit suicide rather than surrender. This mentality was the overwhelming reason for their brutality against POW's and civilians alike. In 1942, American Forces in the Philippines were being decimated by superior and better-equipped Japanese armies and navies. America was not able to replace men or supplies in the Pacific. The limited supplies, soldiers and the ships to move them were being sent to the European theater.

In May of 1942, General Wainwright, commander of American Forces in the Philippines, chose to surrender his troops at Bataan. His reason was to save as many of his men as possible. He negotiated the surrender of all American forces in the Philippines. It was understood his men would be treated honorably under the rules of the Geneva Convention.

No sooner had the Americans soldiers laid down their arms than the maltreatment of the prisoners began. Within a few days, they were forced to start on the infamous sixty-mile Bataan Death March. POW's who tried to get water from potholes in the road or were too weak to go on were bayoneted or shot on the spot and left to die. Our soldiers were not treated according to the Geneva Convention; they were beaten, abused, and murdered to satisfy the sick pleasure of Japanese officers and soldiers.[182]

Approximately 63,000 Pilipino and 12,000 US soldiers were taken prisoner on Bataan by the Japanese Army. Of these 75,000 POWs it is estimated that 5,000 to 11,000 prisoners were brutally murdered in the Bataan Death March.[183]

182   http://www.eyewitnesstohistory.com/bataandeathmarch.htm
183   Marston, Daniel, War in the Pacific, Random House, Osprey, 2006, Page 58-62

Iwo Jima

In April of 1945, during the Battle of Iwo Jima, the Japanese marshaled an army of over 21,000 soldiers. These soldiers were not on Iwo Jima. They were literally inside of Iwo Jima, in a labyrinth of caves stretching for miles. After a little over one month of fighting, only 216 of the 21,000 Japanese soldiers on Iwo Jima were taken prisoner. Most of these POW's were taken after they were wounded so severely that they could no longer fight. This was one of the bloodiest and most costly battles of the Pacific war. U.S. losses were humbling, with over 19,000 wounded and over 7,000 killed. The few Japanese who were taken prisoner were amazed that they were not tortured or murdered but were fed and medically cared for by their American captors.[184]

At the outset of the Pacific war America was behind in aircraft and technology. The Japanese Zero was the dominant attack aircraft of the Pacific theater; in addition her pilots had superior training. The Zero could out climb, out turn and out run the best American Carrier based Aircraft.

At the Battle of the Coral Sea in May of 1942, America gained a slight victory over the Japanese in this first Aircraft Carrier battle. One month later, in June of 1942, America had a decisive victory in its second Carrier battle at Midway. Japanese aircraft were superior; however, the U.S. ships had radar, allowing them a decisive edge in early warning of incoming aircraft. American aircraft, while inferior in speed and agility, were built much more ruggedly and the pilots were protected by armor.

In the end, providence played a large part of this victory. American forces were able to locate the Japanese fleet before the Japanese found the Americans. This allowed the U.S. navy to hit the Japanese early, putting them on the defensive. When the Japanese later located the U.S. ships, the Japanese carriers were already under attack. This substantially reduced the number of aircraft that could be flown against the U.S. carriers.

As the war in the Pacific dragged on, America's industry was

---

184   Leckie, Robert, The Wars of America, Castle Books 1998 page 825

on the fast-track, playing catch up to Imperial Japan and Germany's aircraft and navy technologies.

Early in 1943, the navy began deploying a new, improved aircraft carrier-based airplane: the F6F Grumman Hellcat Fighter. The new fighter was faster and had a better rate of climb than the Zero. It was designed with armor around the pilot and was very tough to shoot down. Hellcats would destroy over 5,200 enemy aircraft during the course of the war.

The United States also started a program of superior pilot training. The best American pilots were routinely sent back to the states to train new pilots. In time, this superior training became paramount. Both Germany and Japan kept their best pilots in the field, thus new pilots could not benefit from the experience of seasoned pilots.

By 1943, America had changed war tactics from defensive to offensive operations. While the country paid a dear price in lives and treasure, American technology and training soon created the best fighting force in the world. Over the four years of America's involvement in the war, her ability to build and arm a massive Army, Navy, and Air Force would decimate the Axis forces of Germany and Japan.[185]

European War

America slowly joined the war in what was almost a warm-up period. Under President Roosevelt's urging, Congress started a Lend-Lease program to Great Britain. This program was really a way to participate by supporting the war with bullets and machines without committing soldiers. Under Lend-Lease, The United States would supply England with the wares of war with the provision that the debt would be paid at the end of the war.

The German machine had systematically been taking down country after country. In the wake of German occupation Jews, homosexuals, and other undesirables, including men, women, and

---

185   http://militaryhistory.about.com/od/worldwariiaircraft/p/f6f-hellcat.htm

children were being murdered or arrested and sent to camps where the Germans could carry out their "Final Solution," which included the murder and incineration of over six million Jews just because of their race.

Hitler's rage did not stop at Jews. It included any religion that preached the brotherhood of man, or the fatherhood of God. While Hitler was castigating the religions of God, he would require his generals to take the following an oath: "I swear before God to give my unconditional obedience to Adolf Hitler, Fuehrer of the Third Reich of the German People, Supreme Commander of the Wehrmacht (Armed Forces), and I pledge my word as a brave soldier to observe this oath always, even at the peril of my life."[186]

In the late 1930s, when Hitler began his war on Europe, he made a non-aggression pact with the Soviet leader, Joseph Stalin. Stalin saw an opportunity to gain control of much of Eastern Europe and so agreed to the pact. The truth is Stalin and Hitler hated each other, but both saw an opportunity to gain ground and place more countries and resources under their respective iron-hand rule.

Hitler was a master at deception. Before starting an engagement, he sent infiltrators into the country to stir up the people. Then he would create an incident that he would construe as aggression against Germany by the target country.

Using this method in 1938, Hitler took over the countries of Poland, Austria, German Sudetenland, and Czechoslovakia. With the blatant takeover of their neighbors, France and Britain not only did not come their rescue, but in a conference in the fall of that year, placated Hitler when he promised to make no more land grabs in Europe.

Britain's Prime Minister, the inept Neville Chamberlain, wrote out a pledge of friendship to Hitler. Chamberlain waved this worthless piece of paper in front a cheering crowd and declared: "I believe this is Peace in our time."

Hitler later stated that, had France and Britain come to the aid of Austria, he would never have aggressed further. But their inaction

---

186   Leckie, Robert, The Wars of America, Castle Books 1998 page 676-677

fed his belief that the Allies would never forcefully challenge him. The Axis powers were further encouraged when they found that a liberal professor at Oxford Union University in England encouraged the students to pass the Joad Resolution, which stated, "This house will in no circumstances fight for King and Country."[187]

America enters the European war

This aggression by Hitler would continue unabated for another three years before the United States concluded that Hitler must be stopped. Within days of the attack on Pearl Harbor, Congress declared war on the Axis powers: Germany, Japan and Italy. As we look at history, we often think of it as a foregone conclusion that the Axis powers would lose and the Allies win. However, World War II was very touch-and-go. It would only be won by the sheer determination and commitment of blood and treasure by the allied nations.

Initial battles were baptisms by fire for the unprepared U.S. forces. In Africa, German troops battered the American 2nd Corps at Kasserine Pass. While the Germans won the day, the American army held their ground and the German forces had to withdraw. In the wake of Kasserine, the army pulled out their old warhorse, General George S. Patton.

General Patton, with general's stars on his helmet and flying his red officer's flag on his specially designed command car, arrived at the 2nd Corps headquarters with sirens blaring. In short order, General Patton put the fear of God into the 2nd Corps. He took the men who had suffered at Kasserine and started them on a crash course to turn them into fighting fanatics. Patton, true to his word, led the men of 2nd Corps on to victory in Africa.

The war would drag on for four more years. General Patton would gain the infamous honor of the general most feared by the German High Command. Patton was an avid historian and a student of war. He understood the true art of war better than any general on

---

187   Leckie, Robert, The Wars of America, Castle Books 1998 page 682-683

either side.

Patton held to two basic strategies:

1. Hold 'em by the nose, and kick 'em in the pants! (There have been several adaptations to this statement.)

2. Attack, Attack, Attack.

Patton would tell his men they were not to hold a position. They were to attack, always attack. While Patton was almost always in hot water with his superiors, they continued to keep him as a commander because he understood, as no other general understood, that to minimize casualties and shorten a war, you must hit the enemy with such extreme violence and make war so terrible that the enemy will sue for peace.

Patton was side-lined by the Allied High Command during the Normandy Invasion in June of 1944, but as the Allied forces become bogged down in France, Patton was taken off probation and given command of the Third Army. Patton led the Third Army across Europe, where he proved his theories of war.

General Patton and the Third Army gained more ground, took more prisoners, and had lower casualties than any other command in Europe.[188] Patton proved that he could shorten the war by following his theory of attacking and engaging the enemy violently.

As the allies closed in on Germany from all sides, General Patton understood that he was in a race with the Russians to reach Berlin first. It seemed Patton alone understood the dangers of Joe Stalin and the Soviet Union. The American and Allied leaders tried to pacify the Soviets, and refused to allow Patton's Third Army to reach Berlin first.

The Soviet Soldiers, like the Japanese, were under orders to inflict as much brutality, pain, and suffering as possible on the conquered people. The Russians were not seen as liberators, but as another evil and brutal regime to be feared. In Germany, Stalin used the excuse that three years earlier the Germans had raped and murdered as they pushed their way into Russia. As a result, Stalin

---

188   O'Reilly, Bill, Killing Patton, Henry Holt, Canada, 2014, Page 27

published a leaflet that was given to his soldiers:

"Kill, Kill! Follow the precepts of Comrade Stalin. Stamp out the fascist beast once and for all in its lair! Use force and break the spirit of Germanic women. Take them as your lawful booty. Kill! As you storm onward, Kill! You gallant soldiers of the Red Army."[189]

As the Russian troops approached Berlin, their reputation preceded them. The German people who had the means made an exodus to the west with the hope of surrendering to the Americans. The poor who had no way to escape were left to the mercy of the Russians, and there was little in the way of mercy from the Russian soldiers.

In April 1945, 2.5 million Russians soldiers ringed Berlin and hammered at the besieged city with more than 40,000 artillery pieces. The Russians rained down more tonnage of explosives on Berlin than the previous four years of aerial bombardments by the United States and Great Britain combined. It is estimated that between 80,000, to 100,000 Berliners were killed in these bombardments.

It was not only the Russians who were looting raping and murdering the Berliners, but Nazi gangs, thugs, and SS units. They were walking the streets looting stores and homes, raping and murdering as they went. There was no law left in Berlin. German SS units were hanging suspected deserters from the lampposts and leaving the bodies to swing in the wind.

In this burning hell, many German soldiers and their commanders deserted the ranks and ran for the American lines to avoid being taken prisoner by the Russians. After several weeks of intense fighting the Russians entered Berlin where soldiers ripped children from their mothers' arms and repeatedly raped the women. They ravaged a hospital where they raped women who were in labor or had just given birth. There were mass suicides by German woman to avoid the rapings, and by those who could not cope with the shame of being repeatedly raped.[190] [191]

189   O'Reilly, Bill, Killing Patton, Henry Holt, Canada, 2014, Page 212
190   O'Reilly, Bill, Killing Patton, Henry Holt, Canada, 2014, Page 252-253
191   Author's Note: There were a few Russian and German men and women who, at the peril of their own lives, not only refused to take part in the

Allied commanders were aware of the atrocities being committed by the Russian army; however, for political expediency, believing they were buying peace, both President Roosevelt and later, President Truman, along with General Eisenhower and, with certain reservation, England's Prime Minister Churchill allowed the Russians to keep half of Berlin and most of Eastern Europe. The lone dissenter in this decision was General George S. Patton.

Russia took Germany and Eastern Europe as a prize to be ruled and enslaved. Unlike Russia, the United States would spend billions to rebuild Germany and allow the German people to govern themselves.

Over the next forty-four years, the United State would spend billions more to man an army with the sole purpose to protect Germany and Europe from the aggressive Russian Bear.

General Patton lobbied against allowing the Russians any foothold in Europe. He understood the brutality and true intent of Stalin. He believed Stalin was as dangerous to world peace as Hitler, the Nazis, and the Japanese Empire. Patton advocated rearming the Nazi army, attacking the Russian "Mongols" and driving them back to their own county. By the end of the war, the United States alone had emerged as the leading military power in the world. The United States had an overwhelming technological advantage in conventional war, and was the only nation that had nuclear weapons.

General Patton pushed for war against Stalin and the communists, correctly stating of the Allied forces, "We have the troops and equipment in Europe. We are here and ready to fight." Unwisely, the United States made a gamble that they almost lost by allowing Russia to gain too much land, too much power, and nuclear weapons. History would prove that General Patton was right. In the real cost of treasure and men it would have been cheaper to have finished the fight against communism in the 1940s.

Over the course of Stalin's life and his successors, millions

---

rapes and murders but did everything within their power to stop the carnage. These men and women should be honored for their outstanding courage.

of people would be imprisoned and murdered. U.S. losses in Korea and Vietnam alone were over 90,000 men.

If the United States had finished the fight in the 1940s, there would have been no Korean War, no Vietnam War, and not the hundreds of smaller wars over the next sixty-five years.

Surrender of Japan

There have been volumes written by authors who were *not* in the Pacific in the last days of World War II. Many of these Monday morning quarterbacks have made the argument that the United States did not have to use the atomic bomb to end the war with Japan. They claim that Japan was ready to surrender prior to the use of the atomic bomb. Most of these claims began to surface in the 1960s, almost twenty years after the surrender.

Archived information declassified in the 1970s demonstrates that using the atom bomb in fact saved millions of Japanese civilians and millions more of both Japanese and Allied soldiers. In the spring of 1945, Japan was low on food and there was no question they were losing the war; however they were far from beaten or defeated. Japan had convinced American war planners that they would not capitulate under any circumstances. Using the available information, America had to consider the following:

1. Japan had never surrendered and had no intention of surrendering to America.

2. She still had a standing army of almost three million men.

3. Japan had plans to draft all able-bodied inhabitances regardless of gender. This would include all men 15 to 60 years of age and all women 17 to 40 years of age.

4. Japan did not have enough guns for all the new draftees but planned to arm them with bamboo spears and use them in a support role.

5. Japan still had over 10,000 aircraft. They planned to use half in conventional combat roles and half in Kamikaze

missions.

6. She had over 27,000 vehicles, tanks, and motorized guns.

7. According to Japan's defense plan Ketsu Go (Operation Decisive) America's morale was brittle and could be broken by inflicting enormous casualties on the American troops. Japan believed Americans politicians and citizens would recoil at the bloodletting, thus putting Japan in position to dictate the terms of a cessation of hostilities and not surrender.

8. A key element of Ketsu Go was this: diplomacy would follow, not precede, the invasion or the bloodletting battles.

9. The United States was aware that the Soviets had entertained representatives from the Japanese Empire. They were also aware the representatives were not proposing a plan to surrender, but a plan to seek Soviet mediation. Later, it was discovered that the so-called peace entrepreneurs in Europe had no authority to speak for Tokyo.

10. The United States joint Chiefs warned that it was doubtful Japan would ever surrender; if they did, it was probable that the army would not accept the surrender but would continue to fight a guerrilla war.

Much of the U.S. information came from Magic. Magic was the name given to the code breaking system the United States had developed before the war started. It was never discovered by the Japanese. The U.S. continued to keep Magic secret for years even after the war had ended.

Alternate plans to obtain the surrender of Japan

1. The allies considered the use of conventional landings with a land war to subdue Japan in the same way the Allies had defeated Germany. The cost in deaths of soldier and civilians was projected to be in the millions. This operation would have demanded the use of both conventional bombs and firebombs on Japanese civilians to soften up the mainland before troops were dispatched in country.

2. The second alternative was a quarantine of Japan. It would involve stopping all shipping, of any kind into Japan. Along with the quarantine, it would require the bombing of all rail lines and highways to stop the major transportation of food and supplies. This would have eventually led to mass starvation of millions of Japanese citizens. Japan had convinced the United States that it would willingly sacrifice its own civilian population, prolonging the war to gain a better position for negotiations.

3. The third alternative was the most humane: the nuclear option. The atom bomb was chosen because it would save millions of lives and millions more in casualties. It would also keep the Soviets out of Japan.

The argument has been made, we could have demonstrated to Japan the destructive capabilities of the bomb, and they would have capitulated. Prior to dropping the bomb, this scenario was considered; however, because of information obtained through Magic, war planners knew Japan would have believed it was an empty threat.

In July of 1945, America sent a communication to Japan that we had a weapon that was destructive beyond belief. We warned Japan that if they did not surrender, we would use the weapon against them. The Japanese took the communication as U.S. posturing and did not believe the United States possessed such a weapon. They refused to surrender.

On August 6, 1945, the first atom bomb was dropped on the Japanese city of Hiroshima. After confirmation of the attack, the Japanese High Command refused to believe it was a nuclear attack. Admiral Toyoda determined that if it was a nuclear bomb, America did not have enough material to build a second one. This demonstrated the futility of a demonstration bomb. The Japanese High Command was so drunk on power and invincibility that they could not comprehend defeat.

Three days later, on August 9, 1945, a second bomb was dropped on the city of Nagasaki. It is estimated that between 100,000 and 200,000 people were killed in the combined bombings.

Within days, the Japanese High Command came to the reality that they had indeed been the recipient of the world's first nuclear attack. Within a week, Japan ceased hostilities.

On September 2, 1945, the Japanese government formally surrendered on the decks of the USS Missouri as it was anchored in Tokyo bay.[192]

The nuclear strike also saved the island of Hokkaido from a Soviet invasion, which would have enslaved the Japanese living there and subjected them to the same indignation of rape and murder which the Soviets had brought upon the German people.

The number of civilians killed by the two nuclear bombs was terrible, but it paled to the number of Japanese soldiers and citizen murdered at the hands of the Soviets when they seized 2.7 million Japanese on the Asia mainland. Over 360,000 Japanese civilians and Soldiers perished at the hands of the Soviets. These numbers being indicative of the death and destruction which followed the Red Army, it is estimated that at least an additional 400,000 civilians would have been murdered by the Russian hordes if they had been allowed occupy the main islands of Japan.[193]

The war is over

"The war is over" blinked a message from the code lights on the United States torpedo bomber, piloted by Ray Hawkins. August 20, 1945, prisoners at the POW camp in Naoetsu Japan received notice from their Japanese captors that the war was over. At first, they were subdued, not knowing if they could believe the information they had long sought. Within an hour of the news, a U.S. torpedo bomber flew low over the camp blinking the message

---

192   Marston, Daniel , War in the Pacific, Random House, Osprey, 2006, Pages 227-245
193   Marston, Daniel, War in the Pacific, Random House, Osprey, 2006, Pages 245

to confirm the war was over.[194] [195] [196] [197]

Over the next few days, United States fighters—then, huge B-29 bombers—flew over the camp dropping pallets of food to the starving prisoners. The POWs had received so little food from their captors that many had lost close to 50 percent of their normal body weight.

After several days of gorging themselves on the first real food they had seen since captivity, these soldiers generously took food to their former tormentors, the prison guards. At first, the guards thought the prisoners had come to kill them and were amazed when they were offered food and not retaliation. After the guards, the POW's began to distribute food to the starving Japanese people.[198] This is the face of the American Soldier! This is the face of America! America would go on to spend billions of dollars to rebuild the countries of their former enemies, Japan and Germany.

By contrast, the Soviet Union would continue to lay waist to the conquered peoples, enslave rape, and murder millions of men, woman, and children who were unfortunate enough to live in the lands that would be occupied by the Soviets.

---

194   A full account of this event is found in Chapter 31 of Hillenbrand's *Unbroken.*
195   Hillenbrand, Laura, Unbroken, Random house, 2010, Page 306
196   Author's Note: Of the 34,648 American POWs held by Japan, 12,935, or more than 37 percent, died at the hands of their captors. By comparison, only 1 percent of Americans held by the Nazis died.
197   Hillenbrand, Laura, Unbroken, Random house, 2010, Page 315
198   Hillenbrand, Laura, Unbroken, Random house, 2010, Page 315-317

Chapter 8

Americas wars in the Middle East:

Elements for reducing the carnage of war

Recognize your enemy and identify them as an enemy with no ambiguity.

1. Reduce the time under fire by making attacks violent. Use the means at hand to inflict maximum casualties in the shortest amount of time. Rapid attacks shorten the time of conflict reducing friendly fire casualties, collateral damage, and enemy combatant deaths.[199]

2. Reduce the time of the conflict by concise and stated goals that destroy the enemy so he knows he is beaten.

3. It is not enough that we believe an enemy has been defeated; the enemy must know he is defeated.

4. No man is beaten until he thinks he is.[200]

The most destructive wars are often preceded by poor, ineffectual leaders who project weakness to international neighbors. The United States is the leader of the international community. American leaders, by their action or inaction, encourage or discourage aggression against the United States and other nations. The penalty for the projection of weakness is war and terrorism, which is always costly in human suffering and treasure.

Operation Desert Storm

In 1990, Iraq President Saddam Hussein rolled tanks and troops into the neighboring country of Kuwaiti with the expressed intent of taking over its oil fields and its gulf port. Hussein like Hitler and Stalin before him was nothing short of a ruthless criminal with an eye on dominating other countries, in this case the Middle East. Hussein had expressed his goal of also taking over his weakly

---

199   Alan Axelrod, Patton, Palgrave MacMillan, Page 103
200   Alan Axelrod, Patton, Palgrave MacMillan, Page 104

protected western neighbor Saudi Arabia.[201] Like Stalin and Hitler, Saddam's soldiers tortured, raped and murdered the captive Kuwaiti civilian.

Because of the atrocities being committed on the citizens of Kuwait and the pressure that was being brought to bear on the world's oil market it was prudently decided to relieve Kuwait and go to war with Iraq.[202] [203] [204]

The mainstream American press projected thousands of American casualties. They predicted American armor and aircraft would cease to work in the desert environment. The press was so intent on losing the war before it started, they did not take the time to look at the real capabilities of the American war machine. Information was readily available to the press, which would later prove to counter almost all of the information they spat out to the American public and the world. The press certainly appeared to be complicit with our enemies in the hopeful defeat of American forces.[205]

Mother of all battles

Saddam thought he was ready to take on America. In anticipation of a tremendous tank battle Hussein declared this war; "Would be the mother of all battles."

President George H. Bush (the 41st president) chose the very capable General Norman Schwarzkopf as his commanding general. General Schwarzkopf, who was affectionately referred to

---

201 Leckie, Robert, The Wars of America, Castle Books 1998 page1121
202 Leckie, Robert, The Wars of America, Castle Books 1998 page 1120-1123
203 Author's Note: While it is true that oil is the root of the problem in the Middle East and if not for oil Hussein probably would have had no reason to invade his southern neighbor the deciding factor that convinced President Bush to relieve Kuwait was that when he obtained and read a report from Amnesty International, the report outlined atrocities including rape, murder, and torture being committed by Hussein's army against the citizens of Kuwait. When asked by a prominent minister to wait and give sanctions a chance to work, President Bush angrily replied that the minister should read the Amnesty report. For Bush this became a moral war first and a war about oil and economics second.
204 Leckie, Robert, The Wars of America, Castle Books 1998 page 1130-1131
205 Leckie, Robert, The Wars of America, Castle Books 1998 page 1125-1126

as "Stormin' Norman" has been said to have encompassed all the virtues and none of the vices of Americas greatest Generals. The general was strict and quick to discipline but very fair and without the vice of playing favorites or harboring grudges.

General Schwarzkopf allowed the press to continue to make fools of themselves and wisely used it to his advantage. U.S. intelligences confirmed Iraq believed the American press and were making their battle plans based on the flawed press reports.

The night of January 16, 1991, the military action of Desert Storm began with what was accurately called "Shock and Awe." Far out at sea, hundreds of Cruise missiles flew off combat ships, inbound for targets deep within Iraq, at the same time thousands of combat aircraft, both navel and land-based, started flights to targets inside Iraq. These aircraft consisted of special fighters designed to detect and destroy enemy radar and anti-aircraft batteries. After blinding the enemy, massive flights of fighters including F-14s, F-15s, F-111s, and F-16s were all used to their best advantages to hit targets in Iraq.

A-10 warthogs were deployed for close air support for ground troops and for their specific roll as tank busters. Helicopter gunships blazed over the Kuwait-Iraq border. General Schwarzkopf's ground troops and tanks did an end-run around Saddam's tanks, and blazed right through Iraq's famed Republican Guard. Like General Patten of World War II General Schwarzkopf was an adamant historian, he understood war and the requirement of rapid, well-planned attacks as the means to reduce causalities of American soldiers, non-combatants, and soldiers of the enemy.

Under Schwarzkopf's capable leadership, this war was prosecuted almost flawlessly. The ground war, which Saddam had said would be the mother of all battles, was essentially over in about 100 hours. America had almost devastated Iraq's military capabilities. Over the coming weeks, America air power would amaze the world by sorting more aircraft each proceeding day than the day before ultimately sorting over 5000 aircraft per-day with a total of 116,000 combat sorties flown in a little over thirty days. The American press was chagrinned by the flawless operation of the battle plan, equipment superiority and ability of the American Combat soldier.

Russian leaders became unhinged as they watched the war unfold as American forces decimated the Iraqi army and air force. The Iraq army had been supplied and trained by the Soviet Union. The Soviets were dismayed as they watched Soviet tanks and aircraft being systematically wiped out by U.S. superiority, which superseded all expectations. They were impressed with the intelligence and tenacity of the United States' all-volunteer soldiers.

Generals learn from history, however, our leaders rarely do. After thirty days of battle with an army of over half a million soldiers, we had the unbelievably low loss of only 147 combat deaths and 145 non-combat deaths. US forces were within one week of marching into the Iraqi capital of Bagdad where we would have taken President Saddam Hussein prisoner, or killed him and obtained an unconditional surrender of all hostile forces.

On February 27, 1991, President Bush suspended ground operations. President Bush declared: "Kuwait is liberated, Iraq's Army is defeated. Our military objectives are met."

President Bush, like Woodrow Wilson one half-century earlier stopped short of finishing the war and killing the leader Saddam Hussein. Because of this short-sighted decision, Saddam Hussein was left in power, and in the coming years the Kurds and other ethnic groups who had supported America's intervention would be raped, tortured, and murdered by the tens of thousands. In a little over ten years, America would be in Iraq again, this time at the cost of thousands of American lives.[206] [207]

Recipe for defeat!

President William Jefferson Clinton (1993-2001) had a charismatic personality. He was young and well-spoken. He also followed in the shoes of President Carter as an apologist of America. President Clinton left a legacy of lying to a Federal Grand Jury and

206   Leckie, Robert, The Wars of America, Castle Books 1998 page 1156-1163
207   http://www.gulflink.osd.mil/timeline/fast_facts.htm Referenced March 9, 2015

investigators. America's enemies were emboldened by his lack of character and his weakness on foreign policy. During Clinton's eight years in office, Al-Qaida killed 346 Americans and wounded over 1500 others in seven separate incidents, including the 1993 car bomb under the World Trade Center, which Osama bin Laden took credit for. In Mogadishu, Somalia, 1993, several US Black Hawk helicopters were shot down and sixteen servicemen killed and fifty-seven wounded. This was dramatized in the movie *Black Hawk Down*.[208]

On October 12, 2000, the USS Cole was attacked in Yemen by insurgents in a small boat loaded with explosives. The explosion ripped a large hole in the side of the ship killing seventeen crewmen.[209] After each of these attacks, there was no substantial response from the weak Clinton administration. These attacks culminated in 2001, in the famed 9-11 Muslim attack on the Pentagon and World Trade Center.

March 19, 2003 (under direction of Republican President George W Bush), America found itself back at war with our old enemy, Iraq. Once again, this war was won in just a few weeks. This time, we did march into downtown Bagdad. However, because of the restrictive rules of engagement, there was a decisive win, but not a decisive victory. This war would drag out through two presidencies for over fourteen years, and past 2016.

Americas first war with African Muslims

The countries of Tripoli, Tunis, Algiers and Morocco were a lose confederacy known by the European nations as the Barbary States. For over two hundred years, these Barbary States had made their living by piracy against European and other Christian nations. They would forcibly stop foreign ships looting, pillaging, and enslaving sailors who dared to sail in the Mediterranean.

---

208   http://soldiers.dodlive.mil/2013/10/never-leave-a-fallen-comrade-veterans-remember-mogadishu-rescue-mission-20-years-later/
209   http://www.nbcnews.com/id/4677978/ns/world_news-hunt_for_al_qaida/t/al-qaida-timeline-plots-attacks/#.VKbX1SvF8rg 2014

The Barbary States would routinely take protection money from these nations, then without provocation, declare war on that nation and continue the pillaging. For years, the United States had paid protection money to these pirates just to have them turn and attack our merchant shipping. In 1801, within months of the inauguration of President Thomas Jefferson, Tripoli declared war on America. Jefferson responded by sending four war ships to the Mediterranean to counter the Barbary Pirates.[210]

Early battles with the Barbary's were conclusive wins by the U.S. However, the U.S. did not punish the pirates into submission. Over the years, lessons were slowly learned by the American Navy. The lessons learned and put into practice eventually put an end to the Barbary wars.

The lesson learned was that Muslims held nothing but contempt for national weakness. They only respect absolute and overwhelming power. After fifteen years of war, the US signed the final treaty with Algiers on December 23, 1816.[211]

At the conclusion of the Barbary war Muslims did not significantly bother America again until the late 1900s. Muslims extremists resurfaced in response to the actions of weak leaders who have put America at risk again.

Insane Rules of Engagement

Since the conclusion of World War II, America has sent our troops into battle with their hands tied. These policies have caused the displacement and deaths of millions of civilians and tens of thousands of American soldiers. Centuries of battles, and volumes of histories have been written about the winning and losing of battles and war. This simple fact is one of the most common rules of war.

---

210   Wheelan, Joseph, Jefferson's War, Carroll and Graff, 2003, Prologue, pages 1-4
211   Wheelan, Joseph, Jefferson's War, Carroll and Graff, 2003, Page 362

Your enemies will dictate the rules of engagement.

Rules of Engagement, decided by political expediency rather than battlefield conditions, prohibit our military's ability to properly prosecute the war. They are killing our soldiers and making it impossible to win the wars we fight.

As of 2016, we have been in Afghanistan and Iraqi for over fifteen years. This continuation of war has cost the lives of over 21,000 Afghan and between 132,000 and 151,000 Iraqi civilians. Over 6,800 American servicemen and women have been killed and thousands more injured. Because of the refusal of the administration to bring the full weight of our military down on hostile targets the carnage to both soldiers and civilians will continue.[212, 213]

As of 2016, President Obama continues to attempt to define the rules of engagement for our servicemen. This inept President through his feel good rules has continued to put America at risk and send our servicemen home in body bags.

Rules for winning and reducing casualties

1. There are no police actions. Accept the fact you are at war.

2. Name the enemy and be willing to call them the enemy. If we are to fight and win over Terrorist Muslims, we have to identify them as an enemy.

3. Accept the fact that there will be civilian casualties, never apologize for them.

4. Collateral casualties are the results of your enemies starting the war.

5. Go where the enemies is, hunt them out and kill them.

6. Fight until your enemies know they are beat.

7. Leave the attorneys at home; they do not belong on the battle field.

212   http://costsofwar.org/article/iraqi-civilians, **accessed January 10, 2015**
https://www.iraqbodycount.org/, **accessed January 10, 2015**
213   http://costsofwar.org/article/afghan-civilians, accessed January 10, 2015

8. Never send troops into a war you don't mean to win.

9. Use all conventional assets, and if necessary unconventional assets to win.

10. Do not use the military to nation-build.

In 2012, the Obama administration changed combat instruction materials that had previously depicted Muslims in combat areas to be prone to violence. Under Obama and the Democrats, we are not allowed to consider the enemy an enemy unless they shoot at or kill our people first.

Military convoys travel in convoys as a means of protection and safety. Under Obama's rules of engagement, convoys in combat areas can no longer display signs that say "Keep Back." convoys are expected to pull over and let traffic pass.[214]

This insane rule makes an attack on a convoy, a target of opportunity.

July 2012, First Lieutenant Clint Lorance was deployed to a hot combat zone in Afghanistan. Lt. Lorance was replacing the platoon commander who had been injured in an attack a few days earlier. He had been in this command for only ninety-six hours when three men on a motorcycle traveling at high speed came directly toward his troopers.

Lieutenant Lorance, with only seconds before the motorcycle would be in position to detonate a bomb against his troops, made the difficult decision to have his men open fire. Two of the motorcyclists were killed while a third was allowed to run away.

For this difficult discussion, which could have saved the lives of his men, he was given the thanks of a grateful Commander in Chief. Lt Lorance was charged with murder and sentenced to twenty-years in prison. This was not a traffic stop in suburban America. This was war, in a combat zone where the enemy knows our Rules of Engagement and uses them to kill American soldiers.[215] [216]

---

214   No Easy Day

215   Fox New, The Kelly File October 18, 2013, 8:16 am

216   https://www.change.org/p/us-army-lt-sentenced-to-20-years-charged-with-murder-for-protecting-his-men-from-taliban/ accessed 1/9/15

United States troops receiving fire are not allowed to level a building where the fire is coming from. They are allowed to only fire on the exact spot where they can verify the sniper is.[217]

President Obama and his administration have followed all the rules to increase the cost in casualties, and treasure and fight a war that can never be decisively won. President Obama has followed his Democrat predecessors in disarming America. The results of his policies are already bearing the fruits of war and violence. Our old enemy, Russia, is on the move with complete disregard and lack of respect for America. Why should they fear us? The international embarrassing Obama has made red lines in the sand that cannot be crossed, while opposing countries continue to cross the red lines without consequence. Radical Islam is on the move and the weakling Obama told America in September of 2014, "I don't want to put the cart before the horse. We don't have a strategy yet."[218]

If America is to survive, we need to review our history and not make choices that put us at risk for war. Other countries need to know we are willing, able, and ready to fight to preserve our freedoms. We need to elect presidents and congressmen who are willing to keep America strong and display a strong presence on the world stage. Walk softly and carry a big stick!

We need to humble ourselves, thank God, and petition him for protection and blessings upon our great land.

---

217   http://www.discoverthenetworks.org/viewSubCategory.asp?id=721 accessed 1/5/2015
218   CNN world News, Obama on ISIS in Syria: "We don't have a strategy yet", By Chelsea J. Carter, Catherine E. Shoichett and Hamdi Alkhshili, accessed 2014

Chapter 9

Attitude of Gratitude

The Bible enshrines charity as the greatest virtue. The charity of a nation reflects the strength of a nation. A nation without charity would be a cold and cruel people, indeed. Charity is the cheerful giving of one's own means to lighten the burdens of another. True charity should bless the giver as well as the receiver.

If charity is the greatest virtue, then one of the greatest vices would be ingratitude. There are many people receiving charity who are truly deserving and thankful for the assistance they receive. There are many who find themselves in temporary situations where they cannot properly provide for the basic needs of food and shelter for their families. These persons and families should be provided for. No person or family who is willing to work should be allowed to go hungry or without proper shelter. These people are thankful for the assistance they receive and work to make the assistance period as short as possible.

Thankful people graciously possess the "attitude of gratitude." Unfortunately, there are many who have become entirely dependent on assistance and have developed an attitude of entitlement instead of gratitude. This attitude of entitlement makes the receivers not only dependent on the givers, but creates animosity between giver and receiver. The attitude that you are entitled to the possessions of another is destructive both physically and morally. To forcefully take the possessions of a man and give them to another is theft.

The chains of entitlement are more binding than chains made of iron.

The Democratic Party has embellished the idea that people with less are entitled to the possessions that others have earned through their own labors. Entitlement is an appropriate word because these people develop the attitude of "what's yours is mine and mine is mine." The attitude and outcome of entitlement has become a political tool to keep an ever-increasing number of the populous enslaved by the system. Pandering to the entitlement crowd, politicians of both parties have become drunk with power and a self-righteous attitude that only they really care about the plight of the poor.

There is no comfort in growth and no growth in comfort.

Those who really care about the poor should be involved in programs that enlighten and educate those in poverty. They should assist them with food and bare necessities but never make them comfortable with their poverty. Those in poverty should be given hope and tools to eventually shed the chains of poverty and entitlement. Only by shedding these chains, can people become truly independent and arrive at their full potential. Those who are allowed to be comfortable in their poverty will rarely be able to enjoy the blessings of an independent and productive life.

Assistance without responsibility creates a loss of accountability. Loss of accountability always leads to loss of freedom. Liberals, socialists, and Leftist try to convince Americans that it is only they who show compassion to the poor. However, research shows a different picture.

Who embraces true compassion with their own dollars? There are two opposing groups of people in America; for clarification we will classify them as Group 1 and Group 2.

Group 1 attends church weekly, rejects government intrusion and government redistribution of wealth, and are often labeled as conservatives.

Group 2 rejects religion and is in favor if higher taxation as a tool to redistribute wealth from those who have a lot to those who have less. This group labels themselves as liberals or progressives.

The results are in the reverse of the political rhetoric they send out. Group 1, the church-attending group, is twice as likely to give and gives at a rate 100 times greater than Group 2, the non-church group who believe in government redistribution of wealth. Group 1 also gives fifty times more to non-church charities than Group 2.[219]

Where is the moral high ground in a system that taxes a country trillions of dollars and steals the labors of its citizens in false efforts to help the poor?

There is an extreme difference between the poor and the needy. The traditional implication of poor has always followed the premise that the poor are at least partly responsible for their long-term circumstances; whereas the needy are in true need because of short-term circumstances.

It is also incumbent on the receiver to make every effort to pull themselves from their poverty and eventually to pay it forward to become a giver rather than a receiver.

Charity dates back to some of the earliest histories of man, it was religious people not socialists who were the founders of charitable works. In the Old Testament, Abraham gave tithes to *Melchizedek, "the" King of Salem*. These tithes were used for charity.[220]

The people were commanded to *voluntarily* give a tenth and other offerings to the poor and fatherless.

"When you finished setting aside a tenth . . . give it to the Levite, the foreigner, the Fatherless, and the widow."[221]

"Whoever is kind honors God."[222]

---

219   Brooks, Arthur C, Who Really Cares, Page 10, Published by Basic Books 2006

220   Genesis 14:18-21

221   Deuteronomy 26:12

222   Proverbs 14:31

In the Bible, the story of Ruth exemplifies charity with dignity. This is illustrated when Ruth gleans or forages in the fields of Boaz to gather enough grain for her mother-in-law and herself.[223]

Gleaning was a very successful welfare system dating back to the days of Moses. The owner of the fields did not pick up grain that dropped to the ground; the fallen grain was left for the poor to gather. Using this system, the rich were blessed because of their *charity,* and the poor were blessed with honorable work to gain their bread.

This system had a built in motivation for the people to work to gain their own business or to find meaningful employment. The system provided enough to eat but not enough to get comfortable.

This charitable system of gleaning was used extensively and successfully in the early days of The Church of Jesus Christ of Latter Day Saints (Mormon Church), and is still used today to provide the essentials of food and sometimes shelter to those in need. Those who receive help from the Mormon Church and are capable are expected to work in church canneries, welfare centers, or other distribution centers operated by the Church.[224] [225] [226]

The less informed believe that because the Bible speaks of giving to the poor, the poor have no responsibility for their own care. The scriptures give guidelines for those who choose to be idle and refuse to labor for their own bread.

"Even when we were with you, this we commanded you that if any would not work, neither should he eat." Now them that are

223   King James Bible, Book of Ruth

224   https://www.lds.org/topics/welfare/the-church-welfare-plan?lang=eng Accessed July 1, 2015

225   Author's Note: The Church of Jesus Christ of Latter Day Saints also has one of the largest distribution systems in the world for disaster relief. They often work in concert with Catholic and Muslim relief organizations throughout the world. This relief system blesses the lives of both members and non-members alike. In addition, during disasters Mormon Church missionaries in the region provide tens of thousands of volunteer hours to assist the people in the affected areas.

226   http://www.mormonnewsroom.org/article/humanitarian-aid-welfare-services-breakdown-donations-costs-resources Accessed Jan 9, 2015

such we command and exhort by our Lord Jesus Christ that with quietness they work and eat their own bread."[227]

Charities

In the Americas, from the sixteen hundreds to the nineteen hundreds, charities were run efficiently by Christian churches. During colonial days, it was understood that charity was temporary and was connected with the recognition that to an extent, the indigent may be partly or fully responsible for their object poverty.

American Founder Ben Franklin, speaking about the poor and the obligation of society to help them, said the following:

> I am for doing good to the poor, but . . . I think the best way of doing good to the poor, is not making them easy in poverty, but leading or driving them out of it. I observed . . . that the more public provisions were made for the poor, the less they provided for themselves, and of course became poorer. And, on the contrary, the less was done for them, the more they did for themselves, and became richer.[228]

This being said, Franklin considered it "a duty to try to relieve misfortunes of others through managed charities."

Like all things in life, charity needs balance. There is a delicate balance between giving charitably and enabling poverty. While the recipient needs to take responsibility for their condition, it is a fact that situations exist beyond our control, and at times, some may need financial help to sustain themselves and or their families with the necessities of food and shelter.

The problem with our present system is that it encourages those who *need* to become those who *greed*. The system of entitlement enslaves the receiver to the benefactor. They become

---

227   Thessalonians 3:10,12
228   http://www.goodreads.com/quotes/search?q=Benjamin+Franklin+poverty.

beholden or enslaved to those who control the purse strings of the products they enjoy.

A government, who can give you anything, is a government who can take everything. Franklin was right. We have a larger percent of people in poverty now than before our benevolent society tried to give everything to the poor.

It is difficult to assess true poverty in the United States because poverty rates are only based on taxable dollars and do not include non-reported income, panhandling, and noncash benefits such as public housing, Medicaid, or employer-provided healthcare.[229]

Entitlements

When did we stop assisting the less fortunate and start enabling them? Was it as simple as a name change? During the Great Depression, the word, "relief" was coined by the government for programs that created government jobs and or ran soup kitchens. Many relief programs were not just handouts. There were countless dams, roads, bridges and buildings constructed to provide work for people who needed employment. This type of relief offered help with dignity. The men involved in these projects took home a paycheck and restored their personal pride and dignity of being the family breadwinner.

My father and mother were married in 1933 in Utah when unemployment rates topped out at over 35 percent.[230] In the words of my father: "You couldn't buy a job." To further complicate my parent's poverty, shortly after they were married, my dad became crippled from a disease that affected his foot and ankle. For the next seven years, my dad was confined to a pair of crutches. During this time, there was no ADA or other government programs for the disabled. My parents received supplemental relief checks for a total of ten dollars per month.

229   http://www.npc.umich.edu/poverty/
230   historytogo.**utah**.gov/**utah**_chapters/from_war.../thegreatdepression.html

My mom worked because my dad couldn't. My dad and mom grew most of their own food a little five-acre farm. Their gross receipts in 1936 amounted to six hundred dollars. My dad told me the little welfare they received was a blessing to them. The welfare checks gave them enough to survive on but only if they grew a garden and had other income. My parents were grateful and thankful for the help they received. But because of the meager support, they were driven to learn new skills to become productive members of society.

My parents taught my siblings and me through example to be grateful for help and always be ready and willing to help others. This was the true lesson of the grateful heart of my parents. My dad and mom would work side by side for the next sixty years.

My parents were truly grateful, and through the years, I watched as my mom and dad often anonymously donated time and money to many individuals and causes to help others as they had been helped.

My parents who started out with so little would die with an eventual net worth of just short of a million dollars. It is interesting to look at period pictures of my parents. It is rare to find a photo of my dad with his crutches. My dad used his crutches as a tool of transportation, not as a means for sympathy.[231]

When governments create dependence, we harness and subdue the human spirit just as surely as if we put them in chains. In 2012, while addressing a group of black Americans, Vice President Joe Bidden made this statement referring to Presidential candidate Mitt Romney and the Republicans: "They're going to put y'all back in Chains."[232]

This statement came from Joe Biden, a champion of welfare programs proven by design to keep the poor chained to the system.

231   http://historytogo.utah.gov/utah_chapters/from_war_to_war/thegreatdepression.html
232   http://abcnews.go.com/blogs/politics/2012/08/vp-biden-says-republicans-are-going-to-put-yall-back-in-chains/

Vice President Joe Biden is either a liar or completely ignorant of facts. The political machine that continues to "put y-all in chains" is the Democratic Party who has made you a dependent of welfare.

Where is the freedom in a system that provides no hope for emancipation from the program? Where is the freedom in a system that provides midnight basketball but no jobs and no incentive to work, a system punishing achievers and rewarding idleness through confiscatory taxation? Where is the freedom in a system that has the greatest rate of obesity of any select group in the world?

In the mid-1960s President Lindon Johnson declared a "War on Poverty." To provide the army for this war, he coined the phrase the "Great Society. Part of the Johnson plan was to take away the stigma associated with accepting money and goods, which a person had not obtained through effort and work. In the years following, to lessen the stigma of welfare, the new word became "entitlement." Like all modern assistance programs, it was sold with guilt, not fact.

Webster's definition of entitlement:

1. The condition of having a right to do, or get something.

2. The feeling or belief that you deserve to be given something (such as special privileges.)

3. The belief that one is deserving of or entitled to certain privileges.

The word entitlement leaves the impression that someone has a right to expect something because of a condition or class. When the giver is required to give, this is not charity, but theft. There are few things in this world that people are entitled to. You may be entitled to a paycheck for labor preformed. But you are not entitled to a paycheck for someone else's labor.

One of the favorite past times of the Left is relabeling, or co-opting words. Each time a word starts to become synonymous with the true intent of a law or behavior, the Left simply changes the word and remarkets it in an attempt to disguise the true agenda.

Entitlement is one of those words. By its very usage, it is designed to deceive not only the public at large, but also the beneficiaries of the program. The beneficiaries are convinced that they are entitled to the spoils of someone else's industry.[233]

Under the presidency of Barrack Obama and the complacency of Congress from 2008 to 2012, America had the single largest jump of people living in poverty and people living on welfare in her history.

Under the failed leadership of President Obama and the establishment, welfare payments jumped to over 1.03 trillion dollars. This represents a 32 percent increase in entitlement spending. This figure excludes Medicare and Social Security, which are paid into by the beneficiaries.[234] Under this president and the Democrat leadership, we have the 2000 model of the 1930 soup kitchens. The only difference is that instead of soup kitchens, we send out food-voucher cards to the recipients.

During this same time-period, real unemployment exploded. When President Obama took office in January of 2009, the unemployment rate was 7.6 percent. This was labeled by President Obama as President Bush's unemployment. However, by 2010, the rate had soared to over 9.7 percent. President Obama refused to take responsibility for the failure of his administration and for the rapid jump in unemployment. He continued to blame President Bush, even though Bush had been out of office for two years.

This reported unemployment rate is considerably lower than the actual rate. It is based on the rate of people who file for unemployment. Small single-employee businesses rarely pay into and are not eligible to file for unemployment. It does not track those

233   Charity…Entitlements…Do Names Matter? Written *by* Shelli Dawdy *on* August 12, 2010
234   http://www.washingtontimes.com/news/2012/oct/18/welfare-spending-jumps-32- percent-four-years/?page=all , Washington Times October 18, 2012 by Stephen Dinan

who gave up looking for a job and moved on to so called entitlement programs.

If all eligible unemployed persons were counted, the true unemployment rate is actually a whopping 38 percent. The last time we approached this rate was under Democrat President Jimmy Carter in 1978.[235] This abject reporting of employment rates would never be tolerated by the press under a Republican president, but under Obama and a complacent media, this is not only tolerated but perpetrated by those who should be the watch dogs of public officials.[236]

The Democratic administration's dismantling of the job market has added to the poverty rate in America. The ruling party Democrats and establishment Republicans can claim all the credit for this dismal state of affairs.[237]

---

235   CNSNews, 62.8 percent: Labor Force Participation has Hovered Near 37 year low for 11 months, By Ali Meyer, March 6, 2015
236   Forbes, Jobs: The 'Real' Unemployment Rate Please? Anyone? , By Dan Dimicco, Feb 13, 2015
237   http://www.ncsl.org/research/labor-and-employment/national-employment-monthly-update.aspx ;
http://www.bizjournals.com/bizjournals/on-numbers/scott-thomas/2012/07/recession-claimed-170000-small.html ;
http://www.motherjones.com/blue-marble/2012/01/america-food-spending-less ;
http://www.ibtimes.com/us-spends-less-food-any-other-country-world-maps-1546945

Chapter 10

America's Poor

A job gives a man hope. Hope makes a man better. A better man is a better husband and father. A better father makes a stronger family. Strong families make strong nations.

America has poor, but how poor is poor by world standards? Here are the facts. In two hundred years, the United States, employing the strength of a Constitutional Republic with a capitalist-free market economy, has created the richest poor people in the world. In this same time we have created the largest middle-class the world has ever produced. The United States has the lowest food at risk population on planet earth. People in the United States spend the lowest percent of income on food of any major county in the world.

U.S. citizens spend an average 6 percent of their monthly income on food. The U.S. food facts include the dollars spent for luxury foods such as lobster, organic grown foods, steak and other meats. Almost all persons in the United States are able to get ample supplies of fruits, vegetables, and all types of meats. Most Americans have a better and more nutritious variety of foods at their local McDonalds than the rich of many other counties enjoy.

Citizens of the great utopia of communist Russia spend 47 percent of their income on inferior foods that would rarely grace the tables of most poor Americans. In the utopia of communist China, citizens spend 40 percent of their income on a diet of mostly rice. The great socialist countries of the United Kingdom and Brazil spend 9 and 25 percent respectively of their national income on feeding their people basic foods.[238]

Contrary to what the American media and politicians say

---

238   http://www.motherjones.com/blue-marble/2012/01/america-food-spending-less;
http://www.ibtimes.com/us-spends-less-food-any-other-country-world-maps-1546945

about the poor, the typical American poor are rich in contrast to world standards.

Over 97 percent of America's poor have at least one television, and over half have two or more TVs. Seventy-eight percent have VCR or DVD players, and over 62 percent have cable or satellite TV.

In America, the homes of the poor are in reasonably good repair. Forty-three percent of the poor own their own homes. The Census Bureau found that the average poor person has three bedrooms, one-and-a-half bathrooms, and a garage. The Census Bureau only considers 6 percent of U.S. housing as overcrowded.

American poor have larger homes and more living space than middle-class citizens living in Paris, London, Vienna, Athens and most other cities throughout Europe.[239]

Of America's poor, 83 percent have air conditioning. Almost eight-in-ten own one or more vehicles, and nearly 31 percent own two or more cars.

Most of the middle-classes of other countries own no automobiles. Middle Class of other countries do not have air conditioning, and of course no dishwashers. Most of the world's poor do not have clean water or indoor plumbing. By contrast, almost all Americans, rich or poor, have indoor plumbing. American sanitation standards are the highest in the world. Very few Americans are without a clean and abundant supply of in-house potable water delivered not by truck or bucket, but by municipal or private water systems.

Prior to the Affordable Care Act, poor Americans could obtain emergency medical care at any hospital.[240]

---

239   Author's Note: Economically, most of these are socialist leaning or communist countries.
240   http://answers.yahoo.com/question/index?qid=20070910113636AAIUFWS

Hunger in America

Photo by the author, location I-15 south of Provo, Utah

There are many websites and highway billboards claiming that 1-in-5 American children are at risk for hunger; however, this is not supported by the facts. If these people are truly at risk, is it because of the lack of funds for food, or a lack of priority for food?

This telling statement is from a former welfare recipient: "Poor people have poor ways."

According to the US Department of Agriculture, the amount of households who frequently skip meals or eat too little is only 3.5 percent of the American population. According to the report, children represent a smaller percent because parents will generally feed their children before they feed themselves.

This USDA figure represents 3.5 of 100 people who are at risk for hunger verses the 20 of 100 represented in the unfounded propaganda of the Left.

According to the USDA, on a typical day in November 2003, it was estimated between 490,000 and 698,000 households or 0.4 percent to .06 percent of all U.S. families could not afford enough food for their families. This number would indicate less than 5 of every 1000 families are really at risk of hunger.[241]

When false information is continually fed to the people, it dilutes the real threat of hunger faced by a small minority. For those who are truly hungry, every effort should be made to insure their food needs are met; however, when we allow those who are not truly needy to suck up precious resources, they are literally taking from the truly needy to feed the greedy.

Even NBC's Today Show star Al Roker stated "It just doesn't make sense. It can't be possible that seventeen million children are going to bed hungry each night. If we choose to believe the seventeen million figures, then we must admit the massive failure of the Washington bureaucrats to administer severally failed programs."[242]

Reducing Poverty

If a nation is truly concerned about reducing poverty, three components need to be included in the conversation.

First is a low cost sustainably food supply. Second is a free market business environment that stimulates business creation in the private sector. Third is a tax system that encourages maximum production by employers and employees and does not punish the population for becoming producers.

Conservatives are not anti-poor; quite the opposite. They believe in the potential of the human spirit. They believe in the person and the people. If it is our desire to raise the poor out of their

---

241   Food Security Research Brief. http://www.worldhunger.org/articles/04/editorials/hungry_us_children.htm
242   http://www.forbes.com/sites/paulroderickgregory/2013/06/02/even-matt-damon-and-beyonce-could-not-sell-the-true-child-hunger-statistic/

impoverished circumstances, there is a proven way. No country in the world at any time has ever reduced poverty by pandering to it. No country has ever reduced poverty by paying the poor to remain poor. The way to reduce poverty is jobs, industry, and the reduction of confiscatory taxation. The present tax system encourages entitlements because it reduces the incentive for lower income workers to seek employment.

Our neighbors to the south have shown how to reduce the human spirit and impoverish an entire nation. Mexico is a natural resource-rich nation, from gold and precious metals to oil and carbon fuels. It has been blessed with a mild climate that is superior to the United States' for food-growing enterprises.

Mexico has a tremendous, hard-working population. Most Mexicans who come to America come to work. Contrary to the popular myth of the lazy Mexican, Mexicans are some of the hardest workers in America. Go to almost any construction site and you will see workers of Mexican decent working hour-for-hour, nail-for-nail and in many cases out-working their lighter skinned counterparts. They are experts as concrete finishers, stucco masons, framing crews and all trades in between. Mexican Americans come from stock that believes in quality hard work.

The Mexican government, through their socialized and corrupt government, has stifled the ability of the Mexican people to move out of their abject poverty. Mexico is a third world country only because of their corrupt socialist government. Resources are not used and enhanced for consumption by the Mexican people in the free market. They are controlled by the corrupt government and black market. By using this control the rulers of the government of Mexico have become wealthy, and the common people have been kept in poverty and slavery.

In Mexico, workers are earning pennies on construction projects. As recently as the early 2000s, Mexican workers were mixing concrete with shovels on the streets for use in commercial buildings. The product was being carried by hand in five-gallon buckets up several stories for installation on high-rise buildings. The installers were using hand tools little different than those used at the turn of the century. This work is done under the guise of providing work for the people.

In the United States, the same project would have had standardized, controlled mix concrete delivered in trucks to the site and pushed to the top of the building with concrete pumps. The plant laborers, drivers, delivery, and install personal would be making hundreds of dollars more than their counterparts in Mexico. With the increased efficiency using the most up-to-date equipment the projects are finished in a reduced time frame with a lower cost and higher quality.

The American workers are left with significantly more money, more leisure time, and benefit packages not imaginable in Mexico. Because of the standardized control of products, the buildings are safer. With the efficient use of labor, the construction company is more likely to secure more jobs, benefiting the labor force by ensuring more high paying projects in the future.

How do we really reduce poverty? The answer is simple: jobs. How do we insure jobs? Stop the government from taxing and regulating the job creators out of business. In short, stop abusing business. It is not the job of business to create jobs, give benefit packages, or insure healthcare. These are a natural result of successful businesses. The job of business is to provide products that make a profit to the owners and shareholders. The higher the productivity rate, the lower the job cost, and the more high paying jobs a business will produce.

Dependency

Dependency on the public dole is having a devastating impact on families, children, and the general welfare and tranquility of the whole nation. In the mid-1960s the number of children born out of wedlock was 7 percent. In 2013, that number had soared to over

40 percent, almost a 600 percent increase. The impact of children born out of wedlock is diminished by the mainstream press and politicians of both parties. If the real consequences of the policies that have created this family breakdown were known, the American public would not tolerate it.

Many entitlement recipients have become a product of the system. Our current tax system encourages many people to stay on welfare. A person earning less than fifteen dollars per hour can often take home more after tax dollars by simply not working.

The cure for both the treasury and as a means to help people get out of the rut of poverty is to rid America of the current incomprehensible income tax system. Income tax is a tax on productivity. To tax productivity is the height of arrogance; and to add insult to injury to tax savings is nothing short of insanity. Prior to 1913, the United States had no income tax and the country was funded with ample financial resources from other taxes which were not reduced when the income tax was instituted.

If politicians and administrators really had the best interest of families and especially children, they would be addressing these problems head on. There is a persistent lie perpetrated by the establishment to keep the American public in the dark. If there was a true conversation concerning poverty, it would have to include diminishing self-respect resulting in incarceration of single-parent children versus the rate for children brought up in two-parent homes.

We would have to have a real conversation about personal responsibility of men. Real Men are the protectors of women, old young, pretty or frail. Men as the stronger sex should shoulder their responsibility to protect a woman's virginity, not exploit it.

Men should rally in their responsibility and opportunity to raise the children they produce. It is not society's responsibility to raise your child. We would have to deal with government overreach and over regulation of the job market. This over-regulation diminishes jobs available for those who choose to work.

We need to recognize that there are always those who choose not to work. Prior to the Great Society, welfare spending in 1961 was under 50 billion dollars per year; by 2008 it had soared to over 700 billion. By 2013, under the mismanagement of the Obama administration, and many in our pathetic Congress, this unsustainable figure had grown to over one trillion dollars.[243] [244]

In 2011, a report from the Census Bureau showed over 108,592,000 people were on some type of means-tested government benefit program. This astronomical number is brought to you by the same politicians who vote for tax increases, federal budget extensions, and job-killing legislation. These are the same people who voted for a tax code so cumbersome that even IRS regulators cannot explain or give consistent answers to tax questions.

The U.S. tax code with existing regulations is over four million words, making the tax code almost five times as long as the Bible.[245]

In 2011, the same Census report showed only 101,716,000 people were employed in full time positions. In nine states over 20 percent of those employed work for a government entity. Nationwide, approximately 15 percent of all workers are employed by a government entity. Some government workers are indispensable, military, police, fire, and intelligence services are vital to our internal and international security; however, there is an endless parade of non-essential government employees who soak up the tax-money paid by poor and middle-class Americans.

Government employees, state or federal, do not of themselves create a product or new money. Considering that only 62 percent of Americans are employed and only 85 percent of those work outside of government, that leaves less than 47 percent of Americans who

---

243   Senate Budget Committee/ Ranking member Jeff Sessions Republican/ CBO
244   http://www.heritage.org/research/reports/2010/06/confronting-the-unsustainable-growth-of-welfare-entitlements-principles-of-reform-and-the-next-steps
245   The Tax Foundation, How many words are in the Tax Code? By Joseph Henchman, April 15, 2014

are creating the products and treasure to sustain the other 53 percent of the population. This trend is not sustainable and is destined to self-destruct.

This same study reported thirty-five states where welfare pays better than working. The study concluded that persons in lower paying jobs would have more money from a welfare benefit than they would enjoy after tax dollars.[246]

Each time a person chooses to take an entitlement rather than become employed, it is a double-edged sword. First, they become a greater burden on society because more money has to be taken from those willing to work to maintain current revenue objectives. Second, they increase the risk for the destruction of their family, divorce, obesity and single-parent households. These single-parent households are far more likely to depend on entitlement programs than to contribute to the work force. The likelihood of incarceration is also substantially increased in fractured families.

There is very limited information published concerning suicide among welfare recipients in the United States. However, Japan has stunning information concerning suicide rates among their welfare recipients. The suicide rate in Japan is double for people on welfare as for the general population. The following is a statement from a forty-two-year-old welfare recipient in Japan that could be echoed in America: "It's no surprise to me, really," said Kichi, who lives at a halfway house in Tokyo. "Being on welfare is soul-destroying, humiliating and degrading." He added that it is easy to lose hope, even with a good support network. Breaking away from poverty that welfare locks you into is not as easy as it seems.[247]

---

246   Business Journals exclusive, By G Scott Thomas, Government employ 20 percent or more workers in nine states May 15, 2012
247   http://www.majiroxnews.com/2011/07/14/suicide-rate-of-welfare-recipients-double-the-national-average/ Suicide rate of welfare recipients double the national average. *07/14/2011, By* Robert Koike

Obesity in welfare recipients

Research conducted from the 1980s to the mid-1990s concluded that homes where food stamps were used, 42 percent of women were considered obese. In comparable homes where women were eligible but not participating in food stamps only 30 percent were obese. This is an increase of 12 percent with the only difference being participation in an entitlement program. A third group of women where incomes were above the eligibility limit only 22 percent were considered obese.[248] [249]

Perceptions of wealth

The press has created a lie to project successful people as an enemy of America. The press is careful not to show why successful people are successful. It creates an impression that all wealth large or small is ill gained unless it is wealth of those who support the Democratic Party. Republicans have been vilified as the rich who don't know what it is like to be poor. Here is a list of some of the richest people on the planet, and they all have one thing in common: they are all funders of the Democratic Party: Bill Gates, Warren Buffett, Michael Bloomberg, and George Soros. Others include Bill and Hillary Clinton, Michael Moore, Al Gore, and most wealthy Hollywood elitists. The Left would have us believe these are not the enemy and somehow they have miraculously gained their wealth but did not take it from the common people. This is the height of hypocrisy.[250]

President and Michelle Obama gained most of their wealth on the backs of hard-working taxpayers, including seniors on fixed incomes, single mothers and fathers, hardworking young families trying to pay for homes, cars, and taxes. President Obama and Michelle live off the people. The fact that President Obama had never

---

248   http://webarchives.cdlib.org/wayback.public/UERS_ag_1/20110903214240/http://ers.usda.gov/AmberWaves/February06/pdf/Feature4February2006.pdf
249   Center on Budget and Policy Priorities (Liberal think tank) Leonard Lance on Monday, April 15th, 2013 in a press release
250   Forbes, Are America's Richest Families Republicans or Democrats?, By Katia Savchuk, July 9, 2014

run a business or made a payroll was never brought up in the 2008 or 2012 campaigns. While President Obama was given a free hand to degrade Mitt Romney who gained his wealth by creating business benefiting millions of people. President and Michelle Obama were taking an unprecedented number of vacations on the back of the taxpayer and acting like spoiled little rich kids but remaining exempt from criticism. All presidents take vacations, but the Obamas set a new standard in fleecing the America public. They behaved without regard to responsibility and stewardship of the ship of state.

In 2012, Michelle Obama spent forty-two days on vacations, including junkets with staff and friends to Florida, Martha's Vineyard, Hawaii, South Africa, Latin America, Vail Colorado and Oregon. The Obama's have ruled like monarchs over the most expensive White House in History, spending over forty-four million dollars of taxpayer money on vacations over the last six years.[251]

If you are a donating member of the Democratic Party, then wealth just goes with the territory; however, if you are a Republican, your wealth has to be ill-gained.

251   http://dailycaller.com/2014/07/05/the-obamas-have-spent-over-44351777-12-in-taxpayer-cash-on-travel/ http://watchdog.org/134687/obama-vacation-hawaii/ accessed January 23, 2015

Chapter 11

Redistribution verses Distribution of Wealth

You can sheer a sheep many times, but you only skin him once.

Redistribution of Wealth, the collective system, and communism are one in the same. It is a constant drumbeat by socialists in our government that to level the playing field, government must take money from successful businesses and people and redistribute it to those people with less. However, this system never has, and never will level the field. It is not designed to create balance; it is designed to install unbreakable powerbrokers in the government. This system is the reason politicians with dismal satisfaction ratings manage to be reelected time and again.

Redistribution of wealth is one the great evils of any society. It steals from those who are the producers and gives the fruits of their labors to powerbroker politicians and those who refuse to work.

Redistribution sounds fair, unless you are the one who is being redistributed. America is the richest and most charitable nation in the history of the world. We did not get here by stealing wealth from the producers. We have been told by the present democratic administration that we are stingy, and the American system has been a failure. We are not told how it failed, just that it failed. Our schools teach that the success of the American capitalist system has been a two-hundred-year fluke. The truth is, there has never been a successful communist regime, ever.

The problem of redistribution is that eventually you run out of someone else's money. The entitlement crowd can never have enough because they have no stake in the production of the money or resources they enjoy. We have discussed the consequences of redistribution on the poor. The poor become dependent on politicians who promise the greatest number of perks for the least amount of effort.

Distribution of wealth

By contrast, distribution of wealth is the natural evolution of successful businesses. Successful businessmen and women do not take their profits home and hide them under the preverbal mattress. Profits are used to invest, or are spent on goods and services. In either case, the money is kept in circulation and is distributed down through the grocer, the car dealer, food producers, and their employees. The distribution of money never stops but continually re-circulates through society.

There is an old saying in business: "Please pay us, so we can pay them, so they can pay you." This is a simple statement, but true. With very little oversight, this natural system of distribution is the ultimate way to distribute income among the people.

Political forces from the early 1900s have been methodically trying to disassemble this natural system of wealth distribution in favor of social engineering. In 1980, after four years of President Jimmy Carter, the United States wallowed in the depression of the late 1970s. In 1980, President Reagan was elected and reintroduced the country to the natural system of wealth distribution. It took several years from 1981 to 1984 before the system began to show a measurable amount of self-healing.

President Ronald Reagan was undeterred when the economy did not immediately spring back. He stayed the course, for he understood that productivity is the only sustainable process to distribute wealth to the people. As the economy improved, economists who had derided Reagan became less enthusiastic, and many started realizing that this was not just a short-term recovery, but was destined to bring the United States back to leadership in the economic world.

Economists refer to the Reagan years, 1983 to 2003, as the longest run of peace-time prosperity in history.[252]

---

252   Forbes, The Obama Economy vs. The Reagan Economy: it's Literally No Contest, By Rick Ungar, Sept 18, 2014

There is a difference between selfishness and self-interest. Self-interest is not the great evil that it is portrayed to be. Selfishness is short-sighted; it deals with interests which can be taken advantage of only a few times. If a company produces inferior products to save money, they may make more money per unit on the few products they sell but will have few repeat customers. If the company produces a superior product, it may cost more per unit, but repeat sales will produce a greater income.

When self-interest is invested in a product, the producer is looking long-term and to repeat and referral customers. Successful people do not play the blame game. Whether you are a successful worker at Wal-Mart, or a successful builder of Staples, people use self-interest to promote their best abilities to make the most of the stewardship they have. The successful Wal-Mart employee may be having a lousy day, but he chooses to smile and work to make your shopping experience pleasant, and Wal-Mart has a satisfied customer. Satisfied customers translate to more sales, and more customers come to Wal-Mart, which insures steady employment for the employee.

It is always easier to make money in someone else's business.

If building a business was easy, anyone could do it. The fact is most people do not want to own a business. Most people would prefer to take a job where the overall headaches belong to someone else.

Almost all employers have been employees; however, few employees have ever owned a successful business or been an employer. Most employees enjoy the freedom of leaving the job when the day is done to go home and relax. There is nothing wrong with those who would rather work for someone else. However, we often see those same people deriding those who are willing to be the employer and job creators.

What does it take to start and run a successful business?

Money: The small business owner is an unsung hero who puts his money, credit, home, and generally his reputation on the line. The financial burden is overwhelming, and if the business fails, the owner may lose his home, savings, reputation and may be years paying back a busted business loan. The banks and investors are not very forgiving to those whom they have trusted to with their money.

Titles: The small business owner not only has to be the inventor of his business; he or she starts out as the boss, foreman, janitor, and laborer, often putting in twelve to eighteen hours a day, six-to-seven days a week. Generally, there is no accident, unemployment, or health insurance and rarely a steady paycheck.

Government intrusion: After making the decision to open a small business and accounting for the financial liability, the new business faces a formidable barrier of government red tape, licensing, bureaucracy and mind boggling regulations. Among the regulations placed on the business is the insane practice of requiring the business to collect withholdings taxes for both state and federal governments and pay them on behalf of the employee.

Businesses are expected to bear the expense of collecting taxes from their employees, prepare the proper paperwork, and pay the appropriate funds to the government. In essence, they become government employees. However, the government does not follow same the rules it sets for businesses. The government does not pay minimum wage or any wage at all. The feds do not have to carry health insurance or give any other benefit for this service. The company is required by law to do this work for free. How arrogant can a government be?

Companies are required to pay for comprehensive insurance to protect the employee. Does the state or federal government pay comprehensive insurance for the company who is collecting taxes for them? The answer is no.

Failure rate: Of one-hundred new businesses that will start

up this year, 70 percent will fail within the first eighteen months. Within five years, after all the exposure, expense, and taxation, between 80 to 95 percent of the remaining businesses will fail. After five years, only 5 to 10 percent of these companies will still be in business.[253]

When hard times hit, the bills still need to be paid. Often, these payments will come out of the owners' personal assets. If the bills don't get paid, the owner gets the phone call. If the business tanks, the owner is held financially responsible to make up any deficit in income and expense. Most employees prefer not to take that reasonability.

Along with the opportunity to fail is the opportunity to succeed. So why would we tax and abuse those few companies and persons who do succeed? If not for successful companies, there would be no employment. And government would truly be broke!

Thomas Jefferson: "I predict the future happiness for America if they can prevent the government from wasting the labors of the people under the pretense of taking care of them."

Our schools teach a revision of our history with distorted facts that even the most timid of study would prove to be not just distorted fact, but outright lies about the Founders of the nation and the system we call capitalism. America has made mistakes and has had growing pains. We have had power mongers who have attempted to monopolize, terrorize and bastardize the American economic system. However, we have also produced the most generous, moral, and richest people the world has ever recorded.[254]

Rich Americans have donated to and build universities,

253   : http://www.businessinsider.com/small-business-owners-are-optimistic-2013-6#ixzz2sg9FOi34;
http://www.ask.com/question/what- percentage-of-new-businesses-fail Accessed March 10, 2014
254   http://america.aljazeera.com/opinions/2014/10/ap-us-history-educationschoolscolorado.html,
 http://www.washingtonpost.com/wp-dyn/content/article/2010/03/17/AR2010031700560.html
Accessed January 23, 2015

hospitals, community centers, Boys and Girls Clubs, thousands of unnamed libraries and other buildings and institutions too numerous to mention. Never has a nation had so many private citizens build and donate more to their communities than America. No nation on earth has given more to other nations than America.

Compare generous donations of any other nation collectively and individually, and no one comes close to the United States as a charitable nation.

The lie is so easy to feed to the low-information voter. It is a lie that you can redistribute wealth and everyone will have an equal amount. It is a lie that just because someone has more, someone else has less. In fact, the opposite is true. In a capitalist society, when businesses are able to keep more of the money they produce through production, they reinvest that capital in the economy much more efficiently than government ever can. This reinvestment creates jobs and distributes income throughout all employees.

The more businesses re-invest the greater the job growth. When jobs are plentiful, the full power of the free market kicks in. When there are more jobs than qualified people to fill them, the employee can demand and get more remuneration for their labor.

How to keep the poor, poor?

Under a collective system, production is penalized. Money is siphoned out of the pockets of the producers and put in the pockets of the elite. The poor or common man is not compensated. When producers are punished for working hard, production diminishes. Employees are less likely to work overtime if the extra money is taxed away. Likewise, when profits are taxed away from business, producers are less likely to reinvest. When businesses choose not to reinvest, there is no growth. With no growth in business, available employees start to outpace available jobs. The net result is stagnant or reduced wages to the employee.

Since 2008, under the elitist system of the Democrats, President Obama, establishment Republicans and their Senate cronies, real job numbers have been decimated. New job growth in 2014 has not caught up with the number of jobs lost in 2008. This translates into a net job loss over a six-year period under the leadership, or lack thereof, of President Obama.[255] During this time, prices have inflated, but because of low job growth most wages have remained stagnant.[256]

Is there a way out of the welfare state?

"The only job below you is failure to try."

There is a viable way to reduce, and eventually eliminate the welfare state. It is not comfortable, but the result would be well worth the effort. The best way to wean the dependent from the system is through self-interest. If it becomes more profitable and people can live a better lifestyle by working as opposed to taking entitlements, eventually we would see a shift from taker to producer.

Income tax is the nemesis to prosperity and the sponsor of poverty. Income tax reduces the incentive for hard work by taxing the extra efforts of the worker at a higher tax rate.

Income tax has inaccurately been called the redistribution tax. It is through income tax that the government disproportionately removes money from working citizens and businesses. This money is then used against the very people who created it. Taxing production works as an incentive for people to languish in welfare, entitlements, and non-productivity.

By eliminating the income tax burden on low and middle-class Americans, it would make it more profitable for most people to work than to accept assistance. Under the present system, the uninformed voter believes that we can tax the rich into submission. The rich pay their fair share.

The dirty little secret is the ultra rich pay little by comparison to poor, middle-class, and even the so-called rich Americans. The

---

255   Real Clear markets, President Obama, and the Myth about 4.5 million New Jobs, By John Lott, August 13, 2012
256   Author's Note: In every socialist and communist country, the middle class is poorer than the poorest poor of the United States.

reason is simple: it is the tax code. Since the introduction of income tax, our political representatives have prostituted themselves to the sirens of money and power.

The income tax code is over four-million words long. It is designed to give huge tax breaks to ultra-rich businesses. These businesses in return give millions to political parties and politicians. This is not as much a reflection on business as on the politicians who have created this monster.[257]

Can we or should we eliminate income tax?

It is not only viable to eliminate income tax, but it would increase personal and business productivity. It would reduce the power of both the congressional and executive branches to interfere in the personal lives of the people. United States citizens were not burdened with personal income tax until 1913, when the Sixteenth Amendment was passed, which mandated the taxation of income.

To change the tide of poverty, government intrusion, and graft, income tax should be eliminated. If the government can show a compelling reason that a tax is still needed to run the basic government and military, it should be replaced with a 7 percent single-time retail tax. This is not to be confused with a value added tax that taxes an item each time its value is enhanced. A retail tax can only be charged at the retail level and only at the final point of retail sales.

Elimination of the income tax is the top priority if we are serious about helping the poor gain back their dignity and freedom and have real opportunity to pull their way out of poverty.

257   http://www.bankrate.com/finance/taxes/tax-deductions-favor-rich-1.aspx

Chapter 12

The Bible And Its Influence On America

"America is great because America is good. If America ceases to be good, America will cease to be great."

The author of this statement, Alexis de Tocqueville, spent several years in post-revolutionary America. He was amazed at the religious background of the people and their superior education, compared to their counterparts in Europe.[258]

De Tocqueville was a well-educated Frenchman. He wrote of his experiences and what he saw as the fundamental fabric of America. That fabric was America's commitment to religion and the Bible in the educational system.

Censorship

The Bible is one of the oldest histories of mankind and the cornerstone of the Constitution. So why does the United States government seek to censor and destroy any reference to this historic text? The answer lies in an agenda-driven government who is not looking for truth, but is willing to compromise truth and light to further a socialist, communist agenda of power and enslavement.

If excellence in education is the true goal of the United States Department of Education, why are educators so afraid of an opposing point of view? For a proper prospective, we need to look to the history of academia. It was the communist influence in the courts that led to the ultimate expulsion of the Bible from schools and eventually from many places in public life.

Since the early 1900s, there has been a communist influence taking hold in the United States. While those who espouse this intrusion on human freedom attempt to soften the truth by using labels such as Progressive or Liberal, their intention is always the same: to control and extinguish personal liberty and freedom.

---

258   http://www.goodreads.com/quotes/67956-america-is-great-because-she-is-good-if-america-ceases, 2013 Author Mansfield, Harvey C. and Winthrop, Delba eds page 22 Democracy in America

Transformation

"We are five days away from fundamentally transforming the United States of America." Barack Obama, October 30, 2008"[259]

In order to accomplish the ultimate goal of changing or transforming America, three major elements of American life had to be controlled:

1. Education
2. Courts and justice system
3. The media and entertainment industries.[260]

Darkness hates light

This agenda of family and religious destruction was implemented because communism and traditional religious values can never coexist. A people who espouse Christianity will not tolerate communism. Religion teaches family-centered national strength, personal responsibility, accountably, agency, and the freedom to choose the course of one's own life.

The Leftists in America have spent billions of dollars to create a political climate that has virtually taken over these three influential areas of our society. With control of education, the justice system, and entertainment, they have tried to eliminate all positive references to God, religion, family, and patriotism.

References to Satan are considered responsible under the banner of the Democratic Party. In his book *Rules for Radicals*, Saul Alinsky, hardly a defender of the Bible, appears to be quite familiar with biblical history as he cites the fall of Satan after his rebellion against God.

Lest we forget at least an over-the-shoulder acknowledgement to the very first radical: from all our legends, mythology, and

---

259   National Review Online, Victor Davis Hanson, Obama: Transforming America, October 1, 2013
260   http://www.free2pray.info/communism.html

history (and who is to know where mythology leaves off and history begins-or which is which). The first radical known to man who rebelled against the establishment and did it so effectively that he at least won his own kingdom-Lucifer.[261]

Alinsky is akin to those ancients in the Bible who believed in Satan but denied God.

These Godless ideas gained a great supporter in the early 1900s under the presidency of Woodrow Wilson; an avowed progressive and socialist. Over the following ninety-five years, the courts of America were carefully reconstructed with Left-leaning judges to progressively implement these ideas.

In universities across the country, conservative professors were systematically replaced by radical leftist educators. Following suit, those educated by these leftists have infiltrated our primary and secondary education system, and our children, as young as kindergarteners, are being taught to hate America, God and family.[262] [263]

From the beginning of the first settlements in America, Bible reading and study had been at the base of the American education system. In 1962, the U.S. Supreme Court circumvented the rights of students to pray or have any religious influence in school. Once in place this policy has continued to move left to include removal of the Ten Commandments from public places, schools, and most all, government-owned property. Ironically, the Ten Commandments are still displayed on the front of the United States Supreme Court building in Washington DC.

From the founding of America in the 1600s, the Holy Bible had been the standard for religious studies in the United States. Throughout the history of the country, almost every school in America started the day with prayer. Since the ruling against God in

261   Rules for Radicals, Alinsky, Saul D, Random House Inc., New York, 1971, library of congress catalog 70-117651, Title page 2
262   Forbes, Higher Education Has A Strong Leftist Bias – But Not Enough For One Prof, By George Leff, May 1, 2014
263   http://atheism.about.com/od/godlessamericaamericans/p/GodlessSchools.htm, Accessed Jan 12, 2016

school, there has been a continuous march against God and Christ in America. This radical censorship stopped almost all religious activities in schools such as Bible reading and school prayer. Over the next few years, the atheist censor police, assisted by the courts, went after prayer in almost every public arena, including city and county council meetings and almost any other place that could be construed as public property.

America's elitists scoff at and ridicule the Bible, and those who believe in it, as naive and intellectually inferior. Most of the Left and academia have made this judgment based on a text they have never studied, examined, or even read. After all, what could be learned from such an ancient text claiming to be the word of God?

The Holy Bible is not only a history of the people of Israel, but is the center point from which most United States law originates. The US Constitution and The Declaration of Independence were founded on principles found in the Old Testament.[264]

Shortly after the Revolutionary War in America, there was the lesser-known French Revolution. The French Revolution had one major difference from the American Revolution. The American Revolution was based on the belief that man had certain unalienable rights, also known as God-given rights (Declaration of Independence)[265]

The French Revolution lacked this basic God-based value. The French revolution degenerated from a rebuke of tyranny to tyranny itself. Lacking the religious base of the American Revolution, The French Revolution used a secular-based government to prosecute their war.[266]

At the conclusion of the Revolutionary War, the United States rushed to repatriate her brethren who had openly supported Britain during the war. By contrast, the French Revolution was a

---

264   First Amendment Center Charles C Haynes June 29, 2012 http://www.
firstamendmentcenter.org/50-years-later-how-school-prayer-ruling-changed-
america
265   Declaration of Independence, July 4, 1776, verse 2
266   The Catholic Thing / By George J Marlin July 14, 2011

disaster and degenerated to mass execution of dissidents.[267]

America's religious base

America is a religious-based country. In America, in spite of seventy years of attacks from the Left, on the Bible and religion, 90 percent of Americans still believe in God.[268]

The Bible is still the most popular book in the United States and the world. It is estimated that 85 percent of American households have Bibles in their home. American homes average 4.5 bibles per household. Sixty-nine percent of Americans believe the Bible provides answers on how to live a meaningful life. Forty-seven percent believe that the Bible has too little influence in today's society.

Research suggests as people get older, bible and religious belief increases, possibly because life's experiences prove biblical wisdom, and as death moves closer to reality, people begin to look to eternity.[269]

The Bible's scientific and literary background

To have a proper understanding of the Bible and its validity, we need to explore references in their proper time-period, original language, text, and proper interpretations. We need to use the best science available to see if it validates or invalidates accounts from the Bible.

The Bible is not a single book with references to God or God's word. The word, "bible" comes from the Greek root, "biblia" or "the books" or a compilation of books. The book we call the Bible is actually a collection of sixty-six different books written by over forty different authors over a period of almost 2000 years.

Each of these authors were inspired by God; most testified of him, and the Messiah or Jesus Christ. Most books also include

---

267   https://history.state.gov/milestones/1784-1800/french-rev
268   Gallup poll June 2011
269   *Barna Research, commissioned by American Bible Study 2012.*
American Bible Society, The State of the Bible 2013 page 9 / researched

references testifying to the validity of the other prophets from different times. Each book in the Bible represents a separate testament or witness of God and biblical truths. There are over 5,600 original New Testament manuscripts existing today, making the New Testament one of most authenticated texts in history.[270]

The Bible and creation:

According to the Book of Genesis, God created the world in six days. At first glance this seems impossible. Words and context hold the secrets of the Bible. It is important to know words and their many meanings within the context of the original text. To do this requires examining how words are used in other scriptural references.

The original language of the Old Testament was Hebrew. Some words, when translated into English, take on similar but different meanings. These will be discussed as they pertain to the following scriptures.

In the Bible, the word, "day" is not always used to designate a twenty-four-hour period of time. It is often used to describe an event or events which may not be time sensitive. Matthew 7:22, Isaiah 4:1, Joel 3:18, Zachariah 12:3: all of these scriptures start with the salutation, "And in that day." In almost every case where scriptures begin with this salutation, it refers to an event that is not time sensitive.

In my research of the Bible, the word, "day" is used less than 25 percent of the time to designate a measure of time indicating a twenty-four-hour time period. In most references, the word indicates an event. These events may involve an hour, a day, or billions of years, depending upon the event and which biblical time-period or dispensation it falls within.[271]

---

270   *Christian Apologetics*, by Norman Geisler, 1976, p. 307; 2) the article *"Archaeology and History attest to the Reliability of the Bible,"* by Richard M. Fales, Ph.D., in *The Evidence Bible*, Compiled by Ray Comfort, Bridge-Logos Publishers, Gainesville, FL, 2001, p. 163; and 3) *A Ready Defense*, by Josh Mcdowell, 1993, p. 45.
271   The Bible is divided into dispensations or time periods of the prophets.

In the book of Genesis, relative to the creation, it appears that the word, "day" is used to describe events taking thousands, and in some cases billions of years; however, each event is described as a day.[272]

Day One: Genesis 1:1: "In the beginning God created the heaven and the earth." In Hebrew the word, "create" means to fashion or to shape.[273]

Genesis 1:2: "And the earth was without form, and void and darkness was upon the face of the deep . . . ."

In the first day or event, God fashioned, or shaped, the earth from material that was without form, probably material from extinct or exploded planets comets and stars.

In the original text of the Bible, there was never any pretense that God created the earth from nothing. Other documents, such as the book of Abraham, discovered in the catacombs of Egypt around 1823 AD, reinforces the fact that God organized the elements to make our planet.[274] [275]

Our planet did not just appear at some point in time. The so-called Big Bang theory suggests tremendous events in space that brought elements together and sent our planet spinning through space for possibly billions of years, culminating in its final position in its present planetary orbit, allowing life to exist on Earth.

In this planetary orbit, we have the sun, the moon and stars. While spinning through space, these heavenly lights probably did not originally accompany the Earth.[276]

Days two and three division of waters: "And God said, "Let the waters under heaven be gathered together unto one place and let the dry land appear."[277]

Ephesians 1:10, the dispensation of the fullness of times.

272   http://enrichmentjournal.ag.org/201204/201204_084_WISE_ROSS. cfm, researched Feb 6, 2015

273   http://biblehub.com/hebrew/1254.htm accessed April 5, 2015

274   http://www.bhporter.com/lebolo.htm

275   Pearl Of Great Price, Church of Jesus Christ of Latter Day Saints, Book of Abraham Chapter 4:1

276   Genesis 1:13-17

277   Genesis 1:6-9

"And God said, Let the Earth bring forth grass, the herb . . . ."[278]

There is abundant evidence that proves that for millions of years the Earth was covered by immense oceans.[279] Eventually, the land and water were separated. After this separation of the waters, dry land plants began to grow, once again, science verifies these changes as our earth grew and developed.[280]

The Southwest is unique because it is one of the few places in the world where we are able to view, as in an hourglass, the history of the Earth.

Because of the climate and forces of nature, water and wind there are sandstone walls that reach thousands of feet upward and in other places thousands of feet downward. This geographical cutout allows us a glimpse into the geographical history of planet earth.

In this fascinating topography, scientists have found the remains of dinosaur bones, prehistoric animal foot prints, plants and the planetary history written in millions of layers of sandstone.

Several years ago, I rode my horse into a remote sandstone canyon. As I stood mesmerized by the sheer magnitude of the immense sandstone walls reaching five-hundred feet straight up toward the sky, I looked closer and could see the individual layers of sentiment that had been deposited over millions and possibly billions of years and compressed by the pressures of the immense oceans that had once covered this area.

I was amazed at the precise definition of each layer of sandstone, some as small as one half-inch, others several inches in depth. Archeological science tells us that each one of these layers represents a season or year. While I was looking into this beautiful wall of time, I saw near the bottom a large rock

---

278   Genesis 1:11

279   http://metro.co.uk/2008/12/31/early-earth-was-covered-in-water-274995/

280   A Brief History of Life on Earth/ By Laura Klappenbach/ Reference Avers C. 1989 Process and pattern in Evolution. Oxford University Press / Leaky R. 1996 The 6th extinction: Patterns of Life and the future of Humankind. Anchor

embedded in the sandstone, and I wondered: if the sandstone is millions of years old, how old is this single, solitary rock. It must date into the billions of years.

Photograph by the author

Day Four (light and dark, seasons): Genesis 14-18:[14]

"And God said, Let there be lights in the firmament of the heaven to divide the day from the night; and let them be for signs, and for seasons, and for days, and years."

Day Four includes the separation of light and dark and the placement of the sun, moon, and stars. Apparently, the placement of the Earth in its in relation to the heavenly bodies took place during this event. Without the exact placement of the Earth in our solar system, life would not be possible. Without the rotation of the Earth and the exact size of this ball of mud, life could not thrive or survive. With all of space and what is known of our solar system, the exact placement of Earth allows life as we know it.[281]

Day Five is one of the least spoken of events of the creation as written in our biblical history. Moses wrote:

20: "And God said: Let the waters bring forth abundantly

---

281   http://www.godandscience.org/apologetics/designss.html, The incredible Design of the Earth and our Solar System, Accessed January 16, 2016

the moving creatures. And fowls that may fly above the Earth in the open firmament of heaven."

21: "And God created great whales, and every living creature that moveth (sic), which the waters brought forth abundantly after their kind."[282]

The scientific community agrees that creatures were first formed and evolved in the waters of prehistoric oceans. Birds or winged animals were the first animals to make their home on earth. Other animals were created in the oceans. Our English Bible uses the term, "great whales." The Hebrew Torah uses the more descriptive word, "tannanim," which literally means the long or stretched ones, or sea monsters. This description strongly indicates what we would describe as dinosaurs.[283]

The fossil history of the world shows that the great whales, and Tannanim, or dinosaurs, inhabited the earth over 140 million years ago. This event takes place before the creation of the animals we see on the earth today. Day five is generally bypassed or conveniently left out of almost every conversation concerning the creation and the Bible.[284] However, the event was of such importance to Moses that it was specified as a specific day or event. The animals created in that event were not the animals we encounter on the earth today.

Day Six: "And God said, let the earth bring forth the living creature after his kind, cattle . . . and beasts of the earth.[285]

On the sixth day came the animals that are common to the earth today. Some of these animals are similar to many prehistoric species, but the fossil history indicates organized creation and not just survival of the fittest. Most of these animals suddenly appeared in their present form with no evidence that they came from and

---

282   Genesis 1:20-23
283   https://books.google.com/books?id=Vy6uBAAAQBAJ&pg=PT89&lp g=PT89&dq=tannanim&source=bl&ots=3693ysK9Ig&sig=pK17OfiOrpvA6t06k MzKxzb8S3k&hl=en&s, researched February 6, 2015
284   Holy Bible Old Testament Geneses 1: 21 foot note great sea-monsters/ Answers in Genesis by Steve Golden, Tim Chaffey and Ken ham, AIG-US. On August 8, 2012 http://www.answersingenesis.org/articles/aid/v7/n1/tannin-hebrew-mean, Accessed February 6, 2015
285   Genesis 1:24

evolutionary source of ancient animals.

"Paleontologists have paid an enormous price for Darwin's argument . . . . The history of most fossil species includes tow (sic) (toe) features particularly inconsistent with gradualism . . . Most species exhibit no directional change during their tenure on earth. They appear in the fossil record looking much the same as when they disappear . . . in any local area, a species does not arise gradually by the steady transformation of its ancestors; it appears all at once fully formed."[286]

This scientific statement confirms the biblical account of intelligent design and completely denigrates the theory of evolution as taught by Darwin.

"And God said, Let us make man in our image, after our likeness: and let them have dominion over the fish of the sea, and over the fowl of the air, and over the cattle, and over all the earth, and over every creeping thing that creepeth (sic) upon the earth.

"So God created man in his own image, in the image of God created he him male and female created he them."[287]

God is silent as to the exact process in creating man and the beasts of the field; however, God was specific when he said "Let **us** make man in **our** own image, in the image of God."[288]

Man is made in the expressed image of God. He is literally a spirit son or daughter of God. Knowing we are sons and daughters of God changes who we are as a people. We are not just an intelligent animal, but the offspring of a loving heavenly father who is interested in each and every person of the human family.

As Paul said to the Athenians: "For in him we live, and move and have our being as certain also of your own poets have said, for we are his offspring."[289]

This is possibly the most important statement in all of scripture. This is a detail that the Left cannot abide. When a person

286   Gould, Stephen J. The panda's Thumb 1980, page 181-182
287   Genesis 1:26-27
288   Holy Bible Old Testament Geneses 1:1-27 King James Version
289   King James Bible, New Testament, Acts 17:28

understands he or she is a child of God, not just a component or attribute of labor as appropriated in "The Capitalist" by Carl Marx.[290] As a child of God, we are responsible for our fellow beings, and we have an eternal soul.

Over the last century, our left-leaning government has left a path of destruction in its attempt to convince the public that the Bible, beginning with the creation, is not a history but an implausible, man-made myth.

Science proves to be an elusive soul-mate to the Leftists and their commitment to Darwinism. Evidence we were so sure of a few short years or months before is often shattered as we are confronted with new information from new sources. Science continues to change the information we have available to us almost daily. Look at the effect of DNA on science in understanding the human body. DNA can tell us where our progenitors came from, or if we will be more or less susceptible to certain diseases.

Too simple and not so fast

"Too simple" and "not so fast" suggests biological anthropologists from the George Washington University and New York University about the origins of human ancestry. In the upcoming issue of the journal, *Nature*, the anthropologists question the claims that several prominent fossil discoveries made in the last decade are our human ancestors. Instead, the authors offer a more nuanced explanation of the fossils' place in the tree of life. They conclude that instead of being our ancestors, the fossils more likely belong to extinct distant cousins."[291]

The famed "missing link" in our human ancestry is not a single link but a series of millions of missing pieces. These missing pieces or links would indicate in science that the theory of evolution is severely flawed. What we do see in the evolutionary roadmap is "species jump." One fossil may indicate an animal with similar

---

290   The Capitalist, Karl Marx 1867 the/ Labor the theory of value
291   Science Daily February 16, 2011 / New York University/ George Washington University/ Bernard Wood, Terry Harrison

characteristic to a modern animal; the next evidence we find is a fully developed species. These jumps in evolution indicate intelligent design, not the flawed Darwinism theory of evolutionary survival of the fittest.

Even Darwin himself understood that unless we found fossil evidence supporting confusion in evolution it would nullify his theory:

"These difficulties and objections may be classed under the following heads: Firstly, why, if species have descended from other species by insensibly fine gradations, do we not everywhere see innumerable transitional forms? Why is not all nature in confusion instead of the species being, as we see them, well defined?"[292]

The fossil history of confusion Darwin descried has never been found, so Darwin was correct: the lack of fossil evidence has debunked his own theory of evolution and survival of the fittest.

Dissenters can leave the Bible, but they cannot leave the Bible alone.

Those who choose not to believe in God or in the Bible are often obsessed trying to disprove biblical events. There are millions of people in nations throughout the world who have similar biblical histories from a variety of sources.

Other sources include the Quran, The Old and New Testament, The Book of Mormon, The Book of Abraham,[293] the Torah, writings of Josephus (Antiquities of the Jews), the Dead Sea Scrolls, oral histories of the Hopi and other American Indians, and histories found throughout the world.[294] [295]

These additional histories confirm that many of the same

---

292   Darwin, Charles, The Origin of the Species, Chapter 6: Difficulties on Theory, paragraph 2, http://www.talkorigins.org/faqs/origin/chapter6.html
293   Book of Mormon, 2nd Nephi 2:14. The Book of Abraham found in the catacombs of Egypt in the early 1820s translated by Joseph Smith, Chapter 4:26/ Isaiah 40:28/ Ephesians 3:9/ Quran 23:12-14
294   https://en.wikipedia.org/wiki/List_of_flood_myths Accessed January 15, 2016
295   http://nwcreation.net/noahlegends.html Accessed January 15, 2016

historical events found in the Bible, such as the creation, the great flood, and histories of men such as Abraham, Moses, and Jesus did happen and the men did exist.

After considering the above accounts as written by Moses and verified by the other sources mentioned, it leaves us with one of three conclusions concerning Moses and his account of the creation.

Conclusion One

Moses was the greatest scholar of all time and was endowed with knowledge the world would not enjoy until modern times.

Moses had to have knowledge that the ancient world was covered by immense seas and oceans, which left a fossil footprint that would not be studied and researched until almost three thousand years into the future. The first recorded dinosaur skeleton was found on the American continent in 1858 by William Foulke, almost 2900 years after Moses had recorded the history in Genesis.[296]

Conclusion Two

Moses was the greatest conman and speculator of all time. He made up and managed to weave a story about the creation and planetary placement. Additionally, Moses made up prophesies about an obscure people (the Jewish nation) who would become a great nation. These fantastic prophesies would prove to be true, many of them reaching centuries into the future.

Conclusion Three

Moses was a prophet of God and spoke with God. As we examine Moses, we find a man with failings, a man of admitted self-weakness, and a man of strength.

Moses was a man chosen by God to be a leader. He was well known to the Pharaoh of Egypt and to the children of Israel. Leading the people from their captivity was not something he chose to do. He was given a task to do, and he fulfilled the task.

---

296   http://www.infoplease.com/encyclopedia/science/archaeology-modern-archaeology.html April 26,2014 Modern Archaeology / http://en.wikipedia.org/wiki/William_Parker_Foulke William Foulke 1816-1865

To consider that Moses was a figure of folklore is inconceivable. The scripture references and oral histories confirm the man and prophet of God by the name of Moses lived. Moses is one of the most notable and written about men in all of history.

He is accepted as a prophet by almost half of the population of the world, including Muslims, Jews, and Christians. He was a prince of Egypt who was next in line to become Pharaoh of Egypt.[297]

Leading Israel from bondage would prove to be a monumental task. The children of Israel had been living in Egypt for about 400 years. During most of that time, they had been living as slaves to the Egyptians. According to the Bible, there were probably in excess of a million people living under the whip of the Egyptians.

One of the most well known of all biblical scriptures is the Ten Commandments. These commandments were revealed to Moses as a basic guide for the people of Israel. The commandments include detailed writings, but few people spend the time to read the entire text for a better understanding and reason behind each commandment. They are generally simplified and shortened to the following.

Who can honestly dispute the wisdom of the Ten Commandments? Which of the Ten Commandments would not make us better parents, better citizens, and a better nation?

1. Thou shalt have no other gods before me.
2. Thou shalt not make unto thee any graven images.
3. Thou shalt not take the name of the Lord thy God in Vain.
4. Remember the Sabbath day and keep it holy.
5. Honor thy father and thy mother.
6. Thou shalt not kill.
7. Thou shalt not commit adultery.
8. Thou shalt not steal.
9. Thou shalt not bear false witness against thy neighbor.
10. Thou shalt not covet thy neighbor's house; thou shalt not

---

297   US News and World Report, Moses is Revered by Three Faiths, by Kira Zalan, Dec 23, 2013

covet thy neighbor's wife.[298]

Commandments 1-3

God is not a god of idle ambition who expects people to admire him as simply a king or ruler who lives to run the lives of man. He is not just a creator who randomly placed people on the earth. He is the Father of the human race. As a father he expects his children to honor him to the best of their ability, according to the best understanding they have available to them.

Many people look at God and his commandments as a restriction on freedom. Contrary to this belief, God is a loving father who gives commandments to his children for their ultimate happiness and personal freedom.

When we choose to respect and worship other gods, they will preside over and take control of our lives. Other gods can be as simple as focusing our lives on things instead of duty to our fellow man. Other gods can be found in drugs, ambitions of power, love of money and the things it buys. It is love of money, not money itself, which corrupts man.

If you take away a man's god, he will create another.

We have ripped religion out from under our children, and the results have been predictable. Many of our young people are turning from traditional religion to the ancient practices of Earth, Star, Animal or Sun worship. These groups are literally earth worshipers. While they have vilified our traditional Christian religions, our children are turning in record numbers to other religions that are politically acceptable such as fundamental Islam and Atheism, the religion of secularism.[299] These two religions enjoy political acceptance while Christianity is shunned by our modern world. Is this the desired outcome we want for our children and our country. [300]

---

298   Exodus 20: 1-17
299   http://www.atheist-community.org/library/articles/read.php?id=742, Accessed January 16, 2016
300   In Focus Quarterly, Wake-Up Europe: Radical Islam is coming for you, By Mitchell Bard, Fall 2014

Chapter 13

American Law and the Bible

The primary reason the first Europeans settlers journeyed to America was to escape religious persecution in Britain and Europe. America was one of the few countries in the history of the world not founded for gain of property or riches, but freedom of religion. When the first pilgrims came ashore on this land we call America, one of the first items of businesses was a day of prayer and thanksgiving for safe passage. These were humble, poor people who in most cases met the natives with much curiosity; extreme caution was prevalent on both sides.[301]

From the pilgrims' first landing in the 1600s to the writing of the Constitution in 1787 and for the next two hundred years, the people of America were a prayerful people who believed God inspired and guided mankind. Even our laws are founded on principles of the Old and New Testaments.

The Founding Fathers and the Bible:

The founding fathers were not casual bible readers. They were scholars of the holy text. They understood that only a moral and God-loving people could handle the freedom that would become the signature of America. They knew that, to be a truly free and great people, our children needed to be taught from their youth proper respect for God, elders, peers, and themselves.

"Our Constitution was made only for a moral and religious People. It is wholly inadequate to the government of any other." John Adams[302]

"No people can be bound to acknowledge and ignore the invisible hand which conducts the affairs of man more than the people of the United States. Every step by which they have advanced to the character of an independent nation seems to have been distinguished

301   America the Last Best Hope copyright 2006 by William J. Bennett page 37 &38

302   The works of John Adams, ed, C.F. Adams, Boston, 1851, page 4

by some token of providential agency." George Washington[303]

The best way to teach children basic beliefs of right and wrong is through proper religious instruction. The Founders knew that religious training in the education system was paramount in keeping the people knowledgeable and free.

"Thou shalt love thy neighbor as thyself."[304] This verse tells us more about how to teach children and adults about proper treatment of their fellow man than all other books ever written. It is a simple lesson that when applied, defeats racism, robbery, thievery, rape, coveting, spousal abuse, and murder. It is one of the most profound statements of all time. It was stated 2000 years ago by a simple carpenter who was Son of God, Jesus Christ.

Our Founding Fathers were well versed in both the Old and New Testaments and the laws of Moses. The Laws of Moses were designed for justice and equity for an honorable and moral people. Our current justice system pales by comparison.

Laws that carried the death penalty were rarely enforced except in the case of murder. Checks and balances of the Law were equitable. In the case of capital crimes, it required the testimonies of two witnesses, and the witnesses were required to cast the first stone when the death penalty was to be administered. This ensured that persons, other than a cold-blooded murderer would be very careful in accusing another of a capital crime.[305]

In cases that we would classify as civil, justice provided for the accused party to make restitution to the victim of the crime not to create revenue enhancement for the state. This system was far superior to the current revolving door revenue system in place in our courts today.

Imposed fines went to the victim, not to the state. Many cases required the guilty party to repay equal, double or triple the damages incurred. This system allowed the victim to regain the remuneration for damages done to him. It allowed the guilty party to repent of

---

303   Third Thousand Years by C. Leon Skousen 1964 Page 356-357
304   Holy Bible, New Testament, Matthew 22:37-39
305   King James Bible, Old Testament, Deuteronomy 17:7

his trespass and kept the government from monetary gain from the justice system.[306]

The corruption of the justice system is in direct response to the fines imposed that enhance the state treasuries. The system is entrenched with judges that are so untouchable only in rare cases of felony actions can a judge be removed from the bench. The sixth Commandment, "Thou shalt not kill," is the most mistranslated of all the commandments. It is used by those who oppose capital punishment as a hammer against those who believe in God and the Bible. However, the original Hebrew text does not use the word, "kill." The Hebrew word used is "Ratsach,"[307] which means to murder, dash to pieces. Other references in Exodus address murder and manslaughter and other offenses. "Thou shalt not murder." [308] He that smiteth (sic) a man so that he die shall surly be put to death."[309]

Manslaughter is when a person through fault but not malice causes the death of another. Manslaughter had different punishments and did not qualify for the death penalty.[310]

Communist influence in American law and education:

"Undermining of the United States' religious foundation and infiltration of the education system will play a major role in the psychological war designed to control and influence American youth." Joseph Stalin

As early as 1924, lectures delivered at Sverdlovsk University in Moscow, Stalin made the point that cultural and educational organizations are valuable allies in the communist battle for world dictatorship. In 1933, communists in America started an extensive infiltration program into U.S. schools and universities.[311]

So how did Godless ideas take root in a free nation with

---

306   King James Bible, Old Testament, Exodus, 22:complete chapter
307   http://biblehub.com/hebrew/7523.htm
308   Exodus 20:13
309   Exodus 21:12
310   King James Bible, Old Testament, Exodus 21: 12
311   From "The Techniques of Communism: Invading Education" Chapter X 1954 by Louis F Budenz

a historical background of religion and freedom? Unlike most countries who have been co-opted by the communists, America is not poor. America is the most productive and wealthy country in the world. America has been the breadbasket of the world. We are a country that produces and exports more food per acre than any other country. It is a country where churches dot the county side as well as the interior of every city.

It was in the universities where conservatives allowed liberals with communist influences to bring their ideas and values. These people brought their new vision of America. However, once they had a foothold in our institutions of learning, they began pushing out all opposing views. There is no tolerance by Communists for accepting other ideas and ideals.

As Leftists became entrenched in the education system they pushed their influence into the primary and high schools; opposing views were not allowed to be taught or even discussed. As these puppet students grew up, they became teachers and judges.

The Left's obsession with the destruction of religion has been a never-ending assault against the Bible and almost all virtuous, traditional, and moral values, and anything with a Christian slant.

It would seem odd that the institutions and people who claim to teach only absolute truth, and accept all diversity would seek to discredit, defame, and censor the Holy Bible. If it were a false record then why are they so scared? The onslaught never stops from attempting to remove the reference to God from the Pledge of Allegiance and taking Christ out of Christmas.

The communists have an agenda to comprise America and it started with removing religion.

The following is taken from Communist Goals Congressional record (1963). These are the forty-five goals as presented in Congress:

1. U.S. acceptance of coexistence as the only alternative to atomic war.
2. U.S. willingness to capitulate in preference to engaging in atomic war.
3. Develop the illusion that total disarmament (by) the

United States would be a demonstration of moral strength.

4. Permit free trade between all nations regardless of Communist affiliation and regardless of whether or not item could be used for war.

5. Extension of long-term loans to Russia and Soviet satellites.

6. Provide American aid to all nations regardless of Communist domination.

7. Grant recognition for Red China. Admission of Red China to the U.N.

8. Set up East and West Germany as separate states in spite of Khrushchev's promise in 1955 to settle the German question by free election under the supervision of the UN.

9. Prolong the conferences to ban atomic tests because the United States has agreed to suspend tests as long as negotiations are in progress.

10. Allow all Soviet satellites individual representation in the UN.

11. Promote the U.N. as the only hope for mankind. If its charter is rewritten, demand that it be set up as a one-world government with its own independent armed forces. (Some Communist leaders believe the world can be taken over as easily by the U.N. as by Moscow. Sometimes these two centers compete with each other as they are now doing in the Congo.)

12. Resist any attempt to outlaw the Communist Party.

13. Do away with all loyalty oaths.

14. Continue giving Russia access to the US Patent Office.

15. Capture both political parties in the United States.

16. Use technical decisions of the courts to weaken basic American institutions by claiming their activities violate civil rights.

17. Get control of schools. Use them as a transmission belt for socialism and communist propaganda. Soften the curriculum and take control of teachers unions. Put the party line in textbooks.

18. Gain control of all student newspapers.

19. Use student riots to foment public protest against programs or organizations which are under Communist attack.

20. Infiltrate the press. Get control of book-review assignments, editorial writing, and policy-making positions.

21. Gain control of key positions in radio, TV, and motion pictures.

22. Continue discrediting American culture by degrading all forms of artistic expression. An American Communist cell was told to "eliminate all good sculpture from parks and buildings, substitute shapeless, awkward and meaningless forms."

23. Control art critics and directors of art museums: "Our plan is to promote ugliness, repulsive, meaningless art."

24. Eliminate all laws governing obscenity by calling them "censorship" and violation free speech and free press.

25. Break down cultural standards of morality by promoting pornography and obscenity in book, magazines, motion pictures, radio, and TV.

26. Present homosexuality, degeneracy, and promiscuity as "normal, natural, and healthy."

27. Infiltrate the churches and replace revealed religion with "social" religion. Discredit the Bible and emphasize the need for intellectual maturity, which does not need a "religious crutch."

28. Eliminate prayer or any phase of religious expression in the schools on the grounds that it violates the principle of "separation of church and state."

29. Discredit the American Constitution by calling it inadequate, old fashioned, out of step with modern needs, a hindrance to cooperation between nations on a worldwide basis.

30. Discredit the American Founding Fathers. Present them as selfish aristocrats who had no concern for the "common man."

31. Belittle all forms of American culture and discourage the teaching of American history on the grounds that it was only a minor part of the "big picture." Give more emphasis to Russian history since the Communists took over.

32. Support any socialist movement to give centralized control over any part of the culture, education, social agencies, welfare programs, mental health clinics, etc.

33. Eliminate all laws or procedures which interfere with the operation of the Communist apparatus.

34. Eliminate the House Committee on Un-American Activities.

35. Discredit and eventually dismantle the FBI.

36. Infiltrate and gain control of more unions.

37. Infiltrate and gain control of big business.

38. Transfer some of the power of arrest from the police to social agencies.[312] Treat all behavioral problems as psychiatric disorders which no one but psychiatrists can understand (or treat).

39. Dominate the psychiatric profession and use mental health laws as a means of gaining coercive control over those who oppose Communist goals.

40. Discredit the family as an institution. Encourage promiscuity and easy divorce.

41. Emphasize the need to raise children away from the

---

312   Author's Note: We are being governed by agencies such as EPA, FEMA, DHS, DPA, DEA...

negative influence of parents. Attribute prejudices, mental blocks, and retarding of children to suppressive influence of parents.

42. Create the impression that violence and insurrection are legitimate aspects of the American tradition, that students and special-interest groups should rise up and use (united force) to solve economic, political, or social problems.

43. Overthrow all colonial governments before native populations are ready for self government.

44. Internationalize the Panama Canal.

45. Repeal the Connally Reservation so the United States cannot prevent the World Court from seizing jurisdiction over domestic problems. Give the World Court jurisdiction over nations and individuals alike.[313]

This is a Godless agenda which has its roots in communism and domination of the American people. The major stumbling block to their scheme is America's Judeo-Christian roots and its stubbornness in clinging to God.

Hypocrisy

Is there hypocrisy in the person who goes to church on Sunday and is less than perfect the rest of the week? This so called hypocrisy is always exploited by those on the Left who believe people attending church believe themselves to be perfect. A truly religious person who attends church realizes there is no one who struggles more than they. The person who truly believes in God is very aware of their own shortcomings and attends church because they find strength in associating with other like-minded people who graciously share their strengths and weakness to ultimately strengthen each other.

313   The communist takeover of America – 45 declared goals/ By Greg Swank December 4 2002/ Communist Goals (1963) Congressional Record—Appendix, pp. A34-A35 January 10, 1963

The real hypocrisy is found in those who to point a finger at the religious person when they themselves refuse to seek moral improvement in their own lives and refuse to play by competitive rules in life and politics. During the 2012 presidential campaign, Senate Majority leader Harry Reid blatantly lied when he told the news media that candidate Mitt Romney hadn't paid any income taxes. In 2015 when Harry Reid announced plans to retire from the Senate he bragged that he had no regrets about lying and accusing Mitt Romney, without evidence, of failing to pay his taxes. Reid told CNN "Well, they can call it whatever they want. Romney didn't win, did he?"[314]

Hypocrisy is profound in people who complain about religious values being taught or professed in public. These same people complain about cheating, bullying, and lack of principles then find no parallel in the Godless moral degeneracy which is preached from the pulpit of Hollywood, public schools, the halls of Congress, the Supreme Court, presidents who lie to the American people, and the never-ending list of anti-religious zealots who scoff at any recognition of a supreme being.

This hypocrisy is manifest in the Supreme Court, which rules to override state constitutions, legally balloted referendums, and statutes such as declaring marriage to be between one man and one woman. Judges reach the height of hypocrisy and arrogance when they legislate from the bench.[315]

When long-standing traditions are in accordance with the Constitution and the moral will of the people, it is not the right of the courts to impose agenda-driven changes against the will of the states.[316] When prayer is condemned because a minus 10 percent minority finds it offensive, this is absolute hypocrisy.

It is supposed to be the liberal ideology of allowing all people to be respected for their individual beliefs, and yet this is the most

---

314   National Review, Harry Reid Defends baseless Romney Claims: 'Romney didn't Win Did He, By Andrew Johnson, March 31, 2015
315   http://www.huffingtonpost.com/2013/06/26/supreme-court-doma-decision_n_3454811.html
316   Deseret News Same-sex marriage decisions in other states argued in Utah case by Dennis Romboy/ Monday April 28,2014

intolerant group in the United States. This intolerance is just another leg of the hypocrisy of the Left. Why is the religion of secularism and Islam protected, while the religion of Jews and Christians is all but outlawed by the government?

Ironically, in modern America, Secularists, Atheists, and Muslims are the only religions who refuse tolerance for other religions and beliefs.[317] [318]

The battle for freedom

The Bible outlines the history of a war that was started in heaven and is still fully engaged here upon the earth. This battle is the battle for the agency of man, the battle of liberty and freedom.[319] Freedom without responsibility is not freedom but anarchy. There is a persistent mentality suggesting, "I can do as I please without consequence."

True liberty carries responsibility for actions. The war against agency and liberty is alive in America. It is unfathomable that in 2012 a majority of the American public voted against liberty and in favor of becoming a ward of the state. They voted against independence and for dependence by allowing President Obama to be re-elected, when by traditional standards, he should have been impeached.

Dependence and slavery was Satan's plan from the beginning. Satan was so persuasive that in the heavens, he was able to convince one third of Gods children, referred to in the scriptures as the stars of heaven, to abandon the plan of agency and follow him. Gods plan was to give the individual the opportunity for growth with the ability to make decisions for good or bad along with the consequences that follow such decisions.[320]

The Bible relates the struggles of people who tried to choose

317   http://www.thereligionofpeace.com/pages/quran/forced-conversion.
aspx Accessed Jan 16, 2016
318   /www.schwarzreport.org/resources/essays/why-communism-kills
Accessed Jan 16, 2016
319   King James Bible, New Testament, Revelation 12:7-17
320   King James Bible, New Testament, Revelation 12:4

slavery over freedom. Before the Israelites escaped from Egypt, they were allowed few choices of their own. The Egyptians were their taskmasters and dictated almost everything in their lives. When Moses led Israel from Egypt, the people had a difficult time adjusting to freedom. Exodus tells us that almost from the day they left the clay pits of Egypt, the people cried to be allowed to return to Egypt and slavery. Exodus 17:2-4

This history is important to our young people because like the Israelites of old, many of our young people today will choose communism over freedom because they have not the vision of freedom.

When our government is given the power to dictate every move in our lives, we have lost our agency and have truly become slaves of the state.

In the early establishment of the United States, larger cities were set up with wards that were geographic areas within each city. These wards were policed by men from that area; consequently, they knew the people for whom they had stewardship. This system was very effective in keeping crime in check.

Most cities have abandoned this simple form of policing and have moved to unified fire and police. This has been fed to the people as a way to save money. Don't believe it. It has moved neighborhood policing to a centralized system that mimics the military more than police.

The office of "Justice of the Peace," which kept the judges and courts close to the people, has been replaced by district courts. District courts move us further from the people and into centralized courts that are not concerned with justice, but with revenue enhancement.

Love and respect for all persons

Jesus Christ commanded, "Love thy neighbor." Whether we decide to take this advice is incumbent upon the individual. One of the hardest commandments given by Christ is to forgive and pray for those who spitefully use you. When we seek to apply these two commandments, love and forgiveness, we stretch ourselves and we grow. When we make a conscious decision to forgive those who have trespassed against us, in time the bitterness dissipates, hate is decreased and our growth out-paces our anger. Forgiving someone does not mean allowing them to forfeit justice or consequences for the damages and/or injustices that they have perpetrated upon an individual or society.

America is a special land. It is a land rich in natural resources, but the real treasure is in the genius of a government system which encourages morality and still allows the maximum amount of freedom to be enjoyed by the greatest number of people in the history of the world. As our people stray further from the God-based morality of the Founders, our freedoms will continue to be eroded at an accelerated rate.

Many who profess to be haters of America and threaten to leave, such as Piers Morgan, Barbara Streisand, and many others, in the end choose to stay in this blessed country. Many of the less-informed vilify our form of government and protest against the very rights that give them the right to protest. Men who dodged the draft in the 1960s and moved to our northern neighbor, Canada have done all they could to be able to return to the county they abandoned. [321]

Many biblical scholars accept America as the Promised Land spoken of by Isaiah, Ezekiel and other prophets. What is the Promised Land? It is a land blessed by God but with a restriction. It is blessed only as long as the people of the land honor the God of heaven. America fulfills and will continue to fulfill many prophesies of the ancient prophets.[322]

"Blessed" is an interesting concept. It does not mean that there will not be opposition. It is only through opposition that the individual is able to grow and become great. Our county was born in conflict; however, the Founders, almost to a man and woman, had a consensus that they and the country were subject to divine guidance.

God does not have to condemn us. We have managed to do

---

321   Salon, Take it back by Carina Chocano, January 25, 2001
322   Book of Mormon, 1st Nephi 14:2

that well enough by ourselves. If we as a nation chose to ignore time-honored rules and commandments of morality and fidelity, the result will be a corruption of the inner spirit of the person and the nation. This may be manifest in an increase in divorce with the result being the destruction of the family and our nation.[323]

Can America afford to continue down the road of a Godless society?

From the advent of moving pictures in the early 1900s to the mid and late 1960s most movie themes promoted strong families, religious values, and patriotism. These were played out in Hollywood entertainment such as *The Ten Commandments*, *The Robe*, *Ben Hur*, and literally hundreds of pro-American war movies. These movies portrayed the triumph and goodness of God and America.

This positive family and religious entertainment has been replaced with entertainment that does not reflect American values, but attempts to remake those values. This unrestrained entertainment has been effective in destroying family and patriotic and religious values. They vilify the very values that have set America apart from the world. This fabric made America the richest, most generous nation the world has ever seen. Without our religious roots, we will lose the blessing and freedoms that have always been synonymous with the very name, America.

---

323   Scripture Ready, America In Bible Prophecy, By Terry James

Chapter 14

School Prayer and the destruction of The First Amendment

How can public schools teach abstinence from God but not abstinence from sex?

One of the basic foundations of a free republic is the right of the people to peaceably assemble, speak and/or protest. It was traditionally the duty of a free press to report on, not for the government. The free press was to assist the people in keeping government transparent by reporting irregularities or criminal offences of public officials without fear of reprisal.

Encompassed with the freedom of speech is the right of the people to freely express their religious preference without interference from the government.

In America, the Founders had seen and heard what happened in England when the government became too cozy with the Church of England. Freedom of religion was lost, and all people were expected to only pay homage to the gods of the King. In America, prior to our written Constitution, some of the colonies had started to use religious preference as tool to control which candidates could run for elected office. In response to this abuse of liberty, Massachusetts, Virginia, and other colonies started putting language in their charters that protected religious liberty.

"The First Amendment was not written to protect people from Religion but to protect religion from the government." Ronald Reagan

The Constitution was designed to protect the people from the intrusion of the government in their personal lives. To strengthen the Constitution and ensure its continuance, the original signers required that a Bill of Rights be added to the Constitution. The Founders believed these rights in the Bill of Rights were not allowed by government but were God-given rights.

The Founders had seen the imperial overreach of government and how rulers would come to believe the people were beholden to them. The Founders had a new concept and called it an "experiment." The concept was self-government, or rule by the governed. In order for this new concept to work, the Founders would set tight restraints on the rulers or "government" and they would be held accountable to the people, or the governed.

The First Amendment was written to insure that the people would retain freedom of religion not freedom from religion. Religion was the first protection of the Bill of Rights. It is not specific to an organized religious group. There is no implication in the First amendment that only Jewish or Christian Churches, protestant, Catholic, Muslim, or Mormon; could be called religions.[324]

Just as many protestant churches have followers who may not be identified on the rolls of the Church, other organizations have followers that are fiercely protective of their agenda and their beliefs. The worry of the Founders was that there may come a time when the federal or state governments would mandate a specific "religion," or set of values which would become mandatory by federal statute.

Intentions have little to do with the consequence!

If a person falls or is pushed off the Empire State Building, the consequence will be the same regardless of the intention. Intention does not affect the facts of the laws of gravity.

In the hurry to make sure we have no God in Government, we have criminally left our children without balance. To truly have balance in our lives, we have to pay attention to and strengthen ourselves in three areas, physical, mental and spiritual. Liberal Democrats in our government have vilified the spiritual leg of our children, leaving them without balance and guidance in the spiritual side of their lives.

Government mandated religion

In 1962, the United States Supreme Court made a decision which had disastrous consequences to the physical and mental well-

---

324   First Amendment to the U.S. Constitution

being of our most precious commodity: our children. This decision abandoned over three hundred years of American educational tradition.

The Court ruled that students were no longer protected by the First Amendment of the U.S. Constitution. Students in government-funded schools would no longer be allowed to pray, vocally or privately. This ruling would be expanded so that there could not even be a moment of silence to respect those who would choose to silently offer their oblations to the supreme being of their choosing.[325]

This was an incredible twisting of the US Constitution. The courts were reversing almost two hundred years of constitutional religious protection. The Supreme Court could not cite any constitutional case law to support this conclusion. This ruling was the opening of the proverbial Pandora's Box. Court Justices for the next fifty years would cite this bastardization of the First Amendment to continue to make rulings further restricting this fundamental freedom of Americans. The courts would continue to restrict traditional religion while allowing the government to institute and later mandate secular religion in schools. These new government religions include Darwinism, manmade global warming, abortion, and gay rights. Religious dissension against gay rights is not tolerated, and anyone caught disagreeing with the gay agenda is accused of "hate speech." In the early 2000s when global warming claims could not be proved and the oceans did not rise, the religion of global warming underwent a name change to Climate Change: same character, same religion, same government mandating. [326]

This 1962 anti-religion ruling by the courts used the fabled Separation of Church and State as its basis for the ruling. This statement is not found in the Constitution but is a sound-bite from a letter which was drafted by President Thomas Jefferson. The letter was written to the Danbury Baptists Church in response to a letter

325   https://www.au.org/resources/publications/prayer-and-the-public-schools, Accessed July 10, 2014
326   http://www.nwf.org/Eco-Schools-USA/Become-an-Eco-School/Pathways/Climate-Change/Curriculum.aspx

from them concerning a tax that they were being required to pay to support another denomination in the state of Connecticut.[327]

The Danbury letter:

Danbury Baptists Association in the state of Connecticut assembled October 7, 1801.

To Thomas Jefferson, Esq., President of the United States of America.

Sir,

Among the many million in America and Europe who rejoice in your election to office; we embrace the first opportunity which we have enjoyed in our collective capacity, since your inauguration, to express our great satisfaction, in your appointment to the chief magistracy in the United States: And though our mode of expression may be less courtly and pompous than what many others clothe their addresses with, we beg you, sir, to believe that none are more sincere.

Our sentiments are uniformly on the side of religious liberty--that religion is at all times and places a matter between God and individuals--that no man ought to suffer in name, person, or effects on account of his religious opinions--that the legitimate power of civil government extends no further than to punish the man who works ill to his neighbors; But, sir, our constitution of government is not specific. Our ancient charter together with the law made coincident therewith, were adopted as the basis of our government, at the time of our revolution; and such had been our laws and usages, and such still are; that religion is considered as the first object of legislation; and therefore what religious privileges we enjoy (as a minor part of the state) we enjoy as favors granted, and not as inalienable rights; and these favors we receive at the expense of such degrading acknowledgements as are inconsistent with the rights of freemen. It is not to be wondered at therefore; if those who seek after power and gain under the pretense of government and religion should reproach their fellow men--should reproach their order magistrate, as an

---

327   Author's Note: The term "Separation of Church and State" is not found in the U.S. Constitution or the Bill of Rights.

enemy of religion, law, and good order, because he will not, dare not, assume the prerogatives of Jehovah and make laws to govern the kingdom of Christ.

Sir, we are sensible that the president of the United States is not the national legislator, and also sensible that the national government cannot destroy the laws of each state; but our hopes are strong that the sentiments of our beloved president, which have had such genial effect already, like the radiant beams of the sun, will shine and prevail through all these states and all the world, till hierarchy and tyranny be destroyed from the earth. Sir, when we reflect on your past services, and see a glow of philanthropy and good will shining forth in a course of more than thirty years we have reason to believe that America's God has raised you up to fill the chair of state out of that goodwill which he bears to the millions which you preside over. May God strengthen you for your arduous task which providence and the voice of the people have called you to sustain and support you enjoy administration against all the predetermined opposition of those who wish to raise to wealth and importance on the poverty and subjection of the people.

And may the Lord preserve you safe from every evil and bring you at last to his heavenly kingdom through Jesus Christ our Glorious Mediator.

Signed in behalf of the association,
Nehemiah Dodge
Ephraim Robbins
Stephen S. Nelson[328]

The response by President Jefferson to this letter was in agreement with the Baptists. Government had no authority to tax the people to support a specific religion or church.

In the following 230-word letter, the courts used ten words out of context to create their false wall of separation between church and state.

---

328   http://www.wallbuilders.com/libissuesarticles.asp?id=65, Accessed July 10, 2014

President Jefferson's response

Gentlemen

The affectionate sentiments of esteem and approbation which you are so good as to express towards me, on behalf of the Danbury Baptist association, give me the highest satisfaction. My duties dictate a faithful and zealous pursuit of the interests of my constituents, & in proportion as they are persuaded of my fidelity to those duties, the discharge of them becomes more and more pleasing. Believing with you that religion is a matter which lies solely between Man & his God, that he owes account to none other for his faith or his worship, that the legitimate powers of government reach actions only, & not opinions, I contemplate with sovereign reverence that act of the whole American people which declared that their legislature should "make no law respecting an establishment of religion, or prohibiting the free exercise thereof," **thus building a wall of separation between Church & State.** (bold added) Adhering to this expression of the supreme will of the nation in behalf of the rights of conscience, I shall see with sincere satisfaction the progress of those sentiments which tend to restore to man all his natural rights, convinced he has no natural right in opposition to his social duties.

I reciprocate your kind prayers for the protection & blessing of the common father and creator of man, and tender you for yourselves & your religious association, assurances of my high respect & esteem.

Thomas Jefferson

Jan. 1. 1802.[329]

This letter builds on the fact that the government, be it federal or state, have only the right of protecting freedom of religion but not to dictate religion and certainly not to abridge the free exercise of religion.

---

329   http://www.wallbuilders.com/libissuesarticles.asp?id=65, Accessed July 10, 2014

Thomas Jefferson, *The Writings of Thomas Jefferson*, Albert E. Bergh, ed. (Washington, D. C.: The Thomas Jefferson Memorial Association of the United States, 1904), Vol. XVI, pp. 281-282.

Darkness hates light

The United States spent over fifty years fighting the Cold War to stop the Godlessness of communism from restricting the freedoms of man. While we were fighting that war, academia and the U.S. Supreme Court were promoting and creating legislation in the United States that was promoting Godlessness, communism, and restricting constitutional freedoms.

Belief in God, constitutional principles and wisdom of the Founders is no longer taught; in their place is the religion of intolerance, racism, and white privilege.[330]

These are preached from the pulpit of public schools and universities across the country. The present day curriculum will not tolerate teachings of God or intelligent design concerning the creation. In this climate, diversity of opinion is not tolerated. Students and parents are no longer given a choice or alternative in education. Government-regulated religion is forced into the minds of unsuspecting students and parents.

Two Supreme Court rulings—Engel vs. Vitale 1962 and Murray vs. Vurlet 1963—virtually gutted the First Amendment's protection of religion. In future years, the word, "God" used in a sacred context would be all but outlawed. However, any use of "God" to defame the holy name would be acceptable and protected.

Reading of the Holy Bible in school was declared unconstitutional. There was not to be a choice in public education. It is secular education, period. However, the banning of religion in favor of secularism is itself religion.

With this religion of secularism, a new morality has been fed to the people of the United States. This morality, or immorality, is promoted and taught by the United States education system, such as sex without responsibility, same gender sex, abortion, and abandonment of monogamy. These have all become the new norm in our education system.[331] This reduction of morality has resulted in

330   http://www.huffingtonpost.com/2013/01/16/white-privilege-class-at-n_2489997.html, Accessed July 10, 2015
331   http://www.sa.sc.edu/shs/cw/students/sexualhealth/puttingcondom/ , Accessed July 10, 2015

skyrocketing divorce rates, illegitimate births, and sexual diseases among children.

No state in the Union allows pre-teen and teens under the age of fifteen or sixteen to purchase ammunition or drive on our highways. No one under the age of eighteen is legal to drink alcohol, smoke tobacco, purchase a firearm, or vote.

And yet society encourages children as young as grade school to investigate and experiment with sexual procreative powers. We expect children who we do not consider mature enough to make coherent decisions about driving a car, or using alcohol and tobacco, to make cognizant and intelligent decisions about the most powerful passion known to man: sex.

Costs to society

The court rulings banning the teaching of traditional religion in school has been a moral, social, scholastic, and financial disaster for the United States. Within a few short years after the 1962 ruling, out-of-wedlock birthrates started to rise and have continued to rise to the present date. In 1965 out-of-wedlock births among whites were at 3.1 percent; among the black population, it was over 24 percent. By 1990, out-of-wedlock births had risen an astounding 170 percent in whites and 250 percent in blacks.[332] The non-marital birthrate in Tennessee increased 252 percent from 1962 to 1994.[333] Prior to the 1960s, teen parenthood was not generally considered a problem in the U.S.[334]

---

332   Brookings, An Analysis of out of wedlock Births in the United States, By Akerlof, George A, August 1996

333   The state of the Child in Tennessee 1995, Tennessee Commission of the Children and Youth Report.

334   : http://host.madison.com/ct/news/local/health_med_fit/ article_96d0ee57-e3dc-59d7-a5ec-e5cbc5b71ffc.html#ixzz1bv38vTf6 , **Youth Risk Behavior Survey** (YRBS), , Accessed July 10, 2015

Poverty of unwed mothers:

The one undeniable implication in the staggering increase in poverty is single parent households. This poverty will continue to be exacerbated by a Godless society and a welfare system that rewards this trend and punishes responsible behavior.[335]

The cost in dollars to the welfare system over the coming years will be phenomenal; however, this will pale to the cost in human dignity and suffering from this massive increase in out-of-wedlock births.

One of the hardest hit demographic groups has been minorities, especially the black population of the United States. This race of people, in spite of immerging from a background of slavery and unbelievable discrimination, had instilled in their children Christian values, love of the Bible, and the sanctity of the family unit. In less than a decade, this population had been decimated and had become the highest percentage for out-of-wedlock pregnancy in the country. This has resulted in the highest single-parent household rate in the nation, translating into the highest percentage of incarceration in the country. In 2010, the incarceration rates by race and ethnicity were astounding, especially in the black population.

Caucasians	360 per 100,000
Latinos	966 per 100,000
Blacks	2,207 per 100,000[336]

Incarceration rates are directly related to the number of out-of-wedlock births. And out-of-wedlock birthrates can be directly tied to the abandonment of religious studies in schools.

Research released by the U.S. Census Bureau's American Community Survey found that states with the highest out-of-wedlock births in 2011 had a significantly higher incidence of poverty. This 2011 survey found that of the four million women who gave birth in the United States, 36 percent were unmarried, this

---

335   http://www.brookings.edu/research/papers/1996/08/childrenfamilies-akerlof, An Analysis of Out-of-Wedlock Childbearing in the United States," which appeared in the May 1996 issue of the Quarterly Journal of Economics.
336   http://www.prisonpolicy.org/graphs/raceinc.html

rate was up 31 percent from 2005.

In 2011, the state of Utah had the nation's lowest out-of-wedlock birthrate at 14.7 percent. This was in contrast to Washington DC who had the highest rate at 50.8 percent. The great socialist state of California came in at whopping 40 percent of all births were out of wedlock.

Poverty rates are tied directly to illegitimate birthrates. Washington DC is rated number 41 nationwide in poverty; California is rated 33. Utah is rated 15.

Both California and Washington DC brag about their caring socialist societies and their dedication to the poor and to higher education. These two socialist states or districts are some of the highest in the country per student for education spending.[337] Yet, their SAT scores are as dismal as or worse than the rest of the country.

States under Democratic control have the highest percentage of illegitimate births. Both California and Washington DC are blue states or districts, populated by Democratic representatives who have the most disdain for Judeo-Christian religious values and espouse and embrace low traditional moral standards.

By contrast, Utah is one of the reddest states in the Union. It has traditionally been governed by Republicans. Utah is known for strong Judeo-Christian religions and traditional moral values.

If reducing poverty and helping the poor attain financial freedom are the ultimate goal of the government, then perhaps they should examine the chief contributors to poverty. It has been said you cannot legislate morality; however, the federal government has done a tremendous job of legislating immorality.[338] Which states really care about reducing poverty and which states are paving the way to increasing poverty? An increase in poverty assures the poor will

---

337   D.C. had the highest rate of out-of-wedlock births in 2011, Utah the lowest, By Steven Nelson, May 6, 2013, http://www.usnews.com/news/newsgram/articles/2013/05/06/census-bureau-links-poverty-with-out-of-wedlock-births
338   http://www.povertyusa.org/the-state-of-poverty/poverty-map-state/#

remain slaves of the government. And as long as the government is able to convince the poor that they are looking out for them, the poor will continue to vote Democratic and continue as slaves of the state.

Trends indicate that in the near future, one in every two babies born in America will be born to a single mother, and illegitimacy will surpass divorce as the main cause of fatherlessness.[339] About 80 percent of unwed teen mothers will end up living in poverty and on welfare. It is estimated that illegitimate births will cost taxpayers over 2.2 billion dollars in welfare and food stamps each year.[340] Welfare indicators show that 30 percent of all welfare recipients start with out-of-wedlock births. Half of all unwed mothers go on welfare within one year of the child's birth. Only about 30 percent of these will get off welfare within five years.[341]

Over 34 percent of teenage girls in the U.S. are becoming pregnant at least once before the age of twenty. This has created a multitude of problems, including psychological problems, lower graduation rates, and greater reliance on social assistance and welfare. These all contribute to higher poverty rates.[342]

Sexually transmitted diseases

Since 1962, sexually transmitted diseases have affected millions of teenagers, leaving many with cervical cancer, HIV, and decreased chance of pregnancy. Cases of gonorrhea are up almost 400 percent among children ten to fourteen years of age. Traditionally, teens in this age group were not known to be sexually active.[343]

Teen pregnancy in girls from ten to fourteen is up 553 percent since 1962. These are little girls, not yet aware of their own bodies,

339   Marshall, Jennifer, and Sanctioning Illegitimacy: Our National Character is a Stake, Family Research Council, 3/28/97
340   Maynard, Rebecca, and Saul D Hoffman, kids having kids
341   Michael Tanner, CATO Congressional Testimony, March 9, 1995
342   http://www.leaderu.com/orgs/probe/docs/epid-std.html
343   . http://www.nbcnews.com/id/23574940/ns/health-childrens_health/t/teen-girls-has-sexually-transmitted-disease/#.VIfPqDHF9i0

who are now bearing children.[344]

STD: Of the 12 million cases of sexually transmitted diseases that occur each year, three million (or 25 percent) are among teenagers. About 13 percent of youth, ages thirteen to nineteen contract STDs each year.[345]

Chlamydia: It is estimated up to 40 percent of girls between the ages of fifteen and nineteen are infected with Chlamydia. Left untreated, it can cause sterility. In 2006, about one million girls and women between the ages of ten to twenty-four were diagnosed with Chlamydia.

Human Papilloma Virus: 15 percent of sexually active teenage girls are infected with HPV. The majority of those infected have a strain that has been linked to cervical cancer.

Genital Warts: May effect as many as one third of all sexually active teenagers. No permanent cure exists. In females, there is an association between G.W. and cervical cancer.[346]

AIDS: In 2010, the Center for Disease Control estimated that youth ages thirteen to twenty-four accounted for 26 percent of all new HIV infections in the United States.[347]

By age eighteen, two of three teenage boys say they have had sex. Research suggests sexually active boys have had an average of five partners by the time they are eighteen years of age.

Rapes perpetrated by thirteen- to fourteen-year-old boys previously unknown have increased by 186 percent. The other side of this coin is the physical risk to young women raped and brutalized by young boys, who themselves become ever more violent in the brutalizing of women, and in many cases, other young boys.[348]

---

344   http://www.inplainsite.org/what_happened_when_the_praying.html,
http://www.skatewhat.com/russhowell/10-EffectsOfThe1962CourtDecision.html
345   http://www.hhs.gov/ash/oah/adolescent-health-topics/reproductive-health/stds.
html
346   http://www.bhg.com/health-family/parenting-skills/teen-challenges/stds-teens-a-reality-check/
347   http://www.cdc.gov/hiv/risk/age/youth/index.html?s_cid=tw_std0141316
348   http://www.cdc.gov/violenceprevention/youthviolence/stats_at_a_glance/

These are called unintended consequences. We have created a society where our children are commended for behavior that is seriously affecting their health with diseases traditionally found only in the brothel, third world counties, or among people with the lowest of moral values.

Rape, one of the most despicable and violent of all crimes is being perpetrated by ever younger teen boys.

Year	Population	Rape per year
1960	179,323,175	17,190
1965	193,526,000	23,410
1970	203,235,298	37,990
1990	248,709,873	102,560
2000	281,421,906	90,178
2012	313,914,040	84,376 [349]

We have taken away childhood innocence and replaced it with child molestation, violence, and rape. Murder, gang rapes, gang fights, by both sexes are increasing in numbers never before seen in America. The correlation between this deviant and dangerous behavior is easy to find.

There is a direct correlation between out-of-wedlock births and the absence of real fathers in the home who teach their children love respect and gratitude. A second factor in the jump of childhood violence and out-of-wedlock births is lack of religion and spiritual guidance in the lives of young people.

---

349   http://www.disastercenter.com/crime/uscrime.htm

Chapter 15

What Happened to Excellence in Education?

"If a Nation expects to be ignorant and free, it expects what never was and never will be!" Unknown[350]

The SAT student score system was initiated in 1926. Until 1962, the United States had never had a down-turn in student SAT scores. After 1962, SAT scores dropped for a record eighteen consecutive years before starting to level off. According to the Department of Education, this is the first time in our history when we are graduating students with less knowledge than their parents had. The total SAT drop has been an astonishing 80 points. American students who have traditionally placed at the top in international scholastic competitions in recent years have often dropped to dead last.[351]

Again and again, educators have tried to find a common reason for the failure of our schools. It seems that with each experiment, our schools get worse. The single common dominator of low SAT scores, violence, and poverty is the lack of religious study and the removal of God from the classroom.

In addition to dismal SAT scores, student suicides are up by over 235 percent. Between 1962 and 1993, violent crime in the U.S. increased by 660 percent.[352] [353]

---

350   While this statement is attributed to Thomas Jefferson, the author found no documentation to support this exact statement.
351   http://www.inplainsite.org/what_happened_when_the_praying.html
352   http://www.skatewhat.com/russhowell/10-EffectsOfThe1962CourtDecision.html
353   America: To Pray or Not to Pray by David Barton. Mr. Barton drew statistics from the Department of Justice, The College Entrance Exam Board, Department of Health and Human Resources, Department of Commerce, the Census Bureau and other official sources.

What happens when students are taught religious values?

In the United States 12.4 percent of all students attend private school; however, 39.2 percent of the nation's top academic scholars come from private schools. Just over 10 percent of students represent almost 40 percent of all scholars. Most of these private schools are run by Christian-based organizations.[354]

The average Christian school only spends 2,200 dollars per student per year. By comparison, the average public school spends 5,400 dollars per student per year. Private schools with less than half the funds are proportionately turning out three times more scholars. Private schools have proven to be superior stewards over the education dollars they receive. They are doing far more with far less than the public education system.

The monetary difference alone should embarrass the public educators of America. If not the monetary then the quality of education should. One of the largest single differences is private schools spend time balancing their students with religious education instead of the hollow shell of political correctness.

It is estimated that after graduating from public school, over 700,000 students could not read their diploma.[355] Government education is one of the few jobs in the world where you can have a 50 percent failure rate and still receive an increase in pay.

When God and prayer were fashionable

Not surprisingly, after almost every school shooting and other violent acts, there are prayers held for the victims and often for the families of the perpetrators. When the worst happens, a phenomenal number of otherwise non-religious people turn back to God.

From the beginning of settlements in the Americas, Judeo-Christian religions and prayers had been part of the interracial fabric of America. Religion and morality was the overwhelming difference between America and the European nations.

---

354   http://www.inplainsite.org/what_happened_when_the_praying.html
355   http://www.inplainsite.org/what_happened_when_the_praying.html

Alexis de Tocqueville wrote *Democracy in America* in 1835. Speaking of America, de Tocqueville said,

> Christian morality is everywhere the same. In the United States the sovereign authority is religious, and consequently hypocrisy must be common; but there is no country in the whole world in which the Christian religion retains a greater influence over the souls of men than in America, and there can be no greater proof of its utility, and of its conformity to human nature, than that its influence is most powerfully felt over the most enlightened and free nation of the earth.[356]

Brilliant minds

The writer's and signers of the U.S. Constitution had studied the great societies of the past 3,000 years. Most of the Founders were fluent in multiple languages. They were also scholars of the Bible and many of the great works of the Greeks, Roman's, and others. Most politicians of today would be considered illiterate by the educational standards of the Founders. They were capable of reading, studying and understanding these great works relating to political systems in the languages of the original text.

Our education system has attempted to reduce these great men to racist bigots who couldn't see or understand our day; however the Founders were brilliant even by today's standards. The Constitution they established was brilliant beyond description. George Washington called it "an inspired document."[357]

When followed, the Constitution is flexible enough to accommodate technological changes but solid enough to maintain the God-given rights we enjoy as a republic. The question is, will we as Americans continue to allow activist judges and a spineless Congress to continue to override constitutional provisions, or will we hold their feet to the fire. Will we realize before it is too late that

---

356   The project Gutenburg Ebook of Democracy In America Volume 1, by Alexis De Toqueville, Chapter 17, Translator Henry Reeve, Date Released January 21, 2006 Ebook #815

357   Letter from Washington to Lafayette, 7 Feb. 1788, quoted in Catherine Drinker Bowen, *Miracle at Philadelphia,* Boston: Little, Brown and Co., 1966, p. xvii.

it is not the Constitution that is outdated, but belligerent leaders who have perverted the original documents and diluted the checks and balances to accommodate their political objectives?

The Northwest Ordinance of 1787

The Founders believed there were three legs to a good education. They were in the following order: religion, morality, and knowledge.

The following is a quote from the Northwest Ordinance: "Article 3: Religion, morality, and knowledge being necessary to good government and the happiness of mankind, schools and the means of education shall forever be encouraged." [358]

No longer a Christian nation

During the first term of the Obama Presidency, President Obama declared to the world that the United States is "No longer a Christian Nation."[359] He later followed up with: "we are nation of Jewish, Buddhist, and Muslims." Either Mr. Obama is ignorant of fact or disingenuous in the reference. We have always been a melting pot of religions, however, the term Christian nation referred to our rule of laws and morality.

In 2004, the official Democratic platform reduced the mention of God to only seven times. In 2008, it was amended and God was removed from six of the seven references. In 2012, the Democratic National Committee (DNC) voted to remove the term, "God" completely from the platform.

The following day, after rebuke from Republicans and the press, the DNC did an about face; with resounding boos from their constituents,

---

358   Encyclopedia of American History, Vol. 2, pp. 395-396.
359   https://www.youtube.com/watch?v=tmC3IevZiik

they reinstated the word God in their official platform.[360] [361] [362]

Speaking of America and Christianity Frenchman Tocqueville stated:

"Christianity is the companion of liberty in all its conflicts - the cradle of its infancy, and the divine source of its claims."[363]

From George Washington's Farewell Address:

Of all the dispositions and habits which lead to political prosperity, religion and morality are indispensable supports.

In vane would that man claim the tribute of patriotism, who should labor to subvert these great pillars of human happiness, these firmest props of the duties of men and citizens? Let it simply be asked, where is the security for property, for reputation, for life, if the sense of religious obligation desert the oaths which are the instrument of investigation in courts of justice? And let us with caution indulge the supposition that morality can be maintained without religion. Whatever may be conceded to the influence of refined education? Reason and experience both forbid us to expect that national morality can prevail in exclusion of religious principle.[364]

The Courts have almost unanimously agreed that distribution of Bibles in elementary schools—either actively or passively—is unconstitutional because young elementary school children are considered too impressionable to make the distinction between

---

360   ABC News, Dems Quickly Switch to Include God, Jerusalem, By Jake Tapper and Amy Bingham, September 5, 2012
361   Author's Note: The resolution required a two-thirds majority vote. The vote was called for three times. It never did receive the votes required; however, the Democratic leadership, realizing they had kicked over a bee's nest, called the vote a majority. By contrast, God is mentioned 12 times in the Republican platform and the Republicans do not apologize for it.
362   Video of the democratic vote can be found at https://www.youtube.com/watch?v=1zYo3yWY-rU
363   The project Gutenburg Ebook of Democracy In America Volume 1, by Alexis De Tocqueville, Translator Henry Reeve, Date Released January 21, 2006 Ebook #815
364   http://avalon.law.yale.edu/18th_century/washing.asp, Quotes from George Washington's Farewell Address, 1796

private religious speech and school-sponsored speech.[365] [366] [367]

Acts of hostility toward people of biblical faith

President Obama has led a general assault on the values and faith of Christians in America:

- April 2008: Obama speaks disrespectfully of Christians, saying they "cling to guns or religion" and have an "antipathy to people who aren't like them."

- April 2009: When speaking at Georgetown University, Obama orders that a monogram symbolizing Jesus' name be covered when he is making his speech.

- May 2009: Obama declines to host services for the National Prayer Day at the White House (a day established by federal law).

- October 19, 2010: Obama begins deliberately omitting the phrase about "the Creator" when quoting the Declaration of Independence, an omission he has made on no less than seven occasions.[368]

All politicians bring their religion to the office

Does it really matter what a politician believes? In the last fifty years, there has been an unabashed biased toward any president or candidate who espouses Christian beliefs, and yet there is no outcry for a president who does not claim to have religious beliefs. All Politicians bring their religion, or the lack of it, to the Oval Office. With secular religion, there is an absence of complaint that they are imposing their religious view on the people, and yet we see it in their every action.

---

365   http://ffrf.org/faq/feeds/item/14034-bible-distribution-in-public-schools
366   Author's Note: It is against the law to distribute Bibles to elementary students because they are impressionable and might be influenced; however, it is acceptable to indoctrinate elementary students and show them how to use a condom and teach sex without responsibility. It is acceptable to teach vague, unproven theories of creation presented as facts of secular theory, but illegal to teach the possibility of intelligent design.
367   http://www.wesjones.com/coyne1.htm
368   http://www.wallbuilders.com/libissuesarticles.asp?id=106938

Redeeming America

We will continue this downward spiral in America until we can regain control of our educational system. The only way we can gain this control is by forcing the federal government out and allowing education to be administered by the individual states. The values of each individual state should be respected, and their desire to include or exclude God in their curriculum should be the choice of that state.

Once the education system is in the hands of the states, we will begin to see competition in education. Without competition among the states, we will continue the dumbing down of education that has been the hallmark of America for the last fifty years.

Education is an industry and competition is the driving force behind excellence.

Chapter 16

Guns and Freedom

The Second Amendment is the most controversial of all our Bill of Rights. It has been vilified by gun control advocates, judges, and government officials who seek to subvert the people. Gun control has never been about crime reduction. In every culture, it is about control and subversion of the people. The power of the Second Amendment is the difference between citizens and subjects.

As the Revolutionary War was being prosecuted, America was losing more men because of poor sanitation and lack of discipline than by direct combat. In addition, many of the soldiers had inferior or antiquated weapons and poor quality munitions. From the prospective of National defense, it was imperative that the militia keep weapons and munitions which were in good condition and common to the military so they could be expected to work in concert with the army as a whole. It was intended that the militia could be called upon and be subject to better discipline if some previous training and access to the best weapons had been invested prior to the need.[369]

The importance of the militia was stressed in the Federalist Papers, Number 29. Alexander Hamilton noted that the state or federal government would be much better served by a citizen's militia who could be called as a posse in times as needed. The militia was understood to be all male citizens over the age of sixteen who were in good health.

"Reserving to the states respectively the appointment of the officers and the authority of training the militia… If the federal government can command the aid of the militia in those emergencies which call for the military arm in support of the civil magistrate, it can the better dispense with the employment of a different kind of force. There is something so far fetched (sic) and so extravagant in the idea of danger to liberty from the militia that one is at a loss

---

369   Leckie, Robert, The Wars of America, Castle Books 1998, Page 122

whether to treat it with gravity of with raillery."[370]

Hamilton outlined the importance of a standing militia being superior to a standing internal army. The militia should be under the direction of the state for training and at the disposal of the federal government in times of national need. While it is a propensity of tyrants to use the power of the military to forcibly subdue the people, Hamilton and the Founders understood that because the militia was a body of the people, the militia posed no similar dangers to the republic.

Gun Control and the myth of safety

Weapon control is not a new concept. It is recorded in the Bible in the book of Judges that the Philistines removed all the smiths (blacksmiths) from Israel so they could not make swords, spears or other weapons of war to defend themselves from their enemies.[371]

The myth that gun control is for the safety of society has been used by tyrannical governments and now by our Government to convince the people that arms, or guns, in the hands of citizens is the reason we have crime.[372] This lie has been taught in our schools and at almost every level of government.[373] History is replete with arms control being translated into civil population control. Arms and gun control has never been about crime control.[374] [375]

---

370   The Federalist Papers, Forward by Willis, Garry, publisher Bantam Book, 1982 Pages 165 and 168
371   King James Bible, Old Testament, 1 Samuel 13:19
372   http://thefederalist.com/2014/01/16/if-guns-cause-more-violence-wheres-the-exploding-crime-rate/ Accessed Jan 10, 2016
373   Boston Magazine, Harvard Publication on Gun Laws Resurfaces As Talks About Firearms Continue, By Steve Annear, August 30, 2013
374   www.firearmsandliberty.com/cramer.racism.html Accessed January 10, 2016
375   The American Rifleman, Japan: Gun Control and People Control, By David B. Kopel, December 1988

Responsibly armed Americans

Of a population of just over three hundred million, it is estimated that 30 to 50 percent of all Americans own one or more firearms. [376]

In the United States there are an estimated 270 to 310 million guns privately owned by U.S. citizens.[377] According to the Center for Disease Control in 2011, the total number of deaths by firearms including suicide, murder and accidents was 11,208. This equates to one death for every 256,622 firearms. Statistically speaking, the sport of shooting is one of the safest sports in the world.[378]

In spite of an overwhelming safety record of firearms owners, there is a continual narrative by government Leftists and the mainstream press about the irresponsibility of gun owners. They shout the same old broken record of the high number of accidental deaths as a result of guns in the home.

While any fatal accident is a terrible loss, accidental firearms fatalities among children under the age of fourteen account for only 1.5 percent of all fatal injuries. Firearms are among the least likely causes of unintentional fatalities among children. In the United States, firearms account for less than 1 percent of unintentional fatalities of adults. Hunting is rated as one of the safest sports in America.[379] Armed Americans have proven to be far more responsible with firearms than federal and state government employees. The American citizen is among of the safest users and bearers of firearms in the world.

Although hunters comprise one of the largest demographic of gun ownership in America, the Second Amendment does not mention hunting. It was written to demonstrate the belief that man has a right and obligation to protect his family, his country, and

376   The Daily Caller, Gun Ownership by the numbers, Contributor Guns and Gear, By Dan Griffin , Nov, 04, 2014

377   http://www.gunpolicy.org/firearms/region/united-states Accessed April 15, 2015

378   http://www.cdc.gov/nchs/fastats/homicide.htm Accessed April 15, 2015

379   http://www.nssf.org/PDF/research/IIR_InjuryStatistics2013.pdf

his property. This right extends to his obligation to be prepared to defend his nation from all enemies, both foreign and domestic.

The largest and best-armed force in the world is the American citizen, at 100 million to 150 million firearms owners. Combined in this number is the American hunter, numbering between 30 to 40 million gun owners across the nation.[380]

World's largest armies by the numbers

Non-hunting American gun owners:	95,000,000
American hunters:	35,000,000
China:	1,250,000
South Korea:	1,240,000
United States	1,125,000[381]

After almost every tragedy where people are killed by guns, the government and its agents of hate and division beat the drums of fear and attempt to create animosity toward all gun owners. These rants are often extended to demean all gun owners and create hate for an entire class of citizens.

The following statement is indicative of the hate that is constantly being vomited by the American Left: "The NRA is a god-awful fear mongering group, and those who support the NRA are pure trash"[382] Mike Dickinson, Virginia Progressive Democrat.

Mike Dickinson is the face of the Democratic Party's far left; he has also made other hate-filled remarks such as the following about those who are anti-abortion: "Anti-choice, abortion haters are

---

380   http://nation.foxnews.com/2013/11/04/american-hunters- percentE2 percent80 percent93-world percentE2 percent80 percent99s-largest-army
381   http://www.globalsecurity.org/military/world/armies.htm
382   The daily Sheeple, Democrat spews Hate at Gun Owners Calling them pure Trash, Lily Dane, April 8, 2014, Accessed April 12, 2015

all basically mentally disabled. They cannot see or reason. It's all bible thumping."

This is the hostile climate that gun owners are in because they believe in a basic God-given constitutional right. There is a reason all educated Americans should fear the anti-gun crowd. Either they are extremely uneducated about basic rights, or they are complicit with the goals of communists and fascists. Consider the following statement by the Chinese communist ruler, Mao Tse Tung:

"All political power comes from the barrel of a gun. The communist party must command all the guns, that way, no guns can ever be used to command the party." Mao Tse Tung [383]

Government Leftists are unabashed in their coldness to use any tragedy to further their communist agendas.

In 2012, in the wake of the Sandy Hook school shooting, the liberal Left used the shooting as a launching pad for their gun confiscation platform. The uninformed and low- information voter was targeted with a barrage of misinformation, creating the image that the Second Amendment and private gun ownership was responsible for the massacre.

The lie continued with headlines by CNN that all firearms owners, especially those owning military-style weapons, were just felons in waiting. The media, attempting to steer public opinion, claimed the shooter had used the intimidating AR-15. The problem was the perpetrator used a hand gun and not an AR-15 rifle.[384]

President Obama, Hillary Clinton, congressional Democrats and the mainstream media, called for immediate registration of all guns, gun owners, and confiscation of high capacity weapons (especially military-type weapons), auto loading pistols, and rifles. Much to the chagrin of these agents of constitutional destruction, the public did not buy the lie. In fact, there was an unintended backlash from citizens across the United States.

Within days, military-style rifles, semi-automatic loading

383   http://www.buckeyefirearms.org/anti-gun-quotes
384   http://www.cnn.com/interactive/2012/12/us/sandy-hook-timeline/ Accessed April 12, 2015

pistols, and compatible ammunition were flying off the store shelves in such numbers that it created a two-year shortage of firearms and ammunition. It was as if President Obama and the Left were on a campaign to facilitate the sale of firearms in the United States.

President Barack Obama should have been given the award of Gun Salesman of the Century. The sale of firearms and ammunition became so brisk that the price of guns doubled, if they could be found. Ammunition would become almost extinct, doubling then tripling in price.

The giant awoke: the American citizen realized the endgame in this ploy. They knew it had nothing to do with crime or mass murder. This was a government ploy to confiscate firearms and or ammunition from the American people. This same game plan had recently been used to take weapons from the Australians, Canadians, and the people of Great Britain.

President Obama and Diane Feinstein were in an all-out battle to see who could come up with the most restrictive firearms laws, both of which would eventually lead to their ultimate desired outcome of total confiscation. Again, the low-information voter was the target. This is the same voter who had never read the true history of America or the rise and fall of Germany and the Nazi party.

Gun confiscation and removal of God and religion from the people were the same steps taken to subdue the nations of Germany, Russia, Italy, China, and Cambodia. This was done under such inspired and charitable leaders as, Hitler, Stalin, Mussolini, and Pol Pot. All of these ended in tyrannical governments where rights of the individual were trampled and destroyed. Those who offended their rulers were imprisoned and/or murdered.

Government ineptitude, Fast and Furious

Under the pretense of "I didn't know, and blame it on Bush" President Barack Obama's Department of Justice (DOJ) head, Eric Holder, authorized the Bureau of Alcohol Tobacco and Firearms

(BATF) to sell guns to the Mexican drug cartel. When the guns were lost and later one was used to kill a border patrol agent, Holder denied knowledge of the incident and created a lie about the guns. He blamed Arizona gun shops for selling the guns to the cartel. This lie was passed to the biased news media and distributed as fact. However, after congressional hearings, the truth about the sales was made public.

It was found that the DOJ had authorized the sales. President Obama admitted his knowledge of the program when he invoked executive privilege and refused to allow Eric Holder to be subpoenaed to testify to Congress about Fast and Furious.[385] [386] [387]

As of 2015, the BATF, Eric Holder, and President Obama have yet to answer for the murder of the agent or the lie they perpetrated on the American people.

---

385   http://www.latimes.com/nation/atf-fast-furious-sg-storygallery.html, Accessed April 8, 2014

386   Townhall, 5 Things The Obama Administration Had No Idea The Obama Administration was Doing, By John Hawkins, November 2, 2013, researched February 26, 2015

387   Author's Note: Each time there was a potential major incident which could have embarrassed President Obama, he would claim he just found out about the problem from the news media and would vow to investigate. The investigations never happened. Obama's second ploy was to blame his predecessor, George W. Bush.

Chapter 17

Citizen and Weapons

Do we need high capacity magazines and military-type auto-loading firearms?

US Supreme Court "United States V. Miller case 307 US. 174 (1939)

The conclusion of the court was that each American male citizen over the age of sixteen was required to own the same type, style, and caliber of weaponry as is common to the military. This was a common practice in the United States for over 250 years.

These armed patriots have served as the defenders of liberty and homeland security. There is evidence that the high percentage of gun ownership may have been one of the major reasons the Japanese chose not to invade California after their successful attack on Hawaii in 1941. They believed their troops would be slaughtered by armed citizens. This was armed America, not unarmed China.

The feared semi-auto loader, AR-15 and other scary weapons

There is a common misconception among non-gun owners that semi-auto loading weapons are machine guns. Only fully automatic weapons are classified as machine guns. Machine guns or automatic weapons are so called because with a single pull of the trigger the weapon will continue to fire on its own power until either trigger pressure is released or the weapon runs out of ammunition. Machine guns and fully automatic weapons have been illegal for private citizens to own without a special license since the 1930s.

A semi-automatic, also referred to as a "semi-auto loader," only fires one round each time the trigger is pulled. The weapon will not fire another round until the trigger is released to the reset position and depressed again

Why are semi-auto loading pistols and long guns, with large capacity magazines the weapons of choice for police and military in the United States?

The answer is simple, most police officers can read, and most departments look at the most efficient way to protect their officers and stop a dangerous suspect. In most cases of officer-involved shootings, police encounter only a single suspect, and yet police use high-capacity hand guns and long guns with magazines of fifteen to thirty rounds and more.

If there is any advanced warning that a gunfight is a possibility, competent police officers will generally come armed with a long gun similar to an AR-15, or fully-automatic weapons. These long guns have magazine capacities of thirty or more rounds, and the officers carry multiple magazines into the combat zone.

When an officer makes a routine traffic stop or visits a restaurant while on duty, they generally have sixteen rounds in their pistol and another thirty to forty-five rounds in loaded magazines on their duty-belt. Why? Because police officers know that if things go south and a gunfight occurs, it may take forty-five rounds or more to neutralize the suspect or suspects.

AR-15 with retractable stock caliber 5.56

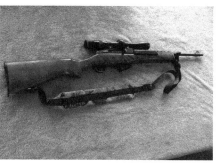

Ruger Ranch Rifle caliber 5.56

Photos by the author

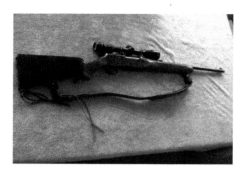

Browning BAR Caliber 30.06

223 / 5.56   30.06

Photos by the author

The above weapons are all semi-auto loading rifles. They differ little in their operation, only in their appearance. They all fire about the same number of rounds per minute. The AR-15 and Ranch Rifle both fire the standard U.S. service round. This 5.56 cartridge is also the same cartridge used in the U.S. military's M-16 rifle.

The Browning 30.06 fires a substantially larger round. The 30.06 is one of the most popular big game hunting rifles in the world. It was also the main rifle caliber used in World War II. Ironically, the 30.06, which most people do not consider an assault rifle, is far more deadly than the AR-15. The popular and vilified AR-15 is a comparatively light rifle round. It is the weapon of choice for home protection because it does not have the penetrating power of a larger caliber. There is less chance for the bullet to pass through a body or walls and cause collateral damage beyond the intended target.

The AR-15 is a great varmint round, but is so light that it is rarely used to hunt big game in North America.

Why carry superior weapons

Research and practical experience has shown the best way to reduce the possibility of a gunfight is to have weapons that are superior to the weapons of the suspect's or opponent's.

Rarely is a person immediately killed or incapacitated by a single round in a combat gunfight. Suspects are often hit by three to six or more rounds before they are neutralized. Combat conditions are completely different than hunting big game. Big game hunters generally stalk their game and take the time to find a steady rest then attempt to place a single shot in a vital area to ensure a clean and humane kill. Even with a well-placed strategic shot, big game often take several minutes or longer to bleed out and die, and at times will run hundreds of yards after taking a hit in a vital area.[388]

In a gunfight, adrenalin may keep a human running and fighting long after being fatally shot. If the shot is not in a vital organ, humans can continue to fight for extended periods of time. In times of war, it is not uncommon for soldiers to fight on for minutes or hours after being mortally wounded.

The trained citizen or police officer will lose an average of 60 percent of his accuracy under combat conditions. This loss of proficiency is caused by the sudden jump in pulse rate resulting from an adrenalin dump that generally happens under combat stress. In combat, an average pulse of about 60 beats-per-minute can jump to 170 beats or even higher. This rush would be similar to a person running a 200-yard sprint then trying to thread a needle.

The stress factor is one of the main reasons police and military are trained to shoot for the center of mass with the hope that each shot will hit something besides air. Using the center of mass as the target, there are only about three locations that may stop a

---

[388]   Author's Note: The author personally shot a deer in the heart and the animal was still able to run almost 100 yards before succumbing to his wounds.

suspect cold with a single shot.

1. Tactical head shot
2. Perfect heart shot
3. A big round into the pelvis to turn it to a mass of jelly, which will stop the suspect from advancing but not from shooting.

In a gunfight, thirty seconds can seem like forever, and thirty or more rounds can be expended in a few seconds. Because of adrenaline and other factors, even trained police officers have been in gunfights at distances of under ten feet and have expended fifteen or more rounds without a single shot hitting the suspect. If a private citizen or police officer has to resort to deadly force, a high capacity magazine in a handgun or in an AR-15 could mean the difference between life and death for the intended victim.[389]

The differences between a police shootout and a citizen shootout are definitive. Police generally have more than one officer on scene, bullet-proof vests, backup in route, and the badge of authority. The private citizen is generally on his own, no backup, no ballistic vest, and no badge of authority. Whether the citizen lives or dies will depend on his weapon, proficiency, and the number of well-placed rounds expended.

When training in self-defense drills, citizens should employ the same tactics as police officers. Train to keep firing until the suspect is neutralized. While some suspects may hit the ground and quit twitching with a single shot, most determined aggressors may walk through multiple, well-placed rounds. Even if you empty your weapon into the suspect, you better be prepared to go hands on to defend yourself until he dies or lapses into unconsciousness.

It is laughable and shows complete ignorance when it is suggested that a victim or a police officer should try to shoot a perpetrator in the leg or just wing him as an option to deadly force. If your gun comes out, you had better be certain the event meets the criteria of deadly force, and that you are mentally and physically

---

389   http://www.virginiacops.org/articles/shooting/combat.htm, Accessed April 8, 2014

prepared to shoot to kill; otherwise leave your gun at home.

The private market drives better weapons

It is the private market that drives advancement of better, safer weapons for police and military. It has always been expected that American citizens should have access to military-style weapons. In the Revolutionary War, many citizen soldiers had had the long rifle, a superior weapon to the military supplied musket. The Kentucky Long Rifle was the AR-15 of its day. The Long Rifle had an effective range of over 200 yards while the typical musket of the day was marginally effective at less than 60 yards.[390]

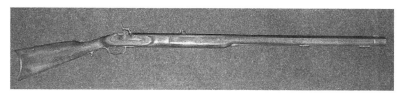

Kentucky Long Rifle – Photo by the author

The debate continues about AR-15s and large capacity magazines. The overwhelming reason for this drummed-up hysteria is a tyrannical government that is scared of the people, especially a well-educated, well-armed and trained militia of private citizens. It is not guns in the hands of the people that is to be feared; it is guns in the hands of federal agents that is the real danger to society.

In the 1970 movie, *Chisum*, the bad guy, Lawrence Murphy, makes this timely statement: "Mr. Chisum is a man who respects the law. Around here, I'm the man who owns the law.

This statement is becoming iconic in regards to the alphabet soup of federal agencies that appear to be increasingly on a rampage to arrest, prosecute, and target American citizens.

As long as the United States respects the Constitution and Americans own weapons such as the AR-15 and similar weapons, we the people will probably never see a time when the government would have to be defended from a tyrannical takeover by a person

---

390   http://www.tngenweb.org/campbell/hist-bogan/KentuckyLongRifle. html, researched February 26, 2015

or party.

However, if the time should ever come when our freedom to own firearms is suspended, we will be ripe for the picking for any tyrant who decides it is his time to subdue the people.

Here are just a few of the branches of the federal government which have well-funded SWAT teams that purchase billions of rounds of hollow point ammunition to use against American citizens.

Department of Homeland security (DHS), Federal Emergency Management Agency (FEMA), Department of the Treasury (IRS), Department of Agriculture (DOA), Bureau of Land Management (BLM), United States Forest Service (USFS), Department of Housing and Urban Development (HUD), Department of Education, Fish and Wildlife, Environmental Protection Agency (EPA), Library of Congress (LOC); and the list goes on. There are over sixty regulatory boards that are not law enforcement-related but have badges, guns and SWAT teams at their disposal to harass and murder American citizens.

In 2010, these out-of-control agencies made thousands of SWAT raids on private citizens and businesses. These are regulatory boards, not police agencies.

Legal verses illegal investigations

In the course of legal investigations, if there is a need for more than a traditional knock-and-talk inquiry, the agency involved should have to demonstrate to a judge why the inquiry could endanger the interviewer. If it is concluded that a raid is appropriate, it should be conducted by the County Sheriff and not some rouge regulatory board who does not answer to the people.[391]

Hollow point ammunition

---

391   Beware the US Education Department Swat Team By; *Brian W. Walsh is a senior research fellow in the Heritage Foundation's Center for Legal and Judicial Studies. Heritage Foundation, Accessed June 15, 2014; Reference:* http://www.foxnews.com/politics/2013/09/14/armed-epa-agents-in-alaska-shed-light-on-70-fed-agencies-with-armed-division, researched February 26, 2015

Hollow point ammunition is forbidden for battle use by the Geneva Convention and cannot be used in war on an opposing nation. Hollow point ammunition can only be used for hunting or against American citizens. FEMA and DHS have purchased over a billion rounds of hollow point ammunition. It is doubtful they purchased this ammunition for general hunting purposes; it was purchased to use against US citizens.

In November of 2012, the author personally spoke with Rep. Jason Chaffetz (R-Utah). Rep. Chaffetz is one of the more conservative members of Congress; however, his response blew me away. Rep Chaffetz informed me these ammunition procurements by DHS and FEMA were only for the agencies to defend themselves when they responded to disasters, and most of the ammunition was for practice. I informed Rep Chaffetz that hollow point ammunition is not generally used for training and could only be used against American citizens.

Rep. Chaffetz told me he did not see a problem with the federal government arming against American citizens. I was astounded that he could not see the obvious implications of German SS style tactics that could and would be used against the American People by a rouge president who may decide to become a dictator. Presently, we have a Congress with no backbone to put the brakes on a president who makes that power grab.[392]

Gun confiscation

In the wake of Hurricane Katrina in 2005, Federal and State agents illegally confiscated guns from the people in New Orleans. These weapons were taken from U.S. citizens with the threat of violence by the government agents involved. The confiscated weapons were never accounted for and were not given back to the citizens.[393]

---

392   http://rt.com/usa/dhs-ammo-investigation-napolitano-645/ Homeland Security under investigation for massive ammo buys, Accessed Jan 14, 2014
393   New York Times, New Orleans Begins Confiscation Firearms as Water Recedes, By Alex Berenson, and Timothy Williams, September 8, 2005, researched February 26, 2015

Today, ammunition supplies, tomorrow our food supply. Would our government and their minions interrupt America's food supply to create food riots?[394]

In 1941, President Franklin Roosevelt (D) used a foreign attack on an American territory to justify the mass confiscation of guns and other property from 127,000 American citizens.[395] Accompanied by a lack of evidence, the federal government deemed Americans of Japanese ancestry as "enemy aliens." These citizens were rounded up and placed in internment camps. They were denied their constitutional rights to face their accusers, legal counsel, or trial.[396] Most property taken from these people was never accounted for or returned.

Medicine to the Dead

"To argue with a person who has renounced the use of reason is like administering medicine to the dead." Thomas Paine.

Utopian dreamers believe they can control crime if they control guns. We live in a world where reason and facts have no place. The only relationship to guns and crime is conclusively, more guns less crime. The ultimate results of gun confiscation and crime can be compared by analyzing statistics from Britain and the United States.

US violent Crime rate   475 per 100,000 citizens, year 2003[397]

UK Violent Crime rate   4,100 per 100,000 subjects, year 2003.[398]

For all of the hype about how Great Britain has a lower gun violence rate than the United States, the odds of being a victim

---

394   American Thinker, President Obama has set in Motion forces he can't handle, Neil Snyder, February 18, 2013

395   www.mtholyoke.edu/~matsu22k/classweb/page1h.html Accessed Jan 10, 2016

396   http://www.policestateusa.com/2014/large-scale-gun-confiscation/, researched February 26, 2015

397   http://www.fbi.gov/ucr/05cius/data/table_01.html), researched February 26, 2015

398   http://www.homeoffice.gov.uk/rds/pdfs04/rdsolr1804.pdf) researched February 26, 2015

of violent crime in Britain are ten times higher than in the United States. While the U.S. has more gun crime, the U.K. has far more violent crimes. Ultimately, the time-proven way to reduce crime is by educating and producing a religious, moral, and armed people.

Chapter 18

Mass Killing and the Blame Game

Littleton Colorado, April 20, 1999. After a year of research and planning, Columbine High School students, Eric Harris 18, and Dylan Klebold 17, went to their school with the intent of killing at least five hundred of their fellow students and teachers. Once at the school, the two went on a twenty-minute rampage of mayhem and murder. This rampage left twelve students and one teacher dead, with another twenty-one persons wounded.

After less than twenty minutes in the school, these two cowards killed themselves. Fortunately, for the students and faculty, a number of bombs the two had placed in the school failed to detonate and the real destruction never happened. Had the bombs detonated, the loss of life could have been in the hundreds.[399]

The Columbine killings were not about bullying, Trench Coat Mafia, politics or any of the other often used rationale. This killing was ultimately about body count, pure evil, and incomprehensible hate and disdain for humanity and human life. Klebold and Harris wanted to be hailed in history as killing the most people in an American terrorist attack.

The two killers made extensive videotapes about their preparation and plans to implement the murders. On these tapes, they told of their intrigue of the media coverage of the Oklahoma City Bombing at the Murrah Federal Building in 1995.[400] [401] [402]

Mass shootings and killings were rarely seen prior to the 1960s. Since the 1960s, foreign and domestic crimes of mass killing have seen a dramatic increase. In earlier years, these mass murders

---

399   http://www.britannica.com/EBchecked/topic/1528263/Columbine-High-School-shootings, accessed Jan 15, 2015
400   http://www.columbine-online.com/etc/columbine-faq.htm Accessed April 12, 2015
401   Author's Note: Prior to the Muslim attack at the World Trade Center on September 11, 2001, the Oklahoma bombing had been the worst terrorist attack on American soil.
402   http://www.history.com/topics/oklahoma-city-bombing Accessed April 12, 2015

were generally perpetrated by political Muslim groups who were seeking news-braking ways to gain name recognition and create terror.

More recently, however, these murderous and cowardly crimes have been perpetrated by individuals or groups who want to go out in a blaze of gunfire and have their names recognized worldwide as the person or persons who committed the most sick and heinous crime of the decade. Often after the crime, there are postings or letters found which have been written by these sick cowards who kill innocent unarmed victims. In the letters and videos they often brag of being ready to go out in a "blaze of gunfire."

After a mass murder or other heinous crime, there is a rush by the press to assign blame and a reason for the crime, other than the pure evil that it is. Crimes of murder, especially mass murder, are often treated like gold to the press and leading psycho-analysts as they seek to create a reason for the crime. It is rare that the criminal is blamed directly; generally a theme is played out which blames everything and everyone but the perpetrator.

In the case of murder by firearms, the blame usually goes to the gun and gun owners in general. How the criminal action is moved from the perpetrator to an inanimate object and a group of persons with no viable connection is always a mystery. The perpetrator planned the action, and obtained the means to carry out the crime. The weapons used could not transport themselves to the crime scene, but still we have a narrative that sounds as though the weapon is responsible for the criminal action.

After intense investigation the press finds that the perpetrator almost always left a trail that showed mental illness or instability. They claim that police, family, teachers or associates should have seen the signs of a potential murderer and notified authorities. However, there are two major flaws with this line of thinking.

First, we live in America. People have the right to be a little crazy. One person's sanity is another person's insanity. Even if someone acts a little crazy or different, without probable cause, the police cannot arrest and punish a person for a crime society thinks he might commit.

If a thousand so-called crazy or odd people were placed in a room for evaluation even the best psychoanalysts in the world cannot with accuracy tell who would commit murder and who would not.

The first step to stopping these despicable crimes is recognizing evil for what it is. Stop making excuses for murderers. Call the perpetrators what they are, evil and cowardly.

Second is the case of aggravated murder, which by a quick definition is any murder where there is another assault-related crime where deadly weapons are used or when two or more persons are killed. Justice demands that those who take a life with malice should forfeit their life as justice for the victim.

Third, sentencing should be carried out in a timely manner. Trials should be carried out as soon as it is possible to get all evidence gathered for presentation to a jury. The suspect should be given every legal consideration to prove his or her innocence in a court of law. However, if guilt is established and a death sentence is applicable, this should be carried out in a timely manner while emotions are still warm. When a death sentence is unduly delayed, emotions cool, sometimes to the point where people begin to second guess the system and forget the severity of the crime. There would be few protests to taking the life of a mass murderer if the sentence were carried out within a year of the crime. Within a year people still remember the physical and emotional hell that the perpetrators put people through. After twelve months, emotions start to cool and the expediency of justice is slowly placed on the back burner of the mind.

There are those who claim the death sentence is not a deterrent to crime that is a question which may never be settled; however, it is a fact that dead men never kill again, and there can be no justice for the victim except the death of the perpetrator.

Motivation for murder

Reporting agencies and the news media like to explore the possibilities of outside influences that changed the person's behavior. Establishing false guilt allows the perpetrator to dodge personal responsibility for his actions.

Leading reasons for mass murder are not that hard to determine. However, the real causes are purposely clouded by Leftists and the media who use each event to further their political agendas.

Mass murder is often encompassed somewhere in two or more of these five basic tenants.

- **Lack of respect for human life**
- **Superiority over others**
- **Name recognition**
- **Political statement**
- **Body count**

Number One: Lack of respect for human life

In a society lacking the moral compass of God and religion, the government cannot build prisons fast enough to hold the perpetrators that such a society produces. When the State becomes the highest moral authority, a sadistic mentality begins to dominate the community or nation. Where there is no accountability, there is no crime. If there is no punishment, no crime has been committed. In a Godless society, there is no punishment or accountability for criminal behavior unless the perpetrator is caught and punished by the state.

Our schools teach our children that they are nothing more than a lower life form that happens to be slightly brighter than the animal kingdom. This idea of being a lower life form is a far-cry from a living, breathing child of God.

If people were to understand that they are children of God, it would generally change their attitude toward the human family. Understanding there will be an eternal judgment for our actions in this earth life, most of mankind would raise to a higher standard of behavior.

"Religion doesn't make the man, but it makes a man better."[403]

---

403   Eugene Palfreyman, 1912-1993

Patriotism and Religion are kin sisters

The Left knows patriotism is a kin sister to religion. Some liberal professors discourage people from taking their children to Fourth of July celebrations because exposure to the American flag may cause them to stop and think, may cause patriotism, and may cause them to start thinking as a conservative.[404] These professors are probably correct: when people are exposed to the American flag, they experience special feelings of patriotism and gratitude to God and America.

Unfortunately through the example of our leaders, our children are taught there is no sin in a lie because there is no consequence. When President William Jefferson Clinton lied to the country on nationwide television, it left an impression of lawlessness upon our children and society.[405] [406]

The conclusion of this action was that character did not matter. This attitude of character, or the lack of it, has had a devastating effect on the morals of our youth. Example is still the best teacher for whatever values you are trying to impress upon people. Political policies have removed God, honor, responsibility, and accountability from the people; they have

404   US News Washington Whispers, Harvard: July 4th parades Are Right Wing, Paul Bedard, June 30, 2011, http://www.usnews.com/news/blogs/washington-whispers/2011/06/30/harvard-july-4th-parades-are-right-wing
405   Author's Note: In 1998 President Clinton was under investigation for sexual harassment and defamation of character from a subordinate named Paula Jones. Jones had worked under then-Governor Clinton in Arkansas. Ms. Jones alleged that in May of 1991 Clinton had crudely propositioned her to be his mistress. He later defamed her when she went public about the incident.
As the investigation proceeded, it came to the attention of investigators that President Clinton was having another affair with a White House intern named Monica Lewinsky. During the Grand Jury investigation, it was found that the President had instructed Ms. Lewinsky to be complicit in his lies to the Grand Jury to conceal their current affair.
The Starr Report concluded that President Clinton had lied to the Grand Jury and had committed at least eleven impeachable offenses. The House of Representatives voted to impeach President Clinton; however, the Democrat-led Senate voted not to terminate Clinton's presidency.
406   http://www.historyplace.com/unitedstates/impeachments/starr-excerpt.htm The Star Report September 9, 1998, researched February 26, 2015

broken the system and have ultimately diminished human life.

No fault abortion

This murder brought to you courtesy of the Atheists of America, and Planned Parenthood

Abortion holds the infamous record as the most used murder weapon in the world, and its victims are the most innocent of all victims. Abortion is one of the main factors in diminishing the value of human life. While there are a small percentage of loving parents who have abortions because of health concerns or are the victims of rape, over 95 percent of all abortions are conducted out of convenience and not for legitimate health concerns.

Of all the efforts of government to devalue human life, Planned Parenthood and the abortion cult has had one of the highest impacts in America and round the world. Since the infamous Roe vs. Wade Ruling in 1973, over 56 million abortions have terminated the lives of unborn children in America.[407]

In the year 2010, the United States aborted / murdered over 756,000 innocent babies. The overwhelming majority of these innocent children had only one crime: being conceived by a female and male who did not want the responsibility that comes with sexual relations. These people are not mothers and fathers; that is an earned title. Planned Parenthood was responsible for over 33 percent of these child murders.[408]

Planned Parenthood was started in 1916 by a flaming raciest Democrat named Margaret Sanger. Sanger believed all undesirables, especially Negros, should be terminated. True to Sanger's plan, Planned Parenthood has continued to target minorities for almost a hundred years. Planned Parenthood has been investigated by the Black Life Coalition for blatant targeting of blacks for extermination.[409]

---

407   Life News, 56,662,169 Abortions in America since Roe vs. Wade in 1973, By Randy O'Bannon PH.D., January 12, 2014
408   Centers for Disease control and Prevention, Surveillance Summaries, November29, 2013, Karen Pazol PHD. Andreen A Creanga MD. , researched February 26, 2015
409   LifeNews.Com, 79 percent of Planned parenthood Abortion Clinics Target

The dynamics of abortion by race show that minorities are the leading targets of this brutal practice with blacks leading the field with an average of 32 per thousand, and whites at only 8.6 per thousand pregnancies terminated by abortion.[410] It is no accident that 79 percent of Planned Parenthood facilities are located within walking distance of black and Hispanic neighborhoods.[411]

Planned Parenthood's ties with the Democratic Party are no secret. In 2013 Planned Parenthood Federation President Cecile Richard's was a keynote speaker at the Democrat National Convention. Planned Parenthood receives in excess of five hundred million dollars per year from our federal government.[412] [413] [414]

Education of murder

Our schools routinely teach our children that murder of the unborn is not a crime, but is a choice. This "choice" to murder our infants is not only acceptable but is sponsored and paid for with our government tax-dollars.

Can children and society really be expected to make a distinction between abortion and murder? Should we think that children can be taught that a mother can kill her child, and it is not murder? And yet, we are appalled when a student bullies, beats another child, or sets out to commit murder? Our children have learned well from our society and our education system.

There is a common thread that almost all non-political mass

Blacks, Hispanics, By Steven Ertelt, October 16, 2012
410   Washington Times, Fewer Abortion Clinics in Minority Communities: Study, By Sheryl Watzstein, Thursday July 10, 2014
411   http://www.protectingblacklife.org/pp_targets/
412   CNSNews.com, Planned Parenthood Got $540.6 Million in Government Grants in FY 2013, By Barbara Boland, January 14, 2014
413   Authors Note: The Democratic Party and Hillary Clinton are major supporters of Planned Parenthood, and in the reverse, Planned Parenthood is a major supporter of the Democratic Party. In 2015, Planned Parenthood President Cecile Richards was caught on hidden camera discussing the black market practice of selling aborted baby parts. In 2014, presidential candidate Hillary Clinton stated that she admired Margaret Sanger.
414   Life New, Hillary Clinton: I admire Planned Parenthood Founder Margaret Sanger, By Steven Ertelt, Sep 23, 2014, researched February 26, 2015

murderers have. They espouse a belief of no god or are involved in some type of satanic worship or cult.

No mass murderer has ever been legitimately tied to a person having active conservative values. Most mass murderers and almost all who have attempted or assassinated American presidents espouse Democrat and communist views. This is expressed in their mentors, the books they read and the entertainment they follow.

Murderers and their politics

Not all Democrats are murderers, but almost all mass murderers are Democrats.

President Lincoln's assassin, John Wilkes Booth, was a southern Democrat who hated President Lincoln because of the Civil War and his role in the abolition of blacks who had been held in slavery. Booth believed he would be hailed a hero for killing President Lincoln. He wanted to see the black race placed back into slavery.[415]

President McKinley was killed by Leon Czolgosz, who was described as an anarchist. Mr. Czolgosz espoused communistic ideals of redistribution of wealth and did not believe that anyone had a right to more than anyone else. After his arrest, Leon wrote a statement where he admitted to the assassination. The statement read, "I killed the President because I done my duty. I didn't believe one man should have so much service and another man should have none."[416]

President Kennedy was killed by Lee Harvey Oswald, a Democrat and avowed communist. Oswald held contempt for the capitalist system because he believed it exploited the people. He preferred the communist system of government. He had lived in Cuba, was an admirer of Fidel Castro, and spoke highly of Cuba. Oswald started to read about Marxism and communism at about the

---

415   http://www.history.com/toics/american-civil-war/john-wilkes-booth,
Researched June, 15, 2015
416   http://www.biography.com/people/leon-frank-czolgosz-235807#early-life
researched February 27, 2015

age of fifteen and held strong convictions about communism. While he was in the U.S., Marine Corp he told fellow soldiers he was a communist.[417] [418]

President Reagan's attempted assassin, John Hinkley Jr., had a history of bizarre behavior and depression. Hinkley had stalked former President Carter and was arrested at the Nashville Airport when a gun was found in his luggage. Hinkley did not espouse any particular political party. However, he was neither religious nor conservative in any sense of the words.[419]

Former Los Angeles police officer Christopher Dorner was a self-proclaimed Obama supporter, anti-gun supporter, and a card-carrying Democrat. In 2008, Dorner was fired from the Los Angeles police department for lying about another officer. On February 3, 2013, Dorner made headlines when he went on a nine-day killing spree targeting police officers and their families. Dorner killed three and wounded three others before he was cornered in a remote cabin where he committed suicide.

Before his death, Dorner made a manifesto and placed it on Facebook.

Following is the short list of Chris Dorner's Manifesto. MSN and CNN chose to censor this material because it didn't fit their template.

- Dorner's statements in support of gun control ("Who in their right mind needs a f_____ silencer!!! who needs a freaking SBR AR15? No one")
- He attacked President Barack Obama's critics ("You question his birth certificate, his educational and professional accomplishments, and his Judeo-Christian beliefs")
- Admiration for Joe Biden ("I've always been a fan of yours and consider you one of the few genuine and charismatic politicians")

417   National Archives, Report of the Presidents Commission on the Assassination of President Kennedy, Chapter 7, Page 338, Interest in Marxism
418   http://www.archives.gov/research/jfk/warren-commission-report/chapter-7.html, researched February 26, 2015
419   http://law2.umkc.edu/faculty/projects/ftrials/hinckley/hbio.htm. researched February 26, 2015

- Criticism of the National Rifle Association ("Wayne LaPierre, President of the NRA, you're a vile and inhumane piece of shit")420

Van Jones CNN Contributor made this point: "Don't focus on Chris Dorner's politics . . . In the wake of a tragedy, it is understandable to ask why this happened. It is appropriate to discuss ways to keep it from happening again. But we should draw the line at suddenly giving an exalted place in our national discourse to the political rantings of a murderer."

In the above article, Jones went to great lengths to cover who Dorner was and his political leanings. The mainstream media did not want any ties to the Left and their party to be newsworthy. Had Dorner ever had any connection with a conservative, it would have been headline news. But CNN tells us politics have no place the discussion on Dorner.[421]

Charleston South Carolina 2015 twenty-one year old Dylann Roof walked into a church where black members were worshiping. Dylann announced he was there to kill black people. Dylann used social media to post pictures of him burning an American flag along with rants about his haltered of blacks and recent black-on-white killings which were not being prosecuted. Dylann cited the lack of an active KKK against blacks and said, "Well someone has to have the bravery to take it to the real world, and I guess that has to be me." Dylann supports the KKK, which was actively supported by the Democratic Party from 1865 to the late 1970s.[422]

Murder has become a part of life, and why not? We spend billions of dollars training our children to respect each other and themselves, but our actions speak much louder than our words. We tell our students to respect life; however, we embrace a political curriculum which includes indoctrinating students that abortion, and murder of the unborn is a right.

---

420   http://twitchy.com/2013/02/07/msm-covers-up-christopher-dorners-hard-left-political-views/, researched February 26, 2015
421   http://www.cnn.com/2013/02/13/opinion/jones-chris-dorner/
422   CNN, Charleston Church Shooting: Who is Dylann Roof, By Ray Sanchez and Ed Payne, June 23, 2015

Left-leaning Hollywood producers and actors make movies embellishing antisocial and murderous behavior. Including movies in which traditional moral values are viewed as old-fashioned, where virtue is not a quality but something to be laughed at. We do not allow the posting of the Ten Commandments because some atheist might be offended. This is the minority imposing their religious views on the majority. For the sake of our children, let the atheist be offended.

We as a Christian Nation are offended at the vain attempt of government to Un-Offend everyone. What about the offence directed at the moral people in America. In the atheist America, Christians have no right to be offended. Christians have no right to honor their God, or to express their view in schools or in a public forum.

The government's war on Christianity bore fruit on October 1, 2015 when a gunman walked on to Umpqua Community College Campus in Oregon. He lined up students and asked their religion. Those who professed to be Christians were shot and killed without mercy. After killing nine and wounding nine, confronted by police this coward took his own life.

Douglas County Sheriff, John Hanlin refused to give the gunman his glory by refusing to give his name in his press release. In honor of the students and Sheriff Hanlin, this author has also refused to name this cowardly scum.[423]

National Rifle Association (NRA)

Each time there is a shooting, conservatives and the NRA are blamed and vilified by the media and the democratic Left. After the shooting at Umpqua Community College in Oregon; Hillary Clinton went on a rampage, blaming the NRA and gun owners for the tragedy.[424]

President Obama blames the NRA each time there is a

---

423   LA Times, Oregon Gunman queried Student on Religion during shootings, By Christine Mai-Duc, Maria L. La Ganga and Matt Pearce, October 1, 2015
424   The Daily Caller, Hillary Clinton Blames NRA for Mass Shootings, by David Bookstead, 10/02/2015

shooting or disturbance of any kind.[425] [426]

In the aftermath of the San Bernardino California shootings in December 2015, the media immediately went on to blame conservative factions. No apology was offered when the shooters fought it out with police and they were found to be Muslims. But once again, President Obama, Hillary Clinton and the Democrats blamed the NRA organization but not the Muslims who did the deed.

Facts about the NRA tell a different story. Of the five million NRA members, there has never been a verified NRA member involved in a mass shooting.[427] NRA members are among the most law-abiding members of our society. By contrast, seven out of ten convicted felons vote Democrat.[428]

It has been the Democrats who are soft on gun crime. The NRA has pushed for stronger gun law to keep guns out of the hands of criminals, along with harsher sentences for criminals who commit crimes with guns. [429]

Atheists of America

This is the official statement from "Atheists.org." This official statement designates Atheism as a religion.

"American Atheists fight to protect the absolute separation of religion from government and raise the profile of atheism in the public discourse."[430]

The religion of anti-religion is a religion. It is the religion being imposed on the American people by the federal government. If

---

425   The Washington Times, Obama Blames NRA for Gun Violence, By Emily Miller, 9/11/2015

426   http://downtrend.com/71superb/obama-blames-everyone-but-the-gunman-for-the-oregon-community-college-shooting/ accessed Dec 8, 2015

427   www.quora.com/Of-the-last-mass-shootings-in-the-US-how-many-shooters-were-known-to-be-NRA-members-and-how-many-of-the-weapons-used-were-legally-owned-by-the-shooters Accessed Dec 8, 2015

428   Washington Examiner, Jail Survey: 7 in 10 Felons register as Democrats, By Paul Bedard Jan 1, 2014

429   Washington Post, Gun Control Battle Behind It, NRA Pushes Effort On Crime Control, By William Claiborne, December 5, 1993

430   http://www.atheists.org, Stand up for your Rights

we are looking for the so-called "smoking gun" or cause of criminal behavior, look no further than the vilification of God and religion.

When asked by Dr. Benjamin Rush if he thought America would succeed, Founder John Adams answered, "Yes, if we fear God and repent of our sins."[431]

Animal rights and Earth worship

As God fearing (God loving) people, we are responsible for proper stewardship of our planet and the animals on it. Proper stewardship is not to be construed as animal rights. As humans, we are the only animal who will work to ensure the continuance of any other species. We should be proper stewards of the world we live in. Animals have been part of the human experience from the earliest writing on canyon walls by ancient man. Horses and dogs have been used by man, performing work and companionship since the dawn of human history.

We love our animals; however, when we pass animal abuse laws where we place animals above humans, we diminish human life. Humans are unique in our ability to think, feel and have concern for others. States pass animal rights laws, but a right requires responsibility. We have a right to own and possess a gun; we have a right to free speech; we have a right to property, but these rights require that we are responsible with our actions in using these rights. How do we explain rights and responsibility to a non-human? The premise that animals are above humans diminishes humanity.

Earth worship, another avenue for diminishing respect for human life, is alive and well in America as a religion. Modern cults have made earth worship a holy calling. Our students and society are taught that man is responsible for climate change and is an evil interloper on earth. Under this line of thinking, man should be subservient to land and animals. Children are taught that to steal a bird's egg is criminal but to abort a baby is moral. And yet we wonder why society has no respect for human life.

431　McCullough, David, John Adams, Simon & Schuster, 2001, Page 160

Number 2: Superiority

Criminals and especially murderers get a high from having superiority over their victims. In the case of the Combine murders, Klebold and Harris believed themselves to be superior to those whom they tormented and killed. Many violent criminals play with and torment their victims before finally murdering them.

Number 3: Name Recognition

The press has been complicit with the killers by making sure every nasty detail about the murderer, his family, and most details of the murders are explicitly reported.

Many of these deviants believe that any event that posts their name to the world, whether it is positive or negative, is acceptable for fame. Every time a mass murder takes place the first thing that the media does is give the perpetrators the name recognition they crave by publishing every fact or rumor, often with little or no fact checking. This name recognition goes on for months, and sometimes years.

Second, they give every sorted detail of the killing including body count, number of injuries, and if possible, how the crime was committed. This information will continue in the news until it has run its course and the public says enough.

By supplying this information and continuing to broadcast it, we reward this sick behavior with the name recognition they desire. If the media was really concerned about slowing or stopping these heinous crimes, they would carefully detail a report with honesty but avoid naming the perpetrator and details that could assist or encourage copycat crimes. Dead or alive, if the perpetrators enjoys no name recognition, one of the main rewards for the crime of mass murder is denied the criminal.

Number 4: Political Statements

Political statements are the primary reason for mass murders committed by Muslim extremists. Across the world, Muslims, following teachings from the Quran, have killed tens of thousands of Christians and homosexuals.[432] Ironically, more Muslims are killed by these Muslim predators than any other group. According to the Combating Terrorism Center at West Point, from 2004 to 2008, only twelve percent of killings by Muslims were against Westerners. The study suggests that about 80 percent of these killings are Muslim-on-Muslim. Muslims likely to be slaughtered by Muslims are doctors, nurses, woman, and children. And this is from the religion of peace?[433]

Their political statement and goal is to rid the world of those who will not live Sharia Law as prescribed in their holy book, the Quran. Militant groups such as the Muslim Brotherhood are openly supported by President Obama and Hillary Clinton. Other groups such as ISIS, Boko Haram, and Al-Qaeda are only given token resistance by President Obama, Democrats, and the federal government.[434]

Congressional Representative Maxine Waters (D-CA) expressed her support of Muslim extremism when she spoke at an Islamic Society of Orange County town hall meeting where she said "Americans are bigots for opposing Sharia Law" By this statement, Ms. Waters openly admits that she supports one of the largest terrorist groups and exporters of mass murder organizations in the world.[435] [436]

If we do not stem the tide, it is only a matter of time before we see insurgent Muslims raining down terror on our home ground here in the United States. In Texas, it has already happened. In May 2015, Muslims tried to shoot up a group who had held a contest for

---

432   http://www.answering-islam.org/Silas/hassaballa_violence3.htm accessed Jan 14, 2016

433   CNN, Who's Killing Muslims, By Dean Obeidallah, January 15, 2015, Accessed May 10, 2015

434   Counterpunch, Muslim Vs. White Mass Murderers, By Matt Peepe, March 31, 2015, Accessed May 10, 2015

435   Freedom Outpost, Maxine Waters: Americans are Bigots for Opposing Sharia Law, Tim Brown, September 12, 2014, Accessed May 10, 2015

436   Author's Note: Sharia Law allows for the beating of women, and beheading of adulators, homosexuals, and all other infidels, including men, women, and children.

drawing pictures of the Prophet Mohammad. Luckily, the shooters were stopped and killed by an on duty police officer.[437]

Number 5: Body Count

Regardless of other reasons for the crime, body count is generally a primary motivator in mass murder. Most mass murderers design their killing to do maximum damage to increase the killed or injured over their predecessors. Statistically, the highest body counts are those where the victims waited for the police to stop the perpetrator. By contrast, the lowest body counts are those stopped by citizens legally carrying their own firearms, and those who—with or without weapons—take action to defeat or interrupt the rampage.

The previously mentioned perpetrators of the Littleton Colorado school killings were armed with guns, knives, and a multitude of bombs. Their plot was to detonate the bombs in the cafeteria at 11:17 a.m. when it could have killed as many as 500 students. The two were not stopped by police, but after twenty minutes of terror, the cowards took their own lives. From their journals, we know this plot was planned over a twelve-month period with the intent of making it the bloodiest attack in history. It was primarily about headlines.[438] Harris wrote in his journal that they hated almost everyone, especially the God Channel. "I hate that channel with all my heart and soul."[439]

How to stop mass murderers

Columbine taught America about mass murder. Prior to Columbine, it was official police policy in almost all jurisdictions to secure the perimeter of the building or area and contain the suspects. Second would be hostage negotiation teams to try to talk the criminal out of murder. And third was to deploy the local SWAT team. After

---

437   http://www.thegatewaypundit.com/2015/05/report-texas-shooters-mosque-controlled-by-muslim-brotherhood-front-group/ Accessed May 15, 2015

438   http://www.columbine-online.com/etc/columbine-faq.htm Accessed April 12, 2015

439   http://history1900s.about.com/od/famouscrimesscandals/a/columbine.htm, Columbine Massacre, Jennifer Rosenberg, Accessed June 10, 2015

Columbine, police across the country reviewed and rewrote their policies; today all departments use guns to stop these crimes.

The first officers on scene immediately deploy into the combat zone. Most jurisdictions do not even recommend waiting for back up. The idea is to take the fight to the criminal. This tactic should be the same, whether it is police or citizen first on scene. Taking the fight to the criminal interrupts their plans and saves lives. It puts the criminal on the defensive and buys time for other assets to get into place.

Conclusion

Because of our continued course in the education of anti-humanity and acceptance of moral decay, our society will likely continue to see an increase in active shooters and mass killings. Despite law enforcement's best efforts, many perpetrators do not have previous records or common indicators that flag them as a potential killer. The armed citizen will not stop the propensity to kill, but armed citizens will significantly reduce the morbidity rate as more people take personal responsibility for their own safety and the protection of others.

Chapter 19

Slavery, the Civil War, and Racism

The history of slavery in America is often shrouded in deliberate miss-information. Most historians paint a picture of slavery that existed throughout the United States prior to the civil war. Before the conclusion of the Revolutionary War in 1783, three states had already passed laws that barred slavery in their borders.

By 1787, before the signing of the Constitution six of the original thirteen colonies had outlawed slavery or provided for gradual emancipation.[440] While the slave states held a seven-to-six majority of what would become the United States, what was referred to as the "Free North" had the largest numbers in terms of overall population.

The Declaration of Independence was signed in 1776. Ten years later, the thirteen original colonies were negotiating the Constitution. One of the largest obstacles was the viability, lawfulness, and morality of slavery in America. As stated above, six of the thirteen colonies had already outlawed this evil practice.

The slave trade was not new when the pilgrims came to America. For thousands of years, almost all nations had engaged in using and trading slaves. In Africa, many slave holders were blacks who held both black and white slaves. Most Africans who were enslaved were captured or traded by African blacks engaged in the slave trade.

In Muslim Africa, many black citizens were run down or trapped by Muslim blacks then sold or traded into slavery; often black Muslim Kings would trade their own people to other nations in exchange for goods. Trading and enslavement was not unique to Africa or to blacks. From the earliest of times, almost all nations made slaves of the citizens of countries they were at war with or ruled over.[441]

---

440   http://alexislloyd.com/tools/slavery_map Accessed May 16, 2015
441   Origins of the African Save Trade, Back to History, by Piero Scaruffi / Race and Slavery in the Middle East, by Bernard Lewis. Accessed Nov. 2014

Egypt enslaved the entire nation of Israel for over three hundred years. This was possibly the only time in history where slaves from another country were led from captivity under their own leaders. This is chronicled in the book of Exodus where Moses leads Israel out of captivity from Egypt.[442]

The African Muslim nations of Tripoli, Tunis, and others engaged in the trading and holding of white slaves, generally from white Christian European and American nations.

England, Europe and America often were engaged in the slavery of Africans as well as some whites. Asian nations fared no better when it came to slavery. The Chinese could enslave anyone except the free Chinese. A convicted criminal's family could be sold and enslaved, and young girls from most countries were bought and sold as sex slaves by the Chinese.[443] [444] Most nations have been guilty of exploiting and placing into slavery persons of other races or national origins.[445]

Before the first European placed a foot on the American continent, the Indians of the Americas were actively involved with raiding other native Indian nations and either trading or placing their captives into slavery. Paiute Indians of the Great Basin of western Utah, some of the poorest of Indians were for centuries the victims of slavery and raiding from the stronger Ute, Shoshone and other neighboring tribes. Many of these slaves were traded to distant lands, never to see their native lands or families again.

Because of their brutality, the Comanche from Texas and the Great Plains area were feared by other tribes. The Comanche often went to war with neighboring tribes and would run them off their own lands. The Comanche were absolutely brutal in their treatment of prisoners; only the lucky ones would avoid torture and murder to become slaves.[446] Because of the strength of the Comanche nation,

---

442   King James Bible, Old Testament, Book of Exodus
443   Britannica, Black History, Slavery, 2014
444   Wheelan, Joseph, Jefferson's War, Carol 7 Graf, 2003 page 33
445   The Root, Did Black people own slaves? , By Henry Louis Gates Jr., March 4, 2013
446   Empire of the Summer Moon, Gwynne, S.C, Simon & Schuster Inc, 2010, page 40, 55

they were considered the scourge of the plains by more peaceful tribes. They were so hated that neighboring tribes often went in confederate with their white neighbors to eliminate the Comanche.[447]

Throughout time, most slaves have been looked upon as inferiors by the slaveholders. The holders rarely saw morality as a viable problem with slavery. This line of thinking is so deranged that many slaveholders convinced themselves that they were doing the slaves a favor. They believed the slaves could never survive without their master to provide for them.

In the American South, slavery was seen as the most economical way to perform the work and chores of large plantations. Slaves were seen as a labor force but the owners could not see that the labor force they had obtained was one of the least effective in history.

The southerners could not see and did not understand that slavery was holding them back, financially. Labor performed by slaves has never been as productive as labor provided by free men, who had a vested interest in obtaining a higher standard of living.

The second tier of this insanity is that slaves received no monetary compensation so they could never become a consumer which is vital in a trading economy.

This inequality of economy and difference of productivity was seen in stark contrast in the superior production standards of the free northern states versus those in the slave south. The United States was a country of immigrants and most of the new immigrants were settling in the free north where there was a higher potential for financial gain and there was no slavery. The result was a much stronger northern economy. Travelers from the North were astounded by the abject poverty that was so prevalent in the South. Ironically, the south was being strangled by slavery, an institution they could not financially afford and believed they could not financially rid themselves of.

---

447   Empire of the Summer Moon, Gwynne, S.C, Simon & Schuster Inc, 2010, page 141

The slave trade has always been fueled by the arrogance of people who believe they hold moral and or physical high ground over others.[448] In almost all nations, slavery has only been terminated by the hostile takeover from another country or when a native people eventually revolt. Slaves have rarely been successful in revolting in a country where they have been transported to.

Because they were brought from another country, it was not probable that freedom was something American slaves could ever obtain for themselves. The slaves were restricted from education, arms, and association of free speech. With these restrictions, it was almost impossible for slaves to form any type of meaningful coalition or organize themselves so they could overthrow their masters. Consequently if the slaves were to ever be free it would fall to people from another race to secure that freedom for them.

In America, people from another race would come to be the benefactors of the slaves. These people would fight what would become a holy war to bring freedom to black slaves in America. That rescue came in the form of millions of white abolitionists from the Free Northern states.

By the year 1860, the United States was a cauldron of pro- and anti-slavery factions. [449] In the election of 1860, slavery was front and center; the country was being split into two with Democrats for slavery and Republicans anti-slavery. This tinder box came closer to igniting as events in Kansas took a turn. In 1860, Kansas was petitioning for statehood; the majority of its citizens (white men & women) wanted a slave-free Kansas. However, Democrat President James Buchanan hoping to appease Southern Democrats, called on Congress to admit Kansas as a slave state. Eventually the will of the people was recognized, and in spite of Buchanan and the Democrats in congress, Kansas was admitted as a free state.[450]

As payment for their anti-slavery diligence the people of Kansas both white and black became the receivers of one of the most brutal acts of the civil war. In 1863 pro slave Democrats, sacked

448   About African History, African Slavery 101, By Alistair Boddy-Evens
449   Team of Rivals, Goodwin, Doris Kearns, 2005 Simon & Schuster, Page 196
450   http://millercenter.org/president/buchanan, Accessed June 10, 2015

the town of Lawrence, Kansas, and killed over 200 citizens, mostly whites, because of their anti-slavery politics.

Freedom

Over the four-year-course of the Civil War (1861-1865), over two million union soldiers (most of them Republicans) went to battle for the freedom of black slaves. During the four years of the war, over 330,000 whites and about 40,000 black Union soldiers were killed and hundreds of thousands more were seriously injured in the bloodiest war in America. The confederate states would lose 260,000 Democrat soldiers trying to defend slavery.[451]

In the end, the ultimate goal of the war was not for riches, land, or fame but to free their black brothers and sisters from the chains of slavery. Never in history had a nation gone to war to free people of another race from slavery; America was the first. After four bloody years of war, the Union anti-slavery forces prevailed and freedom for all people was brought to the land we call America.

Since the Civil War, millions of blacks and whites have chosen to recognize the brotherhood of man and have come together to unite America. Unfortunately, far too many still continue to fight against their brothers and sisters because of the petty offense of color or race.

Whites and blacks alike owe a debt of gratitude to these brave soldiers who fought, and to those who died, to defeat slavery. Whether white or black, when we continue the war of race, it is a slap in the face to those who fought to advance this freedom from racism and bigotry.[452]

Full citizenship for black Americans

A few months after the conclusion of the Civil War, on January 3, 1865, Congress passed the Thirteenth Amendment to the

451   http://www.historynet.com/civil-war-casualties Accessed June 10, 2015
452   http://www.archives.gov/education/lessons/blacks-civil-war/ Accessed May 16, 2015

US Constitution. This amendment made it unmistakably clear that slavery was no longer allowed in the borders of the United States of America. Because of the deaths of hundreds of thousands from the Civil War, America had paid her penance for the abhorrent practice of slavery that she had allowed to go on within her boarders. Even after passage of this critical Amendment, there were powerful political forces in America who were working behind the scenes to continue to keep black American citizens from enjoying all of the blessings of freedom.

It is not a matter of finger pointing but a matter of history that leaders in the Democratic Party clearly did not want the slaves to be freed and fought in congress to keep them in servitude. It was the Republicans who overwhelmingly voted to pass the Thirteenth Amendment, freeing the slaves. Only 23 percent of Democrats voted in favor of this amendment.

The Fourteenth Amendment, which gave blacks the right to vote along with full citizenship, was passed with 100 percent of Republicans voting in favor; however, not a single Democrat voted in favor of this amendment.[453]

The re-writers of history have co-opted the facts of who championed the abolishment of slavery and equal rights for blacks and all Americans. It was the Republicans who abolished slavery and Democrats who voted against abolition and against equality for black Americans.

At the end of the Civil War, and for the next one hundred years, white Democrats continued to believe that they were superior to the black race. They continued to fight for segregation and against integration.

It was southern Democrats who inspired and made up the Ku Klux Klan. Civil War Confederate General Nathan Bedford Forest is believed to be the first Grand Dragon of the KKK. Forest was a powerful Democrat and spoke at the Democratic National

---

453   Politico, GOP Website Touts 14th amendment, By Jonathan Allen, August 4, 2010

Convention in 1868.[454]

Democrats would like to disclaim their connection with the clan. However, their history is tainted with the likes of Senator Robert Byrd (D-WV.) Senator Byrd was a member of the House of Representatives from 1953-1959. In the House, he was voted by the Democratic Party as minority Whip, and later as majority leader. As a Senator (1959-2010) he severed as leader of the Senate Democrat Caucus from 1967 to 1971. Senator Byrd was a leader of the Democratic Party.

After eleven years in Congress, in 1964 he was also a leading member of the KKK in West Virginia. Had Senator Byrd been a Republican, he would have been driven from the Senate for his affiliation with the Klan. Because he was a Democrat, his past was buried and co-opting the black population continued with hardly a bump in the road. Senator Byrd is the hypocritical face of the Democratic Party.[455]

March 17, 1965 is known as "Bloody Sunday." State Troopers and Sheriff Deputies, under orders from Democrat Governor George Wallace, converged on Selma Alabama to stop a legal, non-violent protest. The black protesters were marching fifty-four miles from Selma to the State Capital in Montgomery Alabama in a legal effort to encourage blacks to register and vote.

Under orders from the governor, the police attacked and beat unarmed protestors then released police dogs on unarmed men, women, and children. It was Republican District Judge Frank Johnson who ruled in favor of the protestors to allow them to continue the protest without molestation.[456] [457]

454   Richmond Times Dispatch, Politifact Virginia, State Sen. Stephen Martin says Democratic Party created KKK, By Sean Gorman, June 10, 2013
455   US New and World Report, Byrd's KKK History shows Partisan Double Standard, By Peter Roff, June 30,2010
456   Gateway Pundit, On this Day in 1965 Angry Democrats with Billy Clubs Attacked Selma Civil Rights Marchers, Posted by Jim Hoft March 7, 2015, The learning Network, With the New York Times, March 7, 1965/ Civil Rights Marchers Attacked in Selma, By The Learning Network, March 7, 2012
457   The learning Network, With the New York Times, March 7, 1965/ Civil Rights Marchers Attacked in Selma, By The Learning Network, March 7, 2012

In the late 1950s, the Democratic Party realized they could no longer exclude or control black integration into mainstream America. Democrats made a brilliant move to capture the black vote. The Democratic Party convinced the black population and young American college students that they, the Democrats were the true champions of civil rights.

The narrative included the lie that it was the Democrats and not the Republicans who had been the party for the abolition of slavery. The press was complicit in this cover up and denial of who had opposed equal rights and who the real promoters of equality were. In their effort to cover who they really are, the Democrats have gone so far as to assert that Abraham Lincoln (the first Republican President) was a Democrat.[458]

In 1957, Lindon Johnson, then Senator Johnson, was nobody's fool. He was one of the architects of the Democratic Party who stepped to the front to reinvent the party to black America. Johnson was a devout racist, and the "N" word was an integral part of his vocabulary along with every other vile word in the English language. Johnson was a decisive power in passing the 1957 Civil Rights Bill; however, he referred to it as *the "N----- bill."* While the following statement is attributed to, but not positively identified as coming from Johnson, it stands reminiscent of his sentiments toward black Americans.[459]

"These Negroes, they're getting pretty uppity these days and that's a problem for us since they've got something now they never had before, the political pull to back up their uppityness. Now we've got to do something about this, we've got to give them a little something, just enough to quiet them down, not enough to make a difference . . . I'll have them n____s (explicative) voting Democratic for the next two hundred years."[460]

---

458   The Huffington Post, Abe Lincoln is a Democrat, , By Tyler Kingkade, Nov 07, 2013

459   MSNBC, Lyndon Johnson was a civil rights hero. But also a racist, by Adam Serwer, April 11, 2014

460   http://www.reddit.com/r/AskHistorians/comments/2088gl accessed May 16, 2015

In 1964, following the lead of his predecessors Presidents Eisenhower (R) and Kennedy (D), President Johnson (D) introduced landmark legislation for black civil rights. The 1964 Civil Rights act was passed in the house where over 80 percent of Republicans and only 63 percent of Democrats voted for the bill. In the Senate, Republicans voted 82 percent in favor with 69 percent of Democrats voting in the affirmative. Without the strong support of Republicans, this legislation would have failed in both houses of congress.[461]

Shortly after taking office in the early 1900s President TR Roosevelt (R) showed his conviction for equality by inviting a prominent black man, Booker T. Washington to the White house for dinner. Democrat controlled newspapers denounced the President and even encouraged the killing of blacks "Just to keep them in their place." TR would not be intimidated by these raciest newspaper men, and the dinner went on as planned.[462]

While this may seem small thing, the press then, as today, could make or break Presidents. President Roosevelt stood by his principles and by his black friends. A few short years later President Woodrow Wilson (D) would show his disdain for black Americans by showing in the White House the racist movie, *Birth of a Nation.*[463]

Black leadership

Many of the most effective black leaders did not see themselves as "The Black Leadership" and certainly were not in it for the money. These were just men and women who happened to be black who saw injustice and tried to amend it so justice could prevail.

Dr. Martin Luther King gave all he had to the noble cause of civil rights. He paid not only with his treasure but also with his life.

---

461   The Guardian, Were Republicans really the party of Civil Rights in the 1960's? By Harry J Enten, August 29, 2013
462   Bennett, William J, America the Last Best Hope, Thomas Nelson 2007 page 491
463   Bennett William J, America the Last Best Hope, Thomas Nelson 2007, page 522

Dr. King died with no appreciable assets. [464] Rosa Parks challenged the Democrat backed Jim Crow Law that required that blacks ride only in back seats of city buses. Rosa was a leader, but did not use the position to enrich herself.

Who is fleecing who?

In a recent poll among blacks, only 60 percent believe the black leadership speaks for them. The present so-called black leadership does not appear to be the humble servants of past generations. They have used their position to line their own pockets at the expense of their black brothers and sisters.

Rev. Al Sharpton drives a 475,000 dollar Rolls Royce Phantom and has a net worth of over five million dollars. Al Sharpton also owes a tax bill in excess of four and half million dollars and is a frequent guest in the Obama White House. [465]

Rev. Jesse Jackson has amassed immense wealth as a self-appointed leader of the black community. His wealth is estimated at over ten million dollars. [466]

Maxine Waters, democratic congresswoman from California and self-appointed black leader, has a net worth of between four and six million dollars. [467]

President and Mrs. Obama, who continue to tell Americans to sacrifice, have ruled over the most expensive White House in history. They have accumulated a net worth of over twelve million dollars. The Obamas' wealth has increased over 500 percent since Barack Obama became President. [468]

---

464   African Executive, Poor Dr. King & Rich Civil Rights Leaders, By Rev. Wayne Perryman

465   http://conservative-headlines.com/2014/11/mega-tax-cheat-al-sharpton-drives-most-expensive-production-car-in-the-world/ Accessed May 16, 2015

466   http://www.celebritynetworth.com/richest-politicians/al-sharpton-net-worth/ accessed May 16, 2015

467   Black Enterprise wealth for life, 10 Richest African Americans In Congress, By Richard Spiropoulos, September 16, 2014, Accessed Sept 14, 2015

468   http://www.celebritynetworth.com/richest-politicians/presidents/barack-obama-net-worth/ Accessed May 16, 2015

Hillary Clinton claims to be a poor underdog who can relate to poor people and especially poor blacks. Can she really relate? Hillary's net worth is estimated at around 25 million dollars. The information has been well hidden by the Clintons as they plead poverty to influence their Democrat base.[469]

Louis Farrakhan, another self-appointed voice of the black community, has a net worth in excess of 4.3 million dollars.[470]

There is no sin in having money, but the hypocrisy of these so-called leaders is beyond reality. These millionaires are unique in that they have never owned, managed, or created any business, product, or service. They have accumulated their millions by condemning the wealthy while accumulating immense wealth on the backs of the people they claim to represent.

These self-appointed leaders of the black community have one thing in common: without the hatred and racism which they continue to stir up, their incomes and lifestyle would be negatively impacted.

Under the presidency of Barack Obama, race relations between blacks and whites has become more polarized than at any time since the 1960s. The so-called black leadership uses the black people as pawns to further an agenda of racism, which is by design holding black Americans back financially and politically.

Real leaders in today's world

In 2004 Rev. Wayne Perryman sued the Democratic Party (United States District Court Case No. CV04-2442).

Under oath in court, the Democratic Party admitted their horrendous racism for 150 years under the Party's States Rights claims based on the Democratic Party's Jim Crow Laws and Black Codes. Even with that admission, the Democratic Party refused to apologize because they know that they can take the black vote for

---

469   The Washington Post, $5 million, $50 million or even more- just how rich is Hillary Clinton? Here's why we don't know. By Alexander Becker, July 30, 2014
470   Rich but Broke, Louis Farrakhan's Net Worth is $4,347,156, By Richbutbroke. com, Monday April 16, 2012

granted.

For America, and especially black Americans, Mr. Perryman identifies the Democratic Party as the party of the four Ss: Slavery, Secession, Segregation and Socialism. Democrats started the KKK to lynch and terrorize blacks. Democrats fought against passage of every civil rights law from the 1860s through the 1960s.

Democrats have been running inner cities in America for the past thirty to fifty years. With their failed social policies, they have left a legacy of ruin, despair, and an economic and social wasteland.[471]

---

471   http://www.nationalblackrepublicans.com/index.cfm?fuseaction=pages. DYK-Democrats%20Owe%20Blacks%20an%20Apology Accessed May 16, 2015

Chapter 20

Sacred Documents of the United States of America

Each of the following documents has been taken from the most accurate online sources available. There is a short preview about each document, giving some information about events leading up to the writing and ratifying of these records.

The first shots fired of the Revolutionary War were at Lexington, Massachusetts, April of 1776. Later that year, on July 4th 1776, the historic Declaration of Independence was written and signed by 56 men whom we commonly call the Founding Fathers. These men did not just declare a false hope of independence; they literally backed the declaration with their lives and a pledge: "We mutually pledge to each other our lives, our fortunes and our sacred honor.[472]

Almost all the signers came out of the war with far less money than when it started. Several lost their lives; others lost sons in the war. Some went broke.[473] All remained true patriots. These were not Sunshine patriots but tough, dedicated men who would risk all for the just cause of freedom.

The Declaration of Independence: A Transcription

IN CONGRESS, July 4, 1776

The unanimous Declaration of the thirteen united States of America

When in the Course of human events, it becomes necessary for one people to dissolve the political bands which have connected them with another, and to assume among the powers of the earth, the separate and equal station to which the Laws of Nature and

---

472   Declaration of Independence, July 4, 1776, last line of the document.
473   http://www.constitutionfacts.com/us-declaration-of-independence/about-the-signers/

of Nature's God entitle them, a decent respect to the opinions of mankind requires that they should declare the causes which impel them to the separation.

We hold these truths to be self-evident, that all men are created equal, that they are endowed by their Creator with certain unalienable Rights, that among these are Life, Liberty and the pursuit of Happiness.-- That to secure these rights, Governments are instituted among Men, deriving their just powers from the consent of the governed, --That whenever any Form of Government becomes destructive of these ends, it is the Right of the People to alter or to abolish it, and to institute new Government, laying its foundation on such principles and organizing its powers in such form, as to them shall seem most likely to effect their Safety and Happiness. Prudence, indeed, will dictate that Governments long established should not be changed for light and transient causes; and accordingly all experience hath shewn, that mankind are more disposed to suffer, while evils are sufferable, than to right themselves by abolishing the forms to which they are accustomed. But when a long train of abuses and usurpations, pursuing invariably the same Object evinces a design to reduce them under absolute Despotism, it is their right, it is their duty, to throw off such Government, and to provide new Guards for their future security.--Such has been the patient sufferance of these Colonies; and such is now the necessity which constrains them to alter their former Systems of Government. The history of the present King of Great Britain is a history of repeated injuries and usurpations, all having in direct object the establishment of an absolute Tyranny over these States. To prove this, let Facts be submitted to a candid world.

He has refused his Assent to Laws, the most wholesome and necessary for the public good.

He has forbidden his Governors to pass Laws of immediate and pressing importance, unless suspended in their operation till his Assent should be obtained; and when so suspended, he has utterly neglected to attend to them.

He has refused to pass other Laws for the accommodation

of large districts of people, unless those people would relinquish the right of Representation in the Legislature, a right inestimable to them and formidable to tyrants only.

He has called together legislative bodies at places unusual, uncomfortable, and distant from the depository of their public Records, for the sole purpose of fatiguing them into compliance with his measures.

He has dissolved Representative Houses repeatedly, for opposing with manly firmness his invasions on the rights of the people.

He has refused for a long time, after such dissolutions, to cause others to be elected; whereby the Legislative powers, incapable of Annihilation, have returned to the People at large for their exercise; the State remaining in the mean time exposed to all the dangers of invasion from without, and convulsions within.

He has endeavoured to prevent the population of these States; for that purpose obstructing the Laws for Naturalization of Foreigners; refusing to pass others to encourage their migrations hither, and raising the conditions of new Appropriations of Lands.

He has obstructed the Administration of Justice, by refusing his Assent to Laws for establishing Judiciary powers.

He has made Judges dependent on his Will alone, for the tenure of their offices, and the amount and payment of their salaries.

He has erected a multitude of New Offices, and sent hither swarms of Officers to harrass our people, and eat out their substance.

He has kept among us, in times of peace, Standing Armies without the Consent of our legislatures.

He has affected to render the Military independent of and superior to the Civil power.

He has combined with others to subject us to a jurisdiction foreign to our constitution, and unacknowledged by our laws; giving his Assent to their Acts of pretended Legislation:

For Quartering large bodies of armed troops among us:

For protecting them, by a mock Trial, from punishment for any Murders which they should commit on the Inhabitants of these States:

For cutting off our Trade with all parts of the world:

For imposing Taxes on us without our Consent:

For depriving us in many cases, of the benefits of Trial by Jury:

For transporting us beyond Seas to be tried for pretended offences

For abolishing the free System of English Laws in a neighbouring Province, establishing therein an Arbitrary government, and enlarging its Boundaries so as to render it at once an example and fit instrument for introducing the same absolute rule into these Colonies:

For taking away our Charters, abolishing our most valuable Laws, and altering fundamentally the Forms of our Governments:

For suspending our own Legislatures, and declaring themselves invested with power to legislate for us in all cases whatsoever.

He has abdicated Government here, by declaring us out of his Protection and waging War against us.

He has plundered our seas, ravaged our Coasts, burnt our towns, and destroyed the lives of our people.

He is at this time transporting large Armies of foreign Mercenaries to compleat the works of death, desolation and tyranny, already begun with circumstances of Cruelty & perfidy scarcely paralleled in the most barbarous ages, and totally unworthy the Head of a civilized nation.

He has constrained our fellow Citizens taken Captive on the high Seas to bear Arms against their Country, to become the executioners of their friends and Brethren, or to fall themselves by their Hands.

He has excited domestic insurrections amongst us, and has endeavoured to bring on the inhabitants of our frontiers, the merciless Indian Savages, whose known rule of warfare, is an undistinguished destruction of all ages, sexes and conditions.

In every stage of these Oppressions We have Petitioned for Redress in the most humble terms: Our repeated Petitions have been answered only by repeated injury. A Prince whose character is thus marked by every act which may define a Tyrant, is unfit to be the ruler of a free people.

Nor have We been wanting in attentions to our Brittish brethren. We have warned them from time to time of attempts by their legislature to extend an unwarrantable jurisdiction over us. We have reminded them of the circumstances of our emigration and settlement here. We have appealed to their native justice and magnanimity, and we have conjured them by the ties of our common kindred to disavow these usurpations, which, would inevitably interrupt our connections and correspondence. They too have been deaf to the voice of justice and of consanguinity. We must, therefore, acquiesce in the necessity, which denounces our Separation, and hold them, as we hold the rest of mankind, Enemies in War, in Peace Friends.

We, therefore, the Representatives of the united States of America, in General Congress, Assembled, appealing to the Supreme Judge of the world for the rectitude of our intentions, do, in the Name, and by Authority of the good People of these Colonies, solemnly publish and declare, That these United Colonies are, and of Right ought to be Free and Independent States; that they are Absolved from all Allegiance to the British Crown, and that all political connection between them and the State of Great Britain, is and ought to be totally dissolved; and that as Free and Independent States, they have full Power to levy War, conclude Peace, contract

Alliances, establish Commerce, and to do all other Acts and Things which Independent States may of right do. And for the support of this Declaration, with a firm reliance on the protection of divine Providence, we mutually pledge to each other our Lives, our Fortunes and our sacred Honor.[474]

The Star Spangled Banner

The Star Spangled Banner, or The National Anthem, was written during the War of 1812, commonly called the Second Revolutionary War.

In the thirty-plus years since the Revolutionary War, the British had continued to interfere with American shipping, at times taking and pressing American Sailors into service in the British Navy. On June 1, 1812, Congress declared war on England. Two years into the war in August of 1814, the British entered Washington DC and set fire to the White House and several other government buildings.

A few weeks later, the British fleet proceeded down the Atlantic coast to the Chesapeake Bay with the intent to destroy Fort McHenry and secure the area for British war ships to enter heart of America.

Attorney Frances Scott Key and Government agent John Skinner were given permission to approach and board the British flagship and meet with British admiral, Alexander Cockrane.

Key and Skinner were on a mission to secure the release of Dr. William Beanes, an American who had been taken captive by the English. Key and Skinner were successful in obtaining the release; however, because they had been told information about the British battle plans to destroy Fort McHenry, they were not allowed to leave the ship.

The British had a new weapon in its arsenal, a rocket which was not very accurate but had a longer range than the conventional cannons at Fort McHenry. On September 13, 1814 at 6:30 a.m., the British commenced their twenty-five-hour barrage on the fort and

---

474   http://www.archives.gov/exhibits/charters/declaration_transcript.html

continued all through the day and night.

Key wrote later, "It seemed as though mother earth had opened and was vomiting shot and shell in a sheet of fire and brimstone."[475]

When night came the rockets and cannons continued sending sheets of fire and exploding bombs. Throughout the night when the rockets would explode, lighting up the sky, Key and his companions could see the battle flag still flying above the ramparts (Fortress walls) of the besieged Fort.

As daylight began to lighten the eastern skies, the Commandant of Fort McHenry Major George Armistead ordered the battle flag taken down and the much larger Star Spangled Banner to be hoisted up the ninety-foot flag pole so in the morning light the citizens of Baltimore could see that the fort was still in American hands and the flag was still flying, despite the relentless pounding by the British.

Thus Mr. Key could see "By the Dawns Early Light . . . that our flag was still there." As the morning breeze caught the flag, it began to flutter in the wind and the morning sun captured the full glory of the flag as it unfurled and waved in the morning breeze.

What American who considers the blessing of this beloved land does not get tears in their eyes, and whose heart does not fill with pride when they read these inspiring words?

Mr. Key wrote a poem on the back of an envelope and later published it as the "Defense of Fort McHenry." It was soon renamed the "Star Spangled Banner" and eventually became the National Anthem of the United States.[476]

The original flag, designed to fly over Fort McHenry, was 42 by 30 feet. The battle flag was smaller, measuring 25 by 17 feet. The original poem had four verses; however, the third verse was removed during World War II so as not to offend our British allies. All verses are included in this version.[477]

---

475   http://www.smithsonianmag.com/history/the-story-behind-the-star-spangled-banner-

476   http://www.smithsonianmag.com/history/the-story-behind-the-star-spangled-banner-

477   http://www.si.edu/Encyclopedia_SI/nmah/starflag.htm

The Star Spangled Banner

By Francis Scott Key, 1814

Oh, say can you see by the dawn's early light
What so proudly we hailed at the twilight's last gleaming?
Whose broad stripes and bright stars thru the perilous fight,
O'er the ramparts we watched were so gallantly streaming?
And the rocket's red glare, the bombs bursting in air.
Gave proof through the night that our flag was still there.
Oh, say does that Star-Spangled Banner yet wave
O'er the land of the free and the home of the brave?

On the shore, dimly seen through the mists of the deep
Where the foe's haughty host in dread silence reposes,
What is that which the breeze, o'er the towering steep,
As it fitfully blows, half conceals, half discloses?
Now it catches the gleam of the morning's first beam,
In full glory reflected now shines in the stream:
'Tis the Star-Spangled Banner! Oh long may it wave
O'er the land of the free and the home of the brave!

And where is that band who so vauntingly swore
That the havoc of war and the battle's confusion
A home and a country should leave us no more!
Their blood has washed out their foul footsteps' pollution.
No refuge could save the hireling and slave
From the terror of flight, or the gloom of the grave:
And the star-spangled banner in triumph doth wave
O'er the land of the free and the home of the brave!

Oh! thus be it ever, when freemen shall stand
Between their loved home and the war's desolation!
Blest with victory and peace, may the heav'n rescued land
Praise the Power that hath made and preserved us a nation.
Then conquer we must, when our cause it is just,

And this be our motto: "In God is our trust."
And the Star-Spangled Banner in triumph shall wave
O'er the land of the free and the home of the brave![478]

The Gettysburg Address

The Civil War Battle of Gettysburg was fought on July 1-3, 1863. Union forces of about 93,000 men engaged about 75,000 Southern Confederate forces. When the battle was over, the Union had suffered 23,000 casualties and the South 28,000. Of these, 3,155 Union and 3,903 Confederate soldiers were killed in action. This number only counts those who died on the battlefield, not those who subsequently died of wounds inflicted in the battle.

Gettysburg, Pennsylvania November 19, 1863, President Abraham Lincoln delivered what has become known as, The Gettysburg address. The address was to honor the 23,000 injured and fallen Union soldiers and to insure that their deaths would not be in vain.

The address statement that "all men should be free" was in direct reference to the black slaves held in the south.

Gettysburg is one of those special places where you can feel the spirit of peace and comfort as you walk the hallowed grounds of that immense battlefield.

On June 1, 1865, Senator Charles Sumner referred to the most famous speech ever given by President Abraham Lincoln. In his eulogy of the slain president, he called the Gettysburg Address a "Monumental Act." He said Lincoln was mistaken that "the world will little note, nor long remember what we say here." Rather, the Bostonian remarked, "The world noted at once what he said, and

---

478   http://www.usa-flag-site.org/song-lyrics/star-spangled-banner.shtml

will never cease to remember it. The battle itself was less important than the speech."[479]

The Gettysburg Address

By President Abraham Lincoln, 1893

Four score and seven years ago, our fathers brought forth on this continent, a new nation, conceived in Liberty, and dedicated to the proposition that all men are created equal.

Now we are engaged in a great civil war, testing whether that nation, or any nation so conceived and so dedicated, can long endure. We are met on a great battle-field of that war. We have come to dedicate a portion of that field, as a final resting place for those who here gave their lives that that nation might live. It is altogether fitting and proper that we should do this.

But, in a larger sense, we can not dedicate -- we can not consecrate -- we can not hallow -- this ground. The brave men, living and dead, who struggled here, have consecrated it, far above our poor power to add or detract. The world will little note, nor long remember what we say here, but it can never forget what they did here. It is for us the living, rather, to be dedicated here to the unfinished work which they who fought here have thus far so nobly advanced. It is rather for us to be here dedicated to the great task remaining before us -- that from these honored dead we take increased devotion to that cause for which they gave the last full measure of devotion -- that we here highly resolve that these dead shall not have died in vain -- that this nation, under God, shall have a new birth of freedom -- and that government of the people, by the people, for the people, shall not perish from the earth.[480]

---

479   http://www.abrahamlincolnonline.org/lincoln/speeches/gettysburg.htm
480   http://www.abrahamlincolnonline.org/lincoln/speeches/gettysburg.htm

The Emancipation Proclamation

Here is the story behind the story. In the beginning, the Civil War was about the right of the states to secede from the Union and to take over federal property in the seceding states. Even after the war broke out, President Lincoln understood that under constitutional authority the President did not have the power to make laws. He could not change the laws on slavery without a bill from the congress.

By the second year of the war, President Lincoln had several visionary or revelatory experiences that changed his prospective on the war. By 1862, the purpose of the war for Lincoln changed from saving the Union to abolishing slavery in the United States.[481]

On July 1 and 2 of 1862, President Lincoln called a special cabinet meeting to announce his decision to free the slaves held in the rebellious states. Information had come to Lincoln that the South was using slaves to accelerate the war effort. This use of the slaves to further the war allowed them to be classified as contraband. As commander in chief of the armed forces, the President legally could use his executive authority to release the slaves in the rebellious states from their owners and encourage them to assist the Union.

After President Lincoln read his draft of the Emancipation order to his cabinet it was decided that the Union needed a decisive victory before the order could be announced, or it would look like the last breath of a dying man.[482]

This decisive win would be the Battle of Antietam, September 17, 1862. A few days before that great battle, General Robert E. Lee had drawn up battle plans for the confederate forces. This order was called Special Order No. 191. The few copies were carefully accounted for, and only his top generals were made aware of the top-secret plans.

A few days after the secret meeting and just before the battle (Union) Corporal Barton Mitchell was walking through the soon-to-be battlefield, when he stumbled upon an envelope wrapped around three cigars. The envelope contained Special Order No.

---

481   Ballard, Timothy, The Lincoln Hypothesis, Deseret Book 2014, Page 130
482   Goodwin, Doris Kearns, Team of Rivals, Simon & Schuster, 2005, page 464-469

191. The order was given to Union General George McClellan. The information in the order allowed the Union troops to capitalize on the plan and defeat the Confederate forces at the Battle of Antietam.

Even today, no one has been able to explain how the special order was carelessly left for the Union forces to find. This much is known: according to personal papers written by Abraham Lincoln, he had prayed and made a promise to God that as soon as the Union enjoyed a victory he would publicly proclaim the Emaciation Proclamation. A few days later, on September 22, 1862 President Lincoln, true to his promise to God, announced the Proclamation to America.[483]

Emancipation Proclamation

A Proclamation

Whereas, on the twenty-second day of September, in the year of our Lord one thousand eight hundred and sixty-two, a proclamation was issued by the President of the United States, containing, among other things, the following, to wit:

"That on the first day of January, in the year of our Lord one thousand eight hundred and sixty-three, all persons held as slaves within any State or designated part of a State, the people whereof shall then be in rebellion against the United States, shall be then, thenceforward, and forever free; and the Executive Government of the United States, including the military and naval authority thereof, will recognize and maintain the freedom of such persons, and will do no act or acts to repress such persons, or any of them, in any efforts they may make for their actual freedom.

"That the Executive will, on the first day of January aforesaid, by proclamation, designate the States and parts of States, if any, in which the people thereof, respectively, shall then be in rebellion against the United States; and the fact that any State, or the people thereof, shall on that day be, in good faith, represented

---

483   Ballard, Timothy, The Lincoln Hypothesis, Deseret Book 2014,Page 92-94

in the Congress of the United States by members chosen thereto at elections wherein a majority of the qualified voters of such State shall have participated, shall, in the absence of strong countervailing testimony, be deemed conclusive evidence that such State, and the people thereof, are not then in rebellion against the United States."

Now, therefore I, Abraham Lincoln, President of the United States, by virtue of the power in me vested as Commander-in-Chief, of the Army and Navy of the United States in time of actual armed rebellion against the authority and government of the United States, and as a fit and necessary war measure for suppressing said rebellion, do, on this first day of January, in the year of our Lord one thousand eight hundred and sixty-three, and in accordance with my purpose so to do publicly proclaimed for the full period of one hundred days, from the day first above mentioned, order and designate as the States and parts of States wherein the people thereof respectively, are this day in rebellion against the United States, the following, to wit:

Arkansas, Texas, Louisiana, (except the Parishes of St. Bernard, Plaquemines, Jefferson, St. John, St. Charles, St. James Ascension, Assumption, Terrebonne, Lafourche, St. Mary, St. Martin, and Orleans, including the City of New Orleans) Mississippi, Alabama, Florida, Georgia, South Carolina, North Carolina, and Virginia, (except the forty-eight counties designated as West Virginia, and also the counties of Berkley, Accomac, Northampton, Elizabeth City, York, Princess Ann, and Norfolk, including the cities of Norfolk and Portsmouth[)], and which excepted parts, are for the present, left precisely as if this proclamation were not issued.

And by virtue of the power, and for the purpose aforesaid, I do order and declare that all persons held as slaves within said designated States, and parts of States, are, and henceforward shall be free; and that the Executive government of the United States, including the military and naval authorities thereof, will recognize and maintain the freedom of said persons.

And I hereby enjoin upon the people so declared to be free to abstain from all violence, unless in necessary self-defense; and I recommend to them that, in all cases when allowed, they labor faithfully for reasonable wages.

And I further declare and make known, that such persons of suitable condition, will be received into the armed service of the United States to garrison forts, positions, stations, and other places, and to man vessels of all sorts in said service.

And upon this act, sincerely believed to be an act of justice, warranted by the Constitution, upon military necessity, I invoke the considerate judgment of mankind, and the gracious favor of Almighty God.

In witness whereof, I have hereunto set my hand and caused the seal of the United States to be affixed.

Done at the City of Washington, this first day of January, in the year of our Lord one thousand eight hundred and sixty three, and of the Independence of the United States of America the eighty-seventh.

By the President: Abraham Lincoln

William H. Seward, Secretary of State.[484]

The final nail in the coffin of slavery was the Thirteenth Amendment, ratified December 6, 1865.[485] Legally, the nightmare of slavery was over. America had repented of slavery, and her penance had been paid in the blood of over 600,000 white and 40,000 black Americans dead and untold numbers with serious physical wounds that would never heal. It would be up to the following generations, both white and black, to rise above racial prejudice and become brothers to all men.

---

484   http://www.archives.gov/exhibits/featured_documents/emancipation_proclamation/
485   US Constitution, Amendment 13